THE CORPORAL WAS A PITCHER

THE COURAGE OF LOU BRISSIE

THE
CORPORAL
WAS A
PITCHER

THE COURAGE
OF LOU BRISSIE

Ira Berkow

TRIUMPH
BOOKS

Library of Congress Cataloging-in-Publication Data

Berkow, Ira.
    The corporal was a pitcher : the courage of Lou Brissie / Ira Berkow.
      p. cm.
    Includes bibliographical references and index.
    ISBN-13: 978-1-60078-104-9
    ISBN-10: 1-60078-104-7
1. Brissie, Lou 2. Baseball players—United States—Biography.
3. Baseball players with disabilities—United States—Biography.
4. World War, 1939–1945—Veterans—United States—Biography. I. Title.
    GV865.B716B47 2008
    796.357092–dc22
    [B]   2008041340

This book is available in quantity at special discounts for your group or organization. For further information, contact:

Triumph Books
542 South Dearborn Street
Suite 750
Chicago, Illinois 60605
(312) 939-3330
Fax (312) 663-3557

Printed in U.S.A.
ISBN: 978-1-60078-104-9
Page production by Sue Knopf
Photos courtesy of Lou Brissie unless otherwise indicated.
Front Cover: The 1952 Topps card set forever changed the baseball card industry. The 407-card set featured paintings of players and used team logos on the card fronts for the first time.

For surgeons Maj. Wilbur K. Brubaker
and Maj. Alfred J. Suraci,
and all the military medical personnel,
past and present

Contents

Foreword

By Tom Brokaw

The estimable British military historian John Keegan has described World War II as "the greatest event in the history of mankind." It was fought on six of the seven continents, in the seas surrounding them, and in the skies above. Before it was over more than 50 million people had perished, civilians and combatants alike, a trail of death without parallel in the history of warfare. The size of the battlefield and the consequences of the outcome were so great it is hard even now to imagine it happened in my lifetime.

When I set out to document the experiences of many Americans in that noble but terrible ordeal, I was unprepared for the number of astonishing and inspirational stories I would encounter: The large and small acts of heroism, fraternity, sacrifice on the home-front, the lingering wounds and, of course, the lifelong grief that comes with the loss of a loved one, almost always at a young age.

By now, I thought I had heard all the best stories.

I was wrong.

Ira Berkow introduced me to the courage and the will of Lou Brissie, a young man from the South Carolina textile towns who showed such great promise as a left-handed pitcher as a teenager he attracted the attention of major-league scouts while in high school.

The legendary Connie Mack of the Philadelphia Athletics was particularly interested in young Lou.

Then came the war. Brissie answered the call and found himself in the midst of combat in the Italian campaign; the long, brutal battle to attack Germany from the south while the forces of the Normandy invasion moved on Berlin from the north and west. In his outfit, Brissie's prodigious pitching talent and bright future were well known, but of course it earned him no rear-echelon assignment or orders to report for a battalion baseball team.

He was in the thick of it and one day he paid a terrible price. His squadron was in the crosshairs of a German mortar attack. Lou survived, but just barely, and he was grievously wounded. Frontline surgeons insisted his leg had to be amputated, but he fought them off again and again.

How he recovered from his wounds, saved his legs, hobbled home to his family, and never gave up on his determination to return to baseball is the story of will, medical genius, team play, and one man's dream realized against the greatest odds.

Read about the remarkable life of this modest patriot and remember him, as I will, the next time you hear about an overpaid, undertalented, and self-absorbed athlete complaining that he's not getting a fair shake.

Say to yourself, "Lou may not have made it to Cooperstown, but he'll be in my Hall of Fame every day."

Tom Brokaw
author, *The Greatest Generation*

Acknowledgments

"A man will turn over half a library to make one book," Samuel Johnson said. In many cases, an author, besides upending a goodly part of a library (or libraries), also conducts a plethora of interviews to make a book, some in person and some by telephone, a device not yet devised in Dr. Johnson's 18th-century London. I used all that to compile this book, and much more, including the U.S. Postal Service, e-mail, and, to be sure, the expanded biblioteques known as Google and such other search engines as Factiva and ProQuest. Samuel Johnson would have been shocked to learn of them, but it seems he surely would have found them of terrific help.

For this biography, the best and the single most important source was the subject himself, Leland Victor (Lou) Brissie. We spent hours together and taped interviews at his home in North Augusta, South Carolina, as well in the hotel where I stayed when I visited with him, the Marriott in Augusta, Georgia, across the Savannah River from North Augusta. And we had countless phone conversations, some of them quite long. For a long time, Brissie had turned down previous offers for a full-blown life story, in print and in film, believing that it would call too much attention to him.

I didn't think so, and felt that his story was one of the most inspiring, dramatic, and determined I'd ever run across in my nearly half century in journalism. I first ran across Lou Brissie as a boy of nine and 10 growing up on Chicago's West Side in 1949 and 1950. My friends and I would regularly sneak into ballgames at Comiskey Park and Wrigley Field. The White Sox, of course, played in Comiskey Park, and were hosts to other American League clubs, including the Philadelphia A's. I remember waiting with crowds after the game to get the autographs of the visiting players as they came out of the clubhouse and walked to the team bus. I remember getting Brissie's autograph, as well as such teammates as Eddie Joost, Elmer Valo, Ferris Fain, Carl Scheib, Bobby Shantz, Hank Majeski, and Joe Astroth. I vaguely remembered Brissie pitching with a brace on his left leg. I wasn't aware of his history as a soldier in World War II. I discovered all this in 1960 when I was a junior at Miami (Ohio) University and took out of the library a collection of sports columns, *Out of the Red*, by Red Smith, the great syndicated columnist for the then *New York Herald Tribune*. One column in the book was titled, "Sometimes It Was Discouraging," about the left-handed rookie pitcher, Lou Brissie, trying to make the A's in spring training.

I was moved nearly to tears by the tale of this wounded war veteran seeking to overcome his disability, a virtually shredded left leg. I never forgot the story. In 1994, on the 50th anniversary of his being the victim of a mortar attack by German soldiers in the mountains of northern Italy, Brissie returned to visit the graves of his fallen fellows. I called him and wrote the story of his return in my "Sports of the Times" column in *The New York Times*.

I stayed in touch with Lou, and then approached him about a book. He was reluctant—like a lot of war veterans he wasn't excited about reliving the horrors he experienced—but we talked some more and, with the urging now of his wife and children and some close friends, all of whom felt his story was an important one to tell as completely as possible, he decided to cooperate with me on it. And he did so fully, from recollections to correspondence. Any time I had a question or questions he was always available.

When the book was finished, I sent him the manuscript to check for factual content. And he was scrupulous in that. He had understood that any impressions and interpretations I had, and any impressions and interpretations others who were interviewed had, would remain integral to the book, even if he didn't necessarily agree with the viewpoint.

There is a long list of people who were essential to the writing and reporting of this book, and I want to express my appreciation to all of them, beginning with Lou's wife, Diana; her two children, Adam Smith and Charlotte Klein; Lou's son, Rob; and his daughters, Vicki Brissie Bishop and Jennifer Brissie. I want to thank Carol Brissie, Lou's niece, for her encouragement and support.

A handful of people read the book in manuscript form, some more than once, and I owe each of them, all good friends, a great debt of gratitude. They include two men with whom I worked in journalism: Murray Olderman, former sports editor of NEA who hired me from the *Minneapolis Tribune* and who served in World War II in Europe; and Sandy Padwe, who was deputy sports editor of *The Times* when I joined the paper and who grew up in the Philadelphia area when Brissie was pitching for the A's and "had his baseball cards."

Also, Richard Frederick, my neighbor in Manhattan who can tinker with a sentence as deftly as he does my computer; Dr. Isaac Herschkopf, the eminent Manhattan psychiatrist and my erstwhile pickup basketball companion; Ted Margolis, my attorney and the editor in chief of the *Miami Student*, the student newspaper of Miami University where we both went to undergraduate school and where we met when I wrote a sports column there; and two physicians and friends, Dr. Peter Berczeller, writer and retiree in France, and Dr. Marc Siegel, author and journalist, both of whom I have entrusted not only my manuscript, but literally, at times, my life.

And, Dolly Case, my loving wife, my astute wife, who can tell me in the gentlest way, more or less, that not only don't my socks match the rest of my so-called ensemble, but a particular sentence may not quite say what I planned it to say. I listen, and learn.

A good number of players that were baseball teammates and/or opponents of Lou Brissie in the minor and major leagues were, happily, still with us, and I contacted all I could, and I want to add my appreciation to them for their cooperation: Joe Anders, Joe Astroth, Bob Dillinger, Dom DiMaggio, Bobby Doerr, Bob Feller, Bill Glynn, Charlie Harris, Eddie Joost, George Kell, Ralph Kiner, Morrie Martin,

Charlie Metro, Johnny Pesky, Al Rosen, Bob Savage, Carl Scheib, Bobby Shantz, George Strickland, and Wally Westlake.

I want to thank Doris Harris, Charlie Harris's wife, for her reminiscence of her good friend Dot Brissie, Lou's late wife.

People also instrumental in my research included John Addison, Ernie Montella, and Carl Goldberg of the Philadelphia A's historical society; Baseball Almanac.com; Baseball-Reference.com; John Boyette, sports editor, *The Augusta Chronicle*; Bob DiBiasio, vice president, public relations, the Cleveland Indians; Jim Gates and Bill Francis of the National Baseball Hall of Fame Library; Eric Handler, public relations executive, YES television network; Jeff Idelson, vice president, communications and education, National Baseball Hall of Fame; R. Dave James, reaction therapist assistant, VA Hospital, Augusta, Georgia; Scott Longert of the Society of American Baseball Research (SABR) in Cleveland; Stuart Menaker, longtime friend from Chicago and helpful "Brissie" researcher; Olin Parnell, former American Legion player from South Carolina; Seymour Siwoff, president of the Elias Sports Bureau and World War II veteran who, like Brissie, was wounded in combat in Italy; a longtime Brissie and A's fan, Howard Geltzer; my former *New York Times* sports columnist mate, George Vecsey; and Mary Frances Veeck.

I want to thank my literary agent David Black for his encouragement and support and creativity from the very beginning of the project, and through every stage. And I also want to thank two members of his agency, David Larabell and Gary Morris, for their good guidance.

I want to extend heartfelt appreciation to Mitch Rogatz, president and publisher of Triumph Books, for his enthusiasm for Lou Brissie's story, and giving the book a home, and his caring follow-through in every way for the publication of this book. And from a hands-on standpoint at Triumph, I could not have been in better hands than those of the managing editor Don Gulbrandsen, the acquisitions editor Tom Bast, and the line editor Karen O'Brien.

Prologue

It was an unseasonably cold day in Augusta, Georgia, in early February 2007. On the radio, the weather report warned that temperatures would dip into the teens that night, and to prepare for possible sleet and snow and likely icy roads. But now, in the sunlight that seemed to shed no warmth, a motorist in a black 1991 Ford Ranger truck pulled up to the Marriott Hotel.

He found a parking space and, with difficulty, climbed out. While some others nearby wore sweaters or coats, the gray-haired man wore only a blue sports jacket. A good guess would have been that he had experienced even more piercing cold than this, and in less gentle conditions than this Southern city. The tail of the jacket flapped in the wind as he made his way, on hand-held aluminum crutches and black orthopedic shoes, to the restaurant in the hotel to meet me for lunch. If one looked closely, a small purple battle ribbon with white stripes could be seen in his jacket lapel. His war wounds still necessitated those crutches and those shoes.

The man would be eighty-three years old in a few months, but despite the crutches and the shoes, he appeared of sturdy build. He was tall, around 6'4", and trim. In his day, one could imagine him taken for a quite handsome man. Not matinee idol looks, necessarily, but strong features—good jaw, good cheek bones, a glint of humor in his attentive blue eyes. In fact, he still had pleasing looks. He moved with a certain grace and dignity, even bent over the crutches. He was ever the athlete, though one would hardly have guessed now that in fact he had once been an All-Star major league pitcher.

Neither the hostess of the restaurant—who led him to the booth where I awaited—nor any of the patrons appeared to recognize the elderly man who inched forward on his crutches. The lack of recognition was no surprise, since he had been out of the news for a long time.

He greeted me and, after diligently placing his supports against a wall, maneuvered his body into the booth. When he spoke, he did so with a bit of a drawl that indicated his South Carolina roots.

"The one thing you learn when you're on crutches," Lou Brissie said with an easy smile, "is to never be in a hurry."

1

Left for Dead

ROME, DEC., 1944, NEW YORK TIMES—Members of the House Military Affairs Committee who concluded their tour of European battlefields with a visit to the Italian front expressed shocked surprise at the rigors of the campaign in (northern) Italy. Nothing they had seen in France, they said, could compare with the terrible terrain of the Apennine (mountains), and nothing they had read at home prepared them for the inhuman conditions in which men of the Fifth Army have to fight. The burden of complaint was that they didn't know the Italian battlefield was one of the toughest in the world. They had no idea of the tremendous natural obstacles the G.I.s have to contend with in addition to the stubbornness of the enemy stand on the best defensive positions he holds in Europe....

Stories have been written and they have been printed.... (But) readers don't hear the scream of shells or the thunder of fallen rockets....

As to the (American soldiers) grinding their way up steep escarpments under enemy fire from on top, or slithering through muddy valleys in snow and rain... they display grim endurance and casual courage.

—Anne O'Hare McCormick

AT THE FRONT LINE IN ITALY, DEC. 1944, SCRIPPS-HOWARD—Our troops are living in a way almost inconceivable to you in the States. The fertile black valleys are knee deep in mud....It rains and it rains. Vehicles bog down and temporary bridges wash out....

Thousands of the men have not been dry for weeks. Other thousands lie at night in the high mountains with the temperature below freezing and the thin snow sifting over them.

They dig into the stones and sleep in little chasms and behind rocks and in half caves. They live like men of prehistoric times, and a club would become them more than a machine gun. How they survive the winter misery at all is beyond us who have the opportunity of drier beds in the warmer valleys.

–Ernie Pyle

December 7, 1944, about 10:30, a frigid, gray Italian morning. Snow blanketed the trees and the mountains, a picturesque scene if not for the knowledge that German artillery forces—deadly mortar, machine-gun, and rifle emplacements—were embedded behind some of those lovely, white-laced pines and ridges. Several army trucks moved slowly on a twisting, rocky road through the Apennines, about 10 miles southwest of Bologna. Cpl. Leland Victor "Lou" Brissie, 20 years old, an infantry squad leader in G Company, 351st Infantry Regiment, 88th Infantry Division, Fifth Army, was riding in one of the seven canvas-covered trucks in the convoy.

He sat in the rear of the vehicle with the other members of his platoon. The outfit was returning from a portable shower unit where they had had a shower and a hot breakfast, the first such luxuries they had enjoyed in several weeks. Neither the cold nor the mountains were like anything Brissie had experienced growing up in the small town of Ware Shoals, South Carolina. Brissie wore two woolen shirts and long underwear under his olive drab combat jacket, and two pairs of woolen socks inside his mud-specked boots. A few of the other soldiers had cut off ends of blankets to wear as scarves, and some wore overcoats. Corporal Brissie wore neither. He found both too confining. His helmet was strapped, his M-1 rifle was held lightly between his long, lean legs—he was 6'4½", weighed 205 pounds, and was called "Slim" by his buddies.

As the truck jounced along the rough road, there was apprehension to be sure among the infantrymen. For every mountain you climbed, Brissie had learned, there was a higher one in front. The Germans had dropped back and knew the exact distance to place their guns so their shells reached where you were. The 88th Division had been in Italy for more than a year and to that point had about a 90 percent casualty rate, with some 6,000 men killed, wounded, or missing. The Germans, amply armed, had spent six months digging themselves into caves, wrecked buildings, and rocky ridges. It was treacherous going for the G.I.s—but still there were the lighter moments, the expressions of anticipation when one day—one day—they would return home.

Brissie didn't remember any specific conversation that morning in the back of the truck, but it most likely was little different from some of the exchanges he'd frequently had.

Just the day before, as a group of soldiers sat around cleaning their rifles in a tent, Brissie was asked, "What are you gonna do when this is over?"

"I have a deal with the Philadelphia Athletics to pitch," he replied.

"Do you play with 'em?"

"No, I haven't played with 'em. But I'm gonna play with 'em."

"Well, by God, I better get some tickets, I'll tell you that!" said one.

"When I come to see you, are you gonna let people know that you know me? Or are you gonna go big time on me?" another soldier said.

And someone else piped up, "Yeah, sure, and I'm gonna pitch for the Yankees." It got a good laugh.

"We all have a dream or a hope," Brissie wrote home to his wife, Dot, which was short for Dorothy. They were married in April 1944, just two months before he was shipped out for combat duty, and both were 19 years old. "We all seemed to respect the other guys' dreams," he would recall. "But you always got the typical G.I. comments."

However, a few of his fellow soldiers smiled knowingly when he talked about pitching for the A's. They had seen him throw a baseball with uncommon strength and accuracy at the reception center in Naples where troops from the States landed. He was a left-handed pitcher who had spectacular success in semipro leagues, in college ball, and in organized military ballgames back home, after having enlisted following his freshman year at Presbyterian College in Clinton, South Carolina. A week after he graduated from high school, Brissie, to his great pleasure and apprehension, was invited up to Shibe Park in Philadelphia to throw for Connie Mack, the legendary manager and owner of the A's. Mack had owned and managed the A's since the American League was founded in 1901, leading them to nine American League championships. "Imagine," he thought to himself, "Me in an A's uniform, me pitching against DiMaggio and Williams, pitching against Feller and Ruffing." It was the kind of reverie he embraced since he was a little boy at home in Ware Shoals playing catch in the park with his uncle Robert.

Brissie was a pitching sensation from the time he was 14 years old, when he starred for the Riegel Textile Mill team in the fast and popular factory league. In his very first game for Riegel against the Greenwood Textile Mill—he was the only teenager on his team—he struck out 17 of the first 19 batters he faced. Later, on a good Camp Croft team against other army teams that fielded some major league players, Brissie, before being shipped out in the summer of 1944, compiled a 25-1 record with Camp Croft, averaged 20 strikeouts a game, and the Camp Croft team won the camp army tournament. (It was from his learning of those games that Connie Mack decided that Brissie's future, if there was to be one, lay as a pitcher and not as a first baseman, a position he also played at Presbyterian. Brissie said that it was his clear impression that Mack's view was "when you're able, or think you're able, I'll see that you get an opportunity to pitch for the A's." Brissie said that Mack "never guaranteed me anything. But that was certainly fair enough.")

Tall, lean, soft-spoken, and one of the most respected men in baseball—almost everyone called him "Mr. Mack"—Cornelius Alexander Mack (born McGillicuddy), then 78 and nearing his 60th year in professional baseball as player and manager, still wore a dark suit, the high, starched collar in turn-of-the-century fashion, and a straw hat even on the bench as he managed his teams. He rarely left the dugout during games, wigwagged signals with his scorecard to move his fielders into

4

position, and always sent one of his coaches to the mound when making a pitching change.

Brissie, who had turned 17 the week before that first appearance in Shibe Park, was awed to be in his presence, yet he impressed Mack with his crackling fastball and sharp breaking pitches and poise. Brissie's trip to Philadelphia was the only time he had been out of South Carolina, until he was shipped to Italy. Brissie now carried with him on the front lines of the war in Italy a hand-written letter that Mack had sent to his father, on letterhead that read, "American Base Ball Club of Philadelphia, Office of the President," a letter that Brissie had nearly memorized:

> *Aug 24th 1944*
>
> *Dear Mr. Brissie Sr.*
>
> *Many thanks for your nice letter and I will be more than pleased to write your dear son whom you and Mrs. Brissie should be so proud of. Was nice to have those two trophies presented for his splendid work. As things are looking so good at present time our hopes are that our club can have your son with us next season. It looks also at this time that our club will be greatly improved over this season.*
>
> *With kind regards, Sincerely yours, Connie Mack, president.*

Shortly after that, Brissie, sitting in a foxhole when the guns were silent, wrote a letter to Mack. In it he said that his ambition had always been to be a big-league pitcher for the A's. He told Mack that it looked like the war "could be over this year...." This was when Gen. George Patton, commander of the Third Army, "was going flat out across France," as Brissie expressed it. Like many of his fellow soldiers, he thought that they would be home by Christmas.

The "deal" that Brissie referred to in his earlier conversation with another G.I. was that Mack had agreed to pay for Brissie's three years in college (long enough to get a degree, at that time), and then he would join the A's organization after that, in 1945.

5

Mack responded to Corporal Brissie's letter:

> *Our club is still in need of a left hand pitcher, only hope you will be where you can still do a little work so that when you join our club the fans will forget such pitchers as Rube Waddell, Eddie Plank, and Grove.*
>
> *Note what you say about that fine Infantry you are connected with, only hope you will all survive the war in as good condition as you are now.*

To Brissie, Mack's comments about him and three of the greatest pitchers the A's ever had, came as "a shock." "I never knew I was that kind of prospect," he said.

Whether Mack just meant to lift the soldier's spirits or really meant what he said, there it was in black-and-white for Brissie to read in his foxhole—by now he had experienced numerous encounters with the enemy, often able to make out the outline of the German soldiers in the night by the flash of fire from their weapons.

But by the end of October the weather had gotten so cold, Brissie wrote home that, "they established what they called 'The Winter Line.'" The Americans had stopped trying to push ahead because the cold and the snow and the mud were so bad. At one point, they just couldn't move anything. Only mules could climb the mountains to bring provisions up to the soldiers and take the dead and wounded back down.

In November, Brissie wrote Mack the forlorn news: "Looks like we won't be getting home all that soon."

He wrote that "we were bogged down in France and Belgium. We were stuck for the winter. And after they stopped us in Italy in late October, we knew that there wasn't any way until spring that they were going to make any kind of push into the Po Valley and north." He added that there was no way that he would be getting back "in time for spring training, and getting back to baseball."

In the killing fields, Brissie, along with many of his fellow soldiers, looked forward to receiving the *Stars and Stripes*, the armed forces newspaper. "And the first thing I'd do when I got the paper was to see if it had a Bill Mauldin cartoon," Brissie recalled. "Most of us did the same."

Brissie said that Mauldin, who became particularly known among the troops for his "Willie and Joe" renderings of disheveled but determined G.I.s, "brought the reality of the war, along with a much-needed sense of humor. He knew what it was like. We might be laughing at them as we sat in a water-filled foxhole with rain soaking the paper."

Indeed, Mauldin, in his early 20s but with the youthful face of a teenager, in his army fatigues and steel helmet and drawing pad, traveled with combat infantry troops as they battled their way from Northern Africa, into Sicily, Italy, and France.

Brissie recalled several cartoons that made an impact on him, including one with Willie and Joe, seated among scraggly weeds, helmeted, rifles at rest, unshaven, wearing boots, their feet in mud, and Willie's arm tenderly tossed around Joe's shoulder, with Joe looking morose. "Joe," read the caption, "yestiddy ya saved my life an' I swore I'd pay ya back. Here's my last pair o' dry socks."

Brissie recalled: "Yes, dry socks were a premium. If your feet were wet for an extended period of time, you could get trench foot. In real cold weather, your feet would freeze. It could virtually paralyze you. I never had it, but I saw guys who did. Mauldin caught that reality of guys on the front line. It struck a chord of the harshness of war, but at the same time he was able to bring a smile to your face. He was a great gift to the World War II G.I. He made life more tolerable for every one of us in combat."

Brissie compared Mauldin to Ernie Pyle, the famed war correspondent. "Both of them were there with the troops, every step of the way. Both of them captured the essence of war."

In the first week of November 1944, Brissie and his unit were pulled back from the front for hot meals and a shower in a rest area near Montecatina. After three days, with replacements, they were returned to the front.

One squad out of each platoon in the 351st was sent ahead as what was called "a listening post," a buffer between the main body of troops and the German combat patrol unit.

Whatever reveries or small talk they had in the back of that truck, or existed in the several other trucks in the little convoy that wound its way through the resplendent, snowy Apennines on that December morning, they were suddenly interrupted by the numbing boom of a 170-millimeter artillery volley—the troops called them "bombs," for they were as lethal—and the instantaneous blaze of explosives.

The drivers slammed on their breaks. "Run for cover," Brissie shouted to his men.

They all leaped out of the truck. His group ran to one side of the road; others fled to the opposite side. They knew that that first shell was just to gauge the distance to the target; there was surely going to be another such volley.

Within moments there was: this shell burst with a shriek, the noise shattering to the ear, the earth erupting as if it had been dynamited. Brissie was slammed to the ground by the impact, his helmet knocked off, every button on his jacket sent flying. His clothes and boots were in tatters and in an instant his entire body felt as if it had just been struck with a jolt of electricity. Another howling shell exploded, and another. He couldn't move his left leg—he could see through the ripped pants that it had been nearly shredded from the knee to the ankle—but he had to move out of the line of fire. His only thought was not to be hit again.

He dragged his body along the snow-covered ground some 20 yards to a nearby creek, where the sloping bank gave him some protection. Blood was streaming from his nose and ears. He fought off the terrible pain as he forced his body down the bank and attempted to slosh through the shallow stream. Then he blacked out. He awoke after a period—he didn't know how long. ("My watch stopped at 10:50 AM; I still have it," Brissie recalled.) He crawled some more, and nearly made it out of the creek, but got no farther. He lay facedown in the mud and snow, his upper body on the bed of the creek but his legs still in the shallow creek. He turned and looked down and saw his right boot sticking out of the water, caked with blood and saw nothing of his left foot. He didn't know if the foot had been blown off. "It's hard to describe the feeling of turning over and not seeing your foot," Brissie recalled. He said a prayer for the foot not to be gone and began to hallucinate. He thought about being at his grandparents' home for a holiday dinner, one of the most pleasant memories of his childhood, and everyone in the family sitting around the table, with one empty chair. Everyone, in this dream, was looking at him to take his seat. Then he blacked out again.

He lay there like that for some eight hours.

When the German mortar onslaught finally subsided, medical corpsmen went through the area looking to see what help they could offer. The dead were strewn along the road and the mountainside. In the fading light, several corpsmen, part of what was called a "graves registration team," carrying folded stretchers to the scene and then unfolding them to carry the bodies away, passed a sprawled body lying halfway in the creek, and moved on, leaving it for dead. One medic, however, double-checking, retracing his steps, now noticed something unusual among the bodies. "Hey," he shouted, "this one moved." It was the one half-submerged in the creek.

They carried Corporal Brissie, half-conscious, onto a stretcher, placed the stretcher across the hood of a jeep, and rushed him back for emergency treatment to a battalion aid station about a mile away.

On the road back, however, the jeep was a target of more of the powerful, 88-millimeter German mortar strikes. The air bursts exploded, scattering shrapnel 360 degrees. One of those bursts detonated at the front of the jeep, making the driver swerve off the road and throwing Brissie from the stretcher into a snow bank. He hit the back of his head on a rock, bruised his neck, fractured a vertebrae, and suffered more shrapnel wounds in his right shoulder.

The medics pulled Brissie back on the stretcher, again placed him across the hood of the jeep, and raced to the safety of the aid station.

Brissie went in and out of consciousness. He remembered waking up in the aid station. It was close to dark and a chaplain was kneeling over him. With a Bible in his hand, the chaplain was praying. Brissie was shaken. "I didn't know if he was saying the last rites, or what he was doing," recalled Brissie.

Brissie didn't have time to ask. Doctors appeared and immediately administered blood transfusions. The medical report on his injuries stated that he had been hit with 21 mortar fragments: "Left leg broken between knee and ankle; both feet broken; left ankle broken; contusions in right thigh bone and left thigh bone; shrapnel in each hand and shoulder; concussion."

Then several doctors looked over his left leg with the gaping wound and suspected it was already infested with bacteria. While Brissie had clawed his way to the creek, his leg had become caked with dirt and mud.

"Immediate resuscitation and blood plasma followed by transport to field hospital facilities provided ligatures to the most serious bleed vessels," a field doctor wrote in a monograph. "In the entire history of warfare prior to WWII, this type off massive injury which Brissie sustained at his leg was invariably managed by surgical amputation."

Gangrene, Brissie was told, would likely set in. As he lay on the makeshift operating table, intravenous tubes connected to his arms, the doctors agreed on the decision: The leg could not be saved. Amputation was necessary.

The surgeon broke the news to him.

"No," Brissie protested. "You can't take my leg off. I'm a ballplayer. I can't play on one leg."

"You will die if we don't."

"Doc," he said quietly, "I'll take my chances."

2

Saving a Limb

1.

From the window nearest his bed in a ward in the 300th General Hospital, the large army facility in Naples (it was formerly a tuberculosis hospital), Cpl. Lou Brissie could see the smoke rising from Mount Vesuvius. The ancient volcanic mountain that destroyed the town of Pompeii centuries earlier had lain dormant for years but steamed and rumbled for most of 1944. "How appropriate," thought Brissie. "It's smoking as the battles raged in the area." For Brissie, however, one battle was over—that of the warfare on the front; and another was beginning, that of trying to save his leg so he could somehow realize his dreams of, first, walking again, and, then—clinging to what seemed nearly impossible—becoming a major league pitcher.

Before Naples, Brissie was treated at two hospitals near Florence as well as the aid station where he had first been transported after he was found breathing fitfully in the snow and mud of a creek in the Apennines. Every doctor who observed his wound said the same thing: the leg has to be amputated.

While he was lying in bed in one of the hospitals in Florence, a cadre of officers came by, just as they did for other patients in his ward, and presented him with a Purple Heart with an oak leaf cluster for the wounds he sustained in the two shellings. Later he was given the Bronze Star Medal, awarded to United States fighting men for heroic or meritorious achievement or service in combat.

Brissie recalled: "They pinned the medal on you, and they'd give you the case with it and everything so you could take it off and keep it, or mail it home, or whatever. I always felt I was so lucky to even have made it. I felt as I did when I went into the service, that anything you earned was an honor. It's the way your country says, 'Thanks.' When I left home, my dad said, 'Good luck, son. Do your duty.' I hoped I had."

Brissie looked back on his combat experience that was only weeks behind him and thought about the fears of facing enemy artillery, and the fortitude it took to stand up to it: "I think the feeling of being in that brings out the uncertainty in you, how scared you can be. But I saw some magnificent things. You see guys—and it's true in all wars—that virtually do the impossible under the most horrendous conditions. I guess the classic example would be Audie Murphy. This guy virtually stopped a regimental attack. He crawled up on the back of that tank and it was already burning, and he got a hold of that 50-caliber machine gun and some guy on the radio said to him, 'How close are they?' And he says, 'Well, wait a minute and I'll let you talk to them.' To remain that cool in the face of death was unbelievable." (Murphy became the most decorated U.S. combat soldier of World War II, receiving the Medal of Honor, the military's highest award for valor, along with 32 additional U.S. medals.)

Other soldiers, exposed for the first time to the sights and sounds of warfare—the gunfire, the rubble, and the physical destruction of the Italian countryside—reacted differently from Audie Murphy and Lou Brissie. "I had heard how some guys were so frozen with fear that when it was time to move, they couldn't move," he said. "They'd just hunker down and stay there. Some would run away from battle. Others showed up after a battle and said they'd gotten into the wrong area. Some guys called them 'shy.' Fear was a part of our everyday existence, of everybody's, I believe, though it wasn't something talked about very much. It was felt."

In Brissie's thoughts the stark, recent past intermingled with a cloudy future. And that future had a lot to do with the preservation of his leg. The doctors, against their better judgment, had for the time being given in to Brissie's pleadings to try to save his leg. They felt that he wasn't in immediate danger and that a few days or a week more of examinations would ease the patient's fears to a degree. In fact, however, after several blood transfusions and immobilization of the left leg, he was feeling somewhat improved. He was then flown to Naples and arrived at the military's largest hospital in Italy. Brissie understood that this would be his last chance to save his leg.

It was December 10, just three days after he had been hit by the shell. He was brought into a crowded ward so full there wasn't an empty bed. Outside of every ward was an open deck that allowed patients to sit in sunlight and fresh air, which had been used for TB cases. There were no TB cases now. There were primarily combat soldiers with amputated limbs and severe burns. And Lou Brissie.

The X-rays revealed that all the muscles and tendons in his left leg were gone. And while amputation was still considered the paramount option, doctors were still able to calm the infection with penicillin—the miraculous new antibiotic drug—long enough for specialists in Naples to check over the leg, to see if in fact it could be saved.

It was a question, Brissie reasoned, of whether or not they could find all the parts and figure out how to fit them back where they belonged.

A medic came by to see how Brissie was doing, and told him, "You're lucky, man. All 11 of the guys in your squad are dead. They got it in the throat and the head." Later he received other information that three of the 11 had actually survived, along with him. He learned that one of the four officers in his company, riding in other trucks, had been killed and two others wounded.

He wondered about his luck and felt a stab of guilt, a survivor's guilt that he would experience off and on for the rest of his life. This was a not uncommon emotion among survivors of combat. "Why was I saved and not the others?" he wondered. "And I knew that the families of some of those guys I was with would be getting the medals sent to them, and what kind of solace, if any, would that bring them?"

But now the survival instinct had become Brissie's strongest impulse. And this is what he expressed to the surgeon, Capt. Wilbur K. Brubaker, when the doctor first came to his bedside the afternoon of his arrival in Naples. A dark-haired, well-groomed, rather formal man, Dr. Brubaker picked up Brissie's medical chart and, without looking at the patient, said that amputation appeared the only alternative in order to save his life. Brissie repeated the plea he had made at his several hospital stops, a pleading that drew time and sympathy. He also knew that this conversation would most likely be his last chance at making his case to save his leg.

"I'm a ballplayer and I want to save my leg," Brissie said to Brubaker. "You're not gonna take it off, are you?"

Brubaker never looked up. He kept reading and finally said, "We'll see about that tomorrow." He added, "Now get a good night's rest because I'm going to see you early in the morning." He read some more of the chart, put it down, and said, "See you in the morning. We'll operate and do the best we can do."

And Brissie just lay there, wondering: what's the best they can do?

Brissie's tibia (the main bone of the lower leg) was, as Dr. Brubacker viewed it, essentially a sea of splintered bone fragments swimming in metal shrapnel. The bone was exposed to the surface of a gaping wound, leaving it open to recurrent infection (osteomyelitis) which, fortunately, could be treated with penicillin, the first antibiotic agent to be used successfully in the treatment of bacterial infections in man.

Dr. Brubaker ordered immediate, round-the-clock shots of penicillin. Brissie became the first recipient of the "wonder drug" in the Mediterranean Theater.

Osteomyelitis, in fact, had settled into Brissie's leg. "It's a bacterial infection of the bone," his doctor explained. "If it gets into the blood, it can kill you." Thus the use of penicillin.

The doctors were deeply concerned about osteomyelitis because once it settles into the system, one may never get rid of it. Many doctors prescribe amputation because osteomyelitis can become a chronic debilitating condition.

Osteomyelitis could, said Brissie, get "right painful." The doctors were also worried about circulation—would there be enough in the mangled limb?

Brissie was taken down to the operating room on the morning of December 11, desperately unsure of the results. If they take my leg off, what kind of life will I be able to lead? Would Dot want me this way? "And," recalled Brissie, "I thought, 'If I can't pitch, why live?'"

While he could refuse amputation, he also thought of himself living a slow, painful death from gangrene. What was left for Brissie was simply the hope, the prayer—the miracle—that the doctors could successfully treat the leg wound. He was not aware of anything that transpired after that in the operating room until later that afternoon, when he awoke in his hospital bed in the ward.

He looked down at the end of the bed and saw under the covers two lumps. "I wanted to shout with joy," he said. Instead he lay back on his pillow with a smile on his face. Hip-to-toe plaster casts were applied to both of Brissie's legs. And in his daily rounds, Brubaker told Brissie that all went reasonably well in the operation—it looked like wiring back parts of his leg was effective, but Brubaker knew only time would tell if it would stay that way. While fragments of bone without blood supply had been removed, Brubaker discerned that there would have to be several more operations to try to save the leg. It is likely that Brissie was the first person to ever escape amputation with this kind of injury, because of the penicillin and his elaborate surgeries. "Even though I couldn't walk," recalled Brissie, "I thought this was a very good first step."

Dreams of home, and hopes for a future in baseball, were kept alive, not only in Brissie's imagination but by another letter he received in his hospital bed in Naples from Connie Mack, written on club stationery before the A's owner-manager knew that Brissie had been wounded:

Dec. 12, 1944

Cpl. L. V. Brissie
Co. G, 351 Inf. APO 88
c/o Postmaster,
New York, N.Y.

Dear Lefty:

Was pleased to receive your letter of November 7th
  Attended the World Series at St. Louis, the games were
well played and the best club won although they had to work

15

hard in every game played. Marion was the real star of both teams. The newspapers are now classifying him with Honus Wagner, as a matter of fact, some feel that he is even better, however, I doubt this, due to Wagner being a great batsman as well as base runner.

Am pleased to know that you had a chance to play some baseball....

Occasionally hear from your friend "Chick" Galloway. Gregg is now somewhere in the Armed Service as well as Clyde. Rollins will be my utility infielder this coming year.

Will be pleased to hear from you whenever you can find time to write.

With very best wishes,
Sincerely yours,
Connie Mack,
President

The letters from Dot and his family were of a different nature, telling of the daily occurrences in home life in South Carolina that made him so desirous to return to, as he said, "being normal."

Brissie had met Dot Morgan on a weekend leave when a friend of his at Camp Croft in Spartanburg, South Carolina, where he had been stationed before going overseas, had invited him to his home, which was also in Spartanburg.

"You'll get a home-cooked meal," the friend said.

"Can't turn an offer like that down," said Brissie. "Love to go."

Not only were the meals appealing, but so was the girlfriend of the fellow soldier's sister. "Dot" (full name Dorothy) was tall (about 5'7"), dark-haired, dark-eyed, fair complexion with a slight smattering of freckles, trimly built. Dot and Lou, in his Army uniform, felt a mutual attraction. "It was instantaneous," recalled Brissie. "She had a gift that she was easy to talk to, and understanding. There was this sense of character about her. And she was very good looking."

They dated, mostly on weekends, since his military duties consumed the weekdays, as did her work as a secretary in a law office in town. They went to movies, went to church social hours and the church social "drop-ins" for soldiers, and danced there to songs on the jukebox like "Cheek to Cheek." They took walks holding hands along the Wofford College campus in downtown Spartanburg, went to an occasional restaurant (the less expensive the better in consideration of his private's salary), and had dinners at her parents' wood-frame house on Sunday. And sometimes they'd sit after dinner in the Morgans' family room and listen to the radio, to some of the music and dramas, like *The Shadow* and *The Green Hornet*. There wasn't a great deal of entertainment available in those war-time days. But Dot and Lou didn't need much; they had fallen in love. One night, on a bench on the Wofford campus, under what he remembered was a warm, starry South Carolina night, Brissie proposed marriage, and Dot, with little hesitation, said yes. The 19-year-old teenagers decided not to wait to be married. An underlying, if sometimes unstated, notion surely was that in these dangerous times life may be all too brief.

"They decided to elope," recalled their daughter Vicki Brissie Bishop, years later. "But they didn't go very far." In fact, they stayed in Spartanburg. And on April 16, 1944, at the home of the minister of the Presbyterian Church, where the two had worshiped together, Dot Morgan and Lou Brissie were married. There was no one else in attendance. "I remember my mother telling me that after the ceremony, 'He went back to the army and I went home, thinking, my mother's going to kill me.'"

Brissie understood that he would be assigned to overseas duty in the coming months, after their marriage. Nonetheless Dot suggested that they try to have a child.

"It wouldn't be fair to you or the baby," said Brissie. "If I don't come back, you'd be a single mother bringing up a child."

"You'll come back," she said.

"Let's wait, honey, and hope for the best."

Dot, after thought, agreed. Their letters to and from the Italian front were of a general nature, and underwent scrutiny from military censors—his letters especially being left unspecific. Brissie said: "You couldn't tell anybody where you were or what you were doing, so you wrote about what it's like as far as conditions were concerned and that things were going well and not to worry. You couldn't refer to specific places. You couldn't write that 'I went to St. Peter's and I'm in Rome and it's beautiful.' You might be able to say 'the old buildings here are beautiful.' You really had to generalize a lot of things because you never knew if the letters would be intercepted by the enemy and your locations revealed."

The letters from Dot were, of course, a highlight for him on the combat front, waiting as he did at mail call for one to arrive. She wrote nearly every day. He could picture her at the desk in her bedroom, her auburn hair spilling over her shoulder, and a silver bracelet on her thin wrist jiggling slightly as she held the pen in writing to him.

Brissie listened to the radio when he was at the front; it played American music and was interrupted when Axis Sally cut in. Axis Sally, as she was called by the American soldiers, was the German counterpart to the Pacific Theater's Tokyo Rose. Axis Sally was actually an American born in Portland, Maine, but was studying in Berlin when war broke out and decided to stay and work for the Nazi regime. She had a seductive voice and sought to undermine the American soldiers' morale in Europe by telling them via the scratchy air waves that, among other things, they should be worried about their girlfriends or wives cheating on them at home.

"And some guys did worry," said Brissie. "But that was just their nature. A guy would get a letter and you'd say, 'Is everything okay at home?' And he'd say 'Well, I don't know....' Or 'I think so,' or 'Uh, yeah.' But you really didn't get too personal with very many guys. It was really a strange thing, because even though you and your buddies depend on each other to save one another's lives, essentially, you'd never know when you might lose them. It's difficult when you live next to a guy, hunkered down with him in a foxhole, and then one day he's not there and you gotta leave him laying on the ground. How do you walk away from a guy that's become as close as that to you—who might have saved your life more than once. Then one day he gets hit and you just gotta leave him layin' there. Those are the most difficult times. Some things you couldn't do anything about, and some you might have. You wonder about them. You know, 'Was I right?' It's a terrible feeling. But we'd have some talks. And I know when Axis Sally would play something like the Glenn Miller song, 'Don't Sit Under the Apple Tree with Anyone Else, But Me,' or 'Til I Come Marchin' Home....' that this disturbed some guys, made them think about home in hurtful ways. That was never a concern of mine, not really. I thought from the beginning that Dot and I had a loving—and trusting—relationship.

"But any letter about the family, or what the family was doing, touched you. You could visualize it. 'We went over to Granddad's today and had dinner. And so-and-so, and so-and-so were there and asked how you were doing....' Sometimes, on the front or in the hospital, you could almost smell the cooking back home. It could bring tears to your eyes."

From both ends, the letters would invariably end with, "looking forward" to coming home, and "I miss you."

In moments of reflection, of living nightmares, really, Brissie would relive recent, agonizing experiences. One that continued to play on his mind as he lay on his hospital bed occurred shortly after Thanksgiving Day, only about a week before he was wounded.

His squad had been stationed at an outpost, living in a bombed-out Italian house on the front, when Brissie got a call on his phone from Capt. T.E. Sears, his company commander. He said, "President Roosevelt said that regardless of where their husband, their father, their son, or whatever was assigned, that they'd get a traditional Thanksgiving Day dinner today." There would be turkey and dressing and cranberry sauce. (This was on the last day of November, when Thanksgiving was held on that day, rather than the last Thursday of the month as it is currently observed.) Captain Sears said, "First Sergeant Hodges and I are going to come up and see you after dark, and we're gonna bring you and your guys a turkey dinner." "We're ready for turkey!" Brissie said.

So Sears came up with a couple of soldiers carrying containers that kept the food hot. And there was a young guy with them. Captain Sears introduced him to Brissie with "This is your replacement. Your squad has been operating a man short, operating with only 11 men."

"I said, 'Fine, okay,'" recalled Brissie. "We had our turkey dinner. And, after that, I said to the new replacement, 'I'm going to put you on outpost.' He was going to be a look-out. His name was William Bowen, and he was from a town in Indiana, where he had enlisted. He was slight of build and had a boyish face—he was only about 18, maybe a year or two younger than me. I said to him, 'Now, when it gets close to daylight or thereabouts, if you hear anything, do not walk out to see what you can see. This is what the 85th Division told us, that guys can get shot doing that. And so you just stay where you are and be alert.' I had also put him with our most experienced soldier, a Pfc. named Chase, and the two of them were to stay together. There was a six-foot-high wall that was part of the building which hadn't been destroyed. I told him to stay behind it no matter what, and told Chase to make sure he does it.

"Bowen said he understood. I said to him, 'I'm sure you're a little nervous, but we all are. That's the nature of things here. We have to live with it.' He nodded, and I left it at that.

"Around daybreak, I was sleeping in the basement of the house with the other guys, the safest place to be, when we heard a shot. Then I heard someone calling out, 'Help me! Somebody, help me!' I raced up to see what had happened and there, some 100 feet from the house, that kid lay sprawled in the snow. He'd been shot by a German sniper. I grabbed my helmet and my rifle—I had my boots on, we never took our boots off—and I crawled out to get him. I didn't know if that sniper still had a bead on us, but it was what I had to do; it was what I was trained to do. Sure, I was scared, but we had been fighting all the time and there was always apprehension. We learned: keep your head down, keep low to the ground. That was my only thought. When I got to him I took him by the collar and dragged him back to the house—tried to get to shelter as fast as I could. I heard another shot just as we made it to the building and slid behind a half-broken wall. Bowen had been hit in the chest. We tried to dress his wounds, but we couldn't get anybody up there—there were no medics. All we had was our meager first aid, and that wasn't good enough. There was no way we could get him back to the battalion aid station, which was several hundred yards away. It was open ground. And the fella died within minutes, bled to death. Chase said, 'I tried to tell him not to go out, but he wouldn't listen.'

"I wondered, 'Did I do enough? Was I emphatic enough to him, not to go out when he heard something?' He pretty much died in my arms. I had his blood on my shirt. I've thought about that a lot. It's a painful memory." Such unremitting recollections, along with the throbbing pain of his body, were all part of Brissie's daily life in the hospital ward.

2.

On the evening after the operation, Dr. Brubaker returned to Brissie's bedside to reiterate the precarious state of injury to the leg, and that he would be given regular doses of penicillin. But he reassured him that every possible medical support would be given to try to avoid amputation.

Brubaker said that although there was no solid bone in more than four inches of his left leg, he wired together the torn bone and stitched together the ripped muscles and severed tendons. "It went pretty well," Brubaker said. "But let's see how it goes in the next few weeks."

It seemed a simple, almost unemotional response by the doctor, but he was just the cautious man of science. Brissie understood the implications. He wasn't out of the woods, but surely there was, in sight, a clearing. Brissie brimmed with emotion.

"Thank you, doctor," said Brissie. "Thank you." That was all he could muster.

Brissie endured five operations to his leg in the next four months. With the grafting of bone and other surgical manipulations deemed essential, the leg was left three-quarters of an inch shorter than his right. Brissie was still unable to walk on it and remained bedridden.

Between operations, Brissie wrote from his hospital bed to his uncle George Forrester in South Carolina, who sent the letter to "Scoop"

Latimer, sports columnist of the *Greenville Gazette*, who printed it. Latimer had covered Brissie when he pitched sensationally for a semi-pro team in the Central Carolina League, and followed him as a dominating pitcher with Riegel and at Camp Croft. Latimer—he once called Leland Brissie "Lou" in a column and the name stuck—quoted Brissie in the column. "I'll play again, but it will be quite a while," Brissie wrote. "Don't worry, I want to play ball. If God lets me walk again, I'll play, too. That's my ambition. I'll be O.K. in time."

"You can't beat that kind of spirit and determination in a boy," wrote Latimer. "He is the nephew of George W. Forrester of Mauldin, to whom we're indebted for a note to say that Brissie was 'doing fine,' as a boy of Lou's cheerfulness and undaunted courage would express it."

Each day, with operation following operation, Brissie experienced frustratingly slow recovery, despite his optimism. His goal of pitching for the Athletics, Brubaker understood, appeared remote, at best. But Brubaker sympathized with the young man's ambition. The man of science was hardly so cold as to not be moved by the will and courage of his young patient. Dr. Brubaker would do everything he could to save the leg.

Brissie received encouragement from fellow patients, one of whom was Captain Sears. "He'd come by my bed and we'd visit a bit," said Brissie. "He truly cared about his men, and it was good to see him. He had suffered shrapnel in his foot in the same action as mine and had trouble walking. The last time he came by, he said he was being returned to the States, was going to land in Charleston, and asked for my family's phone number. When he got back, he called them."

In late January, Brissie received another letter from Connie Mack, dated January 16, 1945.

Dear Lefty:

Pleased to receive your letters of December 23rd and 28th, however, regret exceedingly to hear that you met with such a serious injury and am glad that you are getting along so well.

*Am in hopes you will be ready, if necessary, to continue
your baseball and basketball playing this summer. The doctors can do great things today as they have already proven by
their work in helping some of our boys.*

Have heard from Bob Savage who was wounded the
second time. He expected to be able to leave the hospital by
Christmas.*

*It was mighty nice of you to remember me on my birthday
after all you have been through. Would like to have you keep
me posted on your condition, however, do not overtax yourself
by doing too much writing.*

With very best wishes for a speedy recovery.

Sincerely yours,

CONNIE MACK,
President

Fifteen days later, Mack wrote again to his wounded pitching prospect in the Naples hospital, and the familiarity of the salutation "Lefty"
gave way to the respectful "Corporal Brissie" (perhaps in respect and
admiration for the battle he was waging in the hospitals):

January 31, 1945

*Cpl. L. V. Brissie
2618 Hosp. Section APO 698
c/o Postmaster
New York, N.Y.*

Dear Corporal Brissie:

*Was very pleased to hear of your improvement and from
what your doctor states, your recovery is going along very
satisfactorily. Am always pleased to hear from you, more so*

---

* Bob Savage was a rookie pitcher who appeared in eight games with the A's in 1942,
and compiled an 0–1 record before enlisting in the army.

now than ever, so please keep on writing as I am interested in your condition.

Can understand your longing to play baseball, just keep up this feeling as it will go a long way in helping your present condition. You can be assured of our looking after your schooling. Would want you to finish and receive your college diploma before joining our club, therefore, do not worry about the future as you will be well cared for after leaving the Army. The main thing now is your health, just keep on the way you are and everything will turn out as you may desire.

Am sorry to hear that you missed out in seeing Durocher,* Medwick and the boys who made the trip to Italy and France as you would have enjoyed hearing their stories of sporting events that had taken place since you left the States.

Am expecting Earl Brucker to call most any day and will inform him that you intend to do some real pitching for the club in the near future. From all accounts Marchildon is going all right although he is in a German camp. Do not suppose you ran across Dan Savage, he was in a hospital in Italy, wounded a second time and the last I heard from him he expected to be discharged from the hospital last December and expected to rejoin his Company.

With best wishes,

Sincerely yours,

CONNIE MACK,
President

---

* Leo Durocher, the Dodgers' manager, and Joe "Ducky" Medwick, then a Giants outfielder, were giving baseball clinics for American soldiers in Europe to buoy their spirits and give them a taste of home. Phil Marchildon was a right-handed pitching ace for the A's, and went 17–14 in 1942, before enlisting in the army in his home country, Canada. Mack got Savage's first name wrong in this letter, writing "Dan" instead of "Bob."

The reason for Mack's optimism about what the doctors said about the young corporal's improvement came, perhaps, in an overly optimistic letter from Brissie himself—after all, the leg had not been removed. But Mack's return letter "really put octane in my mind," Brissie later recalled. "I was excited and enthused about it. The idea that I would have the 'opportunity' to be a major league pitcher with the A's really lifted my spirits," said Brissie. "What more could anyone ask for than the opportunity? At this point, I believed my leg to be saved. And my thoughts now were not whether I could pitch with a bum leg—but how. I was determined to find a way."

The man in a bed beside Brissie's was Watuda Oye, a member of the 442nd Regimental Combat Team, an Asian American unit (comprised primarily of Japanese Americans) that had fought with great distinction in Europe and North Africa. The 442nd was the most highly decorated unit of its size and length of service in the history of the U.S. Army—even while many of the soldiers' family members, including Oye's, were subjected to internment camps in America.

Oye had been shot in the back with machine gun fire and had lain in bed since September. Brissie and Oye talked in the night about their ambitions for the future. Oye hoped to be a painter, an artist. "We'd be talking in the dark, and on painful nights we shared our complaints, our concerns, our doubts, and our dreams, and thinking this was a private conversation," said Brissie. "We had been through a lot, like all the others had, and then we'd see a flame, with someone lighting up a cigarette. Then another and another. It was like fireflies. And we realized that three-quarters of the ward was listening to us. Oye and I became close, and his courage, patience, and perseverance inspired me during the times I became discouraged. His sense of humor helped, too."

One morning, Brissie recalled, a nurse was changing the sheets on his bed while a medical assistant, Pfc. Manuel Quintana, stood beside her. Oye was lying in the adjoining bed. When the nurse bent over to smooth the sheet Oye reached out and pinched her buttocks, with his toes. The nurse wheeled around and slapped Pfc. Quintana in the face. He was shocked.

"What's that for?" he said.

She glared at him. "Don't you ever do that again!"

"Do what?"

"She was so mad," recalled Brissie, "she wouldn't speak to him."

"The thing about Oye," added Brissie, "was that he could manipulate his toes the way the rest of us work our fingers. And the temptation the nurse presented was just too great for Oye. We laughed for days about that incident."

Meanwhile, 17 fragments of metal had been removed from Brissie's body. Eventually the number of pieces totaled 21. During his three months in Italian hospitals, Brissie underwent 30 blood transfusions and 12 operations: one on his right shoulder, one each on both hands, one on his right foot, one on his right thigh, one on his left thigh, and six on his left leg from his knee to his ankle.

Finally, in late January, Brubaker came to Brissie one night and said, "Things are looking pretty good. You'll be leaving for the States tomorrow."

A friend of Brissie's in the hospital, Joe Kane, who was wounded in the foot and wore a walking cast, said, "Well, Slim, you'll be home in a couple of weeks." "Sooner than that," said Dr. Brubaker. "Lou, you won't be going by ship, you'll be flying home."

A report from Brubaker read: "Repeated operative removal of devitalized bone fragments were necessary but, after 6 weeks of therapy, there came a time when ultimate closure of the leg wound could be accomplished, and a long leg cast applied so that Brissie could be sent to (a) medical facility in Eastern USA."

Before Brissie left the Naples hospital, Brubaker later wrote, he had these thoughts about his young patient: "So vastly did he impress me with his courage and disposition, that I made him a promise: 'I've been a Cleveland rooter all my life, but from now on I'm pulling for you whenever you pitch. Even if it should be against the Indians.'"

Before Brissie left the hospital, he saw his friend Watuda Oye, with whom he had shaken hands and said good-bye, now sitting in his wheelchair on the sunlit porch, mixing his colors and about to paint a picture of Mount Vesuvius. It was the first time in six months that Oye had been out of bed.

As Brissie was being wheeled out of the hospital, Oye happened to turn and saw him. They gave each other a thumbs-up. "I'd never see him again," recalled Brissie. "But I'd never forget him."

Lou Brissie was headed to America, on a stretcher, both legs in casts, in an Army DC-4 transport plane with some 30 other stretcher-bound G.I.s. "They put the more severe medical problems on planes because they didn't want them to be at sea for 14 days," recalled Brissie. "Some of them had arms blown off, others were in severe body casts. And if they needed something they were going to need it right quick on the plane, or when we landed."

On the plane there was, said Brissie, "a high degree of expectation, of anticipation. 'Oh, yeah. We're going home!'"

The transport carrying Brissie and the other wounded soldiers from Naples to Mitchel Air Force Base on Long Island, outside of New York City, in late March 1945 made its first of three stops en route in Casablanca.

"That afternoon there was a nearly cloudless blue sky, and I could see North Africa in the distance from my window on the plane," Brissie recalled. "I wondered if we were near the grave of Robert. He was like a brother to me." Robert Brissie, who was two years older than Lou, and Robert's brother, Gene, five years older than Lou—his father's two youngest brothers—had lived with Lou and his parents through much of Brissie's childhood. "My father had three sisters and six brothers, and when times were hard, my dad took in his younger brothers to help out his parents," recalled Brissie. He was close with both of those uncles. "I was an only child," he recalled, "but with Robert and Gene in the house I never felt that way."

Gene and Robert enlisted in the army right after Pearl Harbor, in December 1941. Lou wanted to enlist, too. "But I was only 17, and my parents wouldn't let me," he said. Two years later, when he was of age, Lou signed up at his local draft board. During the war, Gene was an ensign in the Pacific, serving on both the USS *Arkansas* and the USS *Bunker Hill*, the latter an aircraft carrier that had been the target of a kamikaze attack that killed 400 of the crew. Gene survived. Robert was in the infantry and assigned to combat duty. He died in the North

Africa campaign, in 1943, fighting against the forces of German field marshal Erwin Rommel, the famed "Desert Fox."

Robert was Brissie's "first catcher." As a boy he threw to Robert for hours in the pasture near his home. Their not-so-secret plan was to go to the big leagues together. They talked about it often. "I was determined that one day," recalled Brissie, "I would return to visit Robert's grave."

The DC-4 had been flying for more than eight hours—with stops for refueling in Casablanca, the Azores, and Bermuda—when the nurse on the plane came by and said, "Boys, we're getting close to the mainland and there's a greeting committee of one waiting to welcome you guys home. The major is going to make sure everyone will see it—because Lady Liberty wants to welcome you home."

The plane flew around the Statue of Liberty twice, so that soldiers on both sides of the plane, rising up on their elbows, could see it from their windows. Brissie recalled:

"The soldiers became perfectly quiet. Before this, there was a lot of usual banter. Now there was silence, as though someone had pulled a switch. You could hear a pin drop—not a single word, not even a grunt, all the way around the statue, both ways. It stayed quiet. But it was just too much for us to handle, and the tears came.

"When the plane landed at Mitchel Air Force Base and taxied to a stop, the major and his copilot walked out of the pilot's cabin—huge applause from us! And you had guys there with one hand! They were pounding their chests. When the pilots walked down that aisle, you heard, 'Thank you, Sir, thank you.' And 'Good goin', Major, good goin'.

"It was a thoughtful, thoughtful gesture, going around the Statue of Liberty," Brissie said. "Soldiers who had hidden and shielded their emotions for so long had been gifted with a view of the one thing that symbolized what their country had stood for, what we had fought for. No matter where you were from, no matter your background, no matter your religion, whatever we believed in and wherever we came from, we all knew what that statue represented: home."

3

The Contraband

1.

Following his return to the States, Brissie was taken to Finney General Hospital, in Thomasville, Georgia, near the Florida panhandle. When he arrived at the hospital in early April 1945, one of the nurses rolled his wheelchair from the entrance to Ward B where he was to stay. She stopped at a desk to get his chart to see which bed he was assigned. To the left of the desk was a small kitchen, where a man was eating at a table. The kitchen was where short-orders could be fixed. The nurse saw that Brissie was to be taken to bed 16 and was about to move on when the fellow in the kitchen, a baldish man wearing T-shirt, khaki pants, and paratrooper boots, waved hello to Brissie and got up to greet him.

He was thin with a pale complexion, due perhaps to the pain that Brissie learned that he had endured. His name was Morgan Waters, and he was from Jacksonville, Florida.

He said to Brissie, "You just get here?"

"Yeah," Brissie replied. "I just came from Italy."

"I was in Italy, too—if I know the army they haven't fed you much on the way down here."

"We had a sandwich earlier."

"Hungry? How 'bout a couple of scrambled eggs and some bacon and toast? I'll cook it up for you."

"Sounds good to me," said Brissie.

Brissie was exhausted from the travel, and he was rolled back to his bed to rest. Waters fixed him bacon and eggs and brought them to his bed at about 9:30 at night.

Waters was a private, and about 10 years older than Brissie. Waters may have been busted a few times—he was a free spirit—or, like some soldiers, he just turned down promotions because he didn't want the responsibility. Some men were content to just do their job and not tell others to do theirs. Brissie and Waters, however, never discussed it. Some things were better left unsaid. "But he was a good guy, a really good guy," said Brissie, "and he had been a brave soldier. Had to have been. He'd been in the 82nd and was hit at Anzio in March 1944. Tore out his shoulder and he couldn't raise his arm above his elbow. It was osteomyelitis and just would not heal, drained all the time. And when it starts draining, the odor was terrible.

"Waters and I became tight friends."

After about 10 days in Finney General, the right foot cast was removed while the left leg cast remained, and Brissie attempted to walk with crutches and two hospital aides. "My first steps were awfully painful—after all, I hadn't used those muscles in about four months," he recalled. He made it to the bed next to his, and then stopped. "I couldn't go on. They had to get a wheelchair and roll me back to my bed." But every day he did just a little more, and a little more. His goal was to get himself to the bathroom, which was at the far end of the corridor. He didn't know if he ever would, but he sure was going to try. And while the pain was great as he tried to be mobile again, he endured without pain medication. "I had been given painkillers when I was first injured," Brissie recalled. "But I didn't like them. I felt I had someone else's brain in my head." He never took them again.

"All of us in the hospital were there because of serious injury," said Brissie. "It was a shared community of understanding and empathy. When I thought of guys in the hospital later I thought of them in the context of what we were as a group. We were different when we were together, the guys in the hospital. You could always look in either direction and see a guy who was worse off than you were. We each had our battles, and each one was somewhat different from yours. But there was a togetherness.

"Different kinds of wounds would create different kinds of problems. You had to come to terms with what problems you had, as Waters tried, as I did. Other guys, for example, that were burned, knew that they would never look the same again. But they resigned themselves to that if they wanted to return somewhat to a way of life that they had once known. It was all about dealing with your situation and trying to somehow overcome, to make the best of it. It was everybody's wish to get normal. But we all had our doubts, not only whether we'd get 'normal' again, but how the world outside the hospital would view us."

And Brissie had those thoughts, those doubts about his wife, Dot, and how she would view him now, an invalid. About a week after Brissie had arrived at Finney, Dot and his parents made the some 350-mile drive from Ware Shoals to Thomasville, near the Florida panhandle. It was a long drive in his father's black 1936 Packard, about eight hours along those old roads. Dot had moved from Spartanburg to Ware Shoals after Brissie left for war, and moved in with Lou's parents. "My dad had said to her, 'If things get difficult, feel free to come live with us,'" Brissie recalled. "My parents and Dot had a great relationship. And she said, 'I'd like that.'" And she did. She got a job as a secretary in the Riegel Textile Mill and was working there when Brissie returned from Italy.

"I wondered how Dot would react to me," recalled Brissie. "There I was with both legs in casts from hip-to-toe. I was bedridden, or in a wheelchair, and we didn't know if I'd ever walk again, or be crippled, or walk with a limp. I wasn't the same person that she said good-bye to some nine months earlier. It was a common thought among the guys in the hospital ward, guys like me who'd been shot up. We were damaged goods, we thought. Would our wives or fiancés or girlfriends turn away from us? We understood if they would, but it was a question that we lived with, and not comfortably."

Brissie recalled the last time he saw his wife. It was in the kitchen of their small, off-base apartment in Spartanburg. "I remember that there wasn't a whole lot said," remembered Brissie. "I tried to keep it light. I told her, 'This thing will be over soon and I'll be back before you know it. We'll get it done.' She had trouble saying anything. We hugged and kissed good-bye. She was choked up and there were tears in her eyes, and I could feel her tears on my cheek. I picked up my duffel bag and stopped at the door—my friend, Charlie Robertson, was in a car waiting to take me to the train station, on the way to being shipped out. I remember how pretty Dot looked, her hair done up nice and wearing a flowered summer dress and heels. Before getting into the car, I turned and Dot threw me a kiss. I waved good-bye. I really didn't know if we'd ever see each other again."

And now they would. Brissie's parents decided to wait downstairs in the lobby, believing it was best that the newlyweds had this time alone.

Brissie was sitting in a wheelchair near the head nurse's office when he saw her enter the room. She wore a white blouse and blue skirt and pearl necklace, her brown hair was shoulder length. She stopped when she saw Lou. They stared at each other for a moment, not sure what to say. While she knew his condition, it was another thing to see him this way, much thinner and unable to walk. "Just by the things she said, and the way she said them, I felt that it was going to be okay with her," he said. "We were glad to be together again. There were hugs and kisses and tears and 'I love you' and 'I missed you.'

"I said, 'I've been waiting for this time.'

"And she said, 'I've been counting the days.'

"But I had to ask her, 'Dot, do you still feel the same way?'"

She gave him a funny look. "Why?" she said. "Has something changed?"

"And we laughed, a kind of quiet laugh.

"I told her that the doctors thought I had a good chance to be on my feet—that it was going to be a fairly long process, but that I could surely make it."

About an hour later, Brissie's parents came up to the room to see him. His dad was about 5'9", 150 pounds. "He was deceptive to look at," said Brissie. "He looked small-boned and wore glasses, but he was fairly muscular." His mother was a rather petite woman, but, as Brissie recalled, "she ran a tight ship. When dinner was ready, you'd better be there. And if she asked you to do something, she expected you to do it right away. And she worshiped my father, and she always worked. It was a warm, loving household."

He had remained close to his parents, wrote them regularly from overseas. They were cautious at first in their remarks to him, then they seemed to grow easier with the situation. His parents stayed about five hours with their son at the hospital. "We talked about family and friends, and the war effort in the textile mill in Ware Shoals, and about everything, it seemed, except what had happened to me," said Brissie. "They tried to make the visit as pleasant as possible." And then they made the long drive back to Ware Shoals to work, but Dot remained—she had brought clothes and refused to go back home.

The day after Brissie's family arrived in Thomasville, Brissie was allowed to go onto the hospital grounds with Dot in his wheelchair. Some of the other patients helped Brissie get out of the wheelchair and sit on the grass. "I just wanted to feel the ground again," he recalled. "Dot and I sat on the grass and talked—talked about our future and having a family and my playing baseball again. She was encouraging, though I'm not sure how confident she was that I'd play again, looking at the way I was then. And we didn't talk about the war. It was too painful to discuss it. She surely sensed it, because she didn't ask, though I can imagine that she was curious."

Years later Brissie, reflecting on that time, wrote in a letter to a friend: "Our battles were behind us and our dreams for the future still with us. It seemed so simple, but we would soon realize our battles were just beginning. We had changed and we, not our families, were not prepared for those changes. Our coming home would not be as we expected for we would never be the same again. Many families would understand, many would not, and like all soldiers from all wars, the questions would begin: 'What's wrong?' 'Are you OK?' 'You're so quiet.' 'Why do you always need to go somewhere?' 'Why are you angry?' And we didn't have the answers.

"Some would never be able to leave the war behind and go on with their lives."

Over time, Brissie experienced some or all of those questions, and those concerns.

Dot stayed for some three months, visiting her husband every day. Then she, too, returned to work, coming back, however, for several more visits.

• • •

After Brissie's parents had departed, he reflected on his boyhood, and the significant influence his parents had on him. Brissie had a particularly great admiration for his father. "My mother always treated me like a boy, the way mothers often do," Brissie recalled, "but my dad always treated me like a man." He remembered especially the letters from his father when he was hospitalized in Italy: "Don't give up, son," was their essence.

In fact, Brissie grew up knowing about pain and endurance. He'd seen his father, a motorcycle daredevil who barnstormed at country airports and fairgrounds, tape up a broken hand and say, "Well, you've got to do it."

Brissie saw his father perform on a motorcycle one time, in Greenville, when he was a small boy. "It was frightening," he recalled. "He was to run his motorcycle through a burning wall of planks that had been set up for the purpose of the act. He went through that wall with no iron bar to protect him, like some of those daredevil cyclists have today, and he wore no helmet. And when he went through it, the crowd on the other side that was roped off, pushed past the rope and into his path—but he was able to avoid hitting anyone. It was really an astonishing feat. He took a pretty good lick because he purposely swerved out of the way. Messed up his back and his hands. He hurt his back again when he went over a mountain crevice. He finally retired from thrill-riding, due to injuries and my mother's insistence."

When rheumatic fever crippled Lou's arms at age 10—a damaged heart valve led to scar tissue, which led to a fusing and stiffening of the elbows so severe that he couldn't feed himself—his father gave him two lard buckets full of sand and told him to walk with them every day, until the arms grew straight and strong. It was an early lesson in the way his body could respond after physical harm, as well as in his fortitude in dealing with it.

"Beyond all that, my dad had a great sense of humor," said Brissie. "He'd have a saying for everything. Like one time he asked me to take the trash out. It was very light. I dropped it. He asked, 'Is that too heavy for you?' But he'd do it with a twinkle in his eyes and a smile. If I messed up on something, I remember him saying, 'You're as much help as a stalk of wheat in a hail storm.' We'd laugh. He never made me feel bad about myself. He had a lot of little Latin sayings, too; he was a great reader. He was easy to meet, and got along with most people. And if there was a serious talk, he'd sit you down and it was eyeball-to-eyeball.

"When I was growing up in Greenville we lived in a small house that had four rooms. It was during the Depression and my dad, who was an expert mechanic, was making ends meet from his cycle shop that he owned with his partner and friend, a black man named Hunt.

"I don't know if that was his last name or his first name. He was just always called 'Hunt.' Surnames always came first. Everybody called my mother 'Brissie.' Everybody called me 'Brissie.' My father and Hunt met when they were barnstorming. There weren't restaurants like there are now. Maybe there was a café or something out of town that would open at 7:00 in the morning and close at 7:00 at night—and if they closed up early there was only a roadhouse that might have food. I know about a night when they were both going to sleep at an airport somewhere in Alabama the night of the show. My dad was there and Hunt came along and they got to visitin', and somehow in the conversation it came up about a meal, and Hunt was limited as to where he could go to eat. He didn't know where to go. And my dad said, 'I'll go get us something.' He went and got them something and brought it on out. It sort of developed that 'I'm going back into Georgia on my way home,' and Hunt said, 'Well, I'll tag along with you.' Hunt was from somewhere in the South. I was about six months old when we moved to Greenville. I was born in Anderson and lived in Greenville until I was 11."

Brissie's father lost his business in Greenville—they were tough times in the mid-'30s—and he eventually got a job in Ware Shoals, shortly after the business ended.

"It was very unusual in the South to have a black man and a white man in business together," said Brissie. "They were like Mike and Ike. Hunt would say, 'He's the funniest white guy I ever knew.' And my dad would say, 'He's the funniest black guy I ever knew.' They got a lot of rapport from somewhere. They just got along terrific."

As a boy Brissie had fear of the Ku Klux Klan—he had known of their lynchings of blacks, their whippings of others, had seen these sometimes violent white supremacists ride in pickup trucks through town in white-hooded sheets and brandishing rifles. People said they were fearful of talking to one another about the Klan because no one was sure who they were talking to, a Klan member or not, or a Klan sympathizer or not.

Brissie recalled: "My father would say that he believed in the Declaration of Independence, and that 'All men are created equal.' He said that that meant blacks as well as whites. Some people—there's always hate-mongers—didn't like my father's views. And the fact that he was in partnership with a black man was enough of a strike against him, in the eyes of some.

"I remember my mother and father whispering at the kitchen table, talking about things they didn't want me to hear. But I would catch snatches of it. It was about colored folks, and about Hunt, and some people's reactions to what my dad did and how he felt.

"One day three guys came into his shop. They started some kind of row over Hunt, making threats and raising their voices. My dad picked up a monkey wrench and told them to get out of the store.

"That night, two cars pulled up in front of our house. My dad was on the front lawn. A bunch of men in white hoods and sheets jumped out and grabbed my father and started to beat him up. I was just coming back from City Park, which was a few blocks away. One of the men grabbed me by the neck and made me watch the beating. My mother was in the doorway screaming, screaming for them to let me go, screaming for them to stop the beating. They punched and kicked my father to the ground, and beat him with a whip, screaming 'nigger lover.' When it ended, they let me go, cursed my father, and they plunged a wooden cross into our lawn and set it on fire. They got back in their cars and drove off. I was shaking with terror. I can still feel the Klan guy's grip on my neck.

"My father was lying on the ground when the Klan left. My mother and I helped him into the house. We didn't take him to a hospital. He refused to go.

"I felt that my father got off relatively light, which is a strange thing to say. I mean, they could have broken his arms and legs, or killed him. But I think because so many people liked my mother and him, maybe even some of those guys in the hoods, they just beat him and whipped him. My parents were active churchgoers and just good people. But my dad wouldn't change his views of blacks. He suffered broken ribs in the beating, and needed stitches in his head and face, but he wouldn't change. He continued to speak about the equality of everyone. I'm not sure where he got it from, maybe his mother, who told me on her deathbed, when I was about 10, that I should live by the Golden Rule: 'Do unto others as you would have them do unto you. And especially the black folks. They need it more than anybody.'"

Hunt soon departed Greenville and left the business to Lou's father. Hunt said that he was going to the big city. "I don't know if it was Philadelphia or Chicago," Brissie recalled. "My dad had several postcards from him, and then they stopped. My dad tried to locate him, but there were only dead ends. My dad assumed he passed away. Whatever it was, he never heard from Hunt again."

But the cycle shop went under a short time later. Brissie's father knew townsfolk were afraid to patronize it because of the Klan's influence.

Young Brissie had fistfights in grade school in Greenville, almost "every day," as he recalled. "There were these bullies, the same group of kids who would jump me in the school yard. It was all about my father and what he stood for. They heard their parents talk, and they learned to hate. I never told my dad about those fights. My clothes would be ripped, but when I came home I'd say, 'Tore 'em playing, Dad.'"

One day when in the first grade, Brissie was walking home from school when a man confronted him with remarks about his father. "I got scared and started to run," said Brissie. "He chased me and then threw a liquor bottle at me that hit a wall and splintered, the neck of the bottle bouncing back and sticking in my head. I ran home and the bleeding wouldn't stop. My mother grabbed a handful of soot from the chimney and piled it on my head to stop the bleeding."

His father, who was of Scotch-Irish descent like many of his neighbors and could trace his family back to the 1700s (sometimes the spelling was also Brisse or Brissey), worked at odd jobs for a while, doing mechanic work when and where he could. He was even a temporary bus driver for the Eagle Lines, which had stops in Greenville, Columbia, and Charleston. But when Brissie was 12, his father moved the family to the textile mill town of Ware Shoals. Brissie's father went to work in Ware Shoals in January 1936. He was chief mechanic for the entire fleet of vehicles—tractors, trucks, and company cars for the Riegel Textile firm, which had its headquarters in New York.

In Ware Shoals, it seemed that his father's views of blacks were, if not fully accepted by the people of the community, at least tolerated in a way they weren't in Greenville. Perhaps it was that Ware Shoals was a town essentially owned and operated by the mill, and any actions disruptive of the community would end in the firing of those involved. But there was still separation of the races, to be sure. Blacks used different bathrooms, different water fountains, sat separately in the movie theater, went to a different school. The janitor in Brissie's school was a black man named Will Rice. Brissie became friends with him, and respected him as an impressive man who not only could help young Brissie with his homework when needed but could throw a football farther than Lou had ever seen. Lou was friends with Rice's son, Welvin. They played catch and would shoot baskets together in Brissie's school gym when Rice opened it for the two of them.

"Will used to talk about dreams," Brissie recalled. "He said to me, 'We all have dreams, and why shouldn't my son be able to dream?'" recalled Brissie. "He never asked me to comment about it. He put it in a way that if both Welvin and me wanted to be ballplayers—and we did, but blacks were not allowed to play in the major leagues—or if we wanted to do anything else, shouldn't we both be able to? It wasn't something that was strange to me, and I agreed with it. I was brought up to understand that. It was something real because I saw my dad go through it with Hunt."

All the mills fielded baseball teams—white players and black players on separate teams—and by 14 Brissie, already as big as a grown man, at 6'2", had become an ace pitcher in the company of men, some of whom had played in the minor leagues. His reputation spread. Scouts from the major leagues made trips to South Carolina to see the young star for themselves, and they came away hugely impressed. Several teams offered to sign him, and the Dodgers offered the most, $25,000, a huge amount in those days, when an average salary for a working man was $2,500. But Brissie's father had other plans.

"Don't worry about the money," he told his son. "Don't do anything until Mr. Mack sees you."

Mack's outward kindness was widely reported, and people across the country rooted for his A's. He had won world championships with players like first baseman Jimmie Foxx, pitcher Lefty Grove, catcher Mickey Cochrane, and third baseman Home Run Baker, but that was years ago. When Lou was just a boy, his father told him, "You're going to grow up and you're going to help the old man win another championship." The father also admired Lou Gehrig, the quiet, powerful first baseman for the New York Yankees. "He's a gentleman," Brissie's father told his son. "You could do a lot worse than follow his example."

His mother was less an influence in one way, but significant in another. "She was a little controlling, and she didn't say a lot, but when she did, you listened—she was a very principled person," said Brissie. In Ware Shoals, his mother was employed as a secretary in the textile mill, as was Brissie's wife, when they came to see Brissie at Finney General.

His mom never was delighted with the idea of his father being a motorcycle daredevil, but it was what he wanted and she went along with it. But she was happier when he settled down to a business in Greenville.

But both parents always said to him, "I love you," as they did now when they greeted their son in the hospital, and when they said good-bye.

2.

For Brissie, it seemed there was no end to the surgeries at Finney General—surgeries to continue to remove shell and bomb fragments that remained stubbornly embedded in his legs, as well as some other parts of his body. Swelling and bleeding and oozing puss continued to be problems that not only frustrated Brissie, but frustrated the surgeons as well. He had been unable to walk for six months, from December 1944, when he was wounded, to June 1945, about a month after the war in Europe ended.

"I heard the news in the hospital and felt a sense of relief, but it wasn't over," said Brissie. "You had a nation united to do one thing: defeat the German and Japanese military machines. And now the country could concentrate on the Pacific side of things. And I don't know if any of us in the hospital thought about what we'd done individually in this effort. We were all in it together. We just felt good that it looked like this terrible thing was coming to an end."

Brissie had been unable to stand because he had a cast on each leg. However, in June, when the cast on his right leg was removed, he tried to walk every day, and every day a little farther. "It was tough," he recalled, "I'd count the steps. And when I felt I couldn't walk any farther, I told myself to walk one step farther than I did yesterday."

One day he told Waters that he wanted to walk to the PX, which was about a quarter of a block up the ramp from his hospital ward.

"I was finally out of a wheelchair," recalled Brissie. "I wanted to walk on the crutches." Waters said to him, "You just got that cast off yesterday. I'll get you a chair. You can't walk that far."

"I said, 'Sure I can. I feel pretty good.' I got out of the ward and started up the ramp along the wall—the cast on the left leg was up to my hip—and then I just started to fall, sliding along the wall to the floor.

"Morgan Waters shook his head. I must have had a very sheepish look on my face. 'Brissie,' he said, 'I told you I should have rolled you up there. Now, stay down there. I'll be right back.' And he came back with a wheelchair, lifted me into it, and rolled me up to the PX."

Brissie made attempts to get out of the wheelchair and walk, without much success. A few steps and he was exhausted, and in pain. He persisted. He rose early every morning and took longer and longer walks with hospital staff members. The skin on the leg was so thin it was like tissue paper. He remembered that his legs were as skinny as broomsticks. Slowly he began to gain some strength in his legs.

He endured hot baths regularly to increase circulation. He spent long hours with physical therapists. Every day. Week after week. Month after month. His baseball dreams driving him. Not only was it painful, he still risked amputation. A fall or a bump to his leg could set off a potentially lethal infection.

To give his left leg the strength of his right one—the right one had also been wounded during the German onslaught but had healed—he was fitted with a bulky aluminum brace that made the lower leg look as thick as a fence post.

In spite of all that, he decided to try to throw a baseball to a hospital aide on the hospital grounds. He threw while balancing himself on one crutch. It was just good to feel the ball—its hardness, its upraised stitching, how it fit so comfortably in the clutch of his long fingers—to catch the ball in a baseball glove on the toss back, to imagine the day when he wasn't having to do it by balancing himself on a crutch. There was that easy whip of the arm as he released the ball, and it plunked into the mitt of the aide. Would it ever happen that he'd pitch in a game again, let alone in the major leagues? Could it ever happen? One day a time, he said to himself, one day at a time.

A week earlier, Brissie was informed that he would be shipped to Northington General Hospital in Tuscaloosa, Alabama, the center for reconstructive plastic surgery. Brissie needed to heal and strengthen his leg to the extent that he could finally be released from hospital care. He read the newspapers, listened to the radio, and followed the baseball season—especially the fortunes of the Philadelphia A's. He imagined himself in an A's uniform, with the styled letter "A" prominent on the cap and the left chest of the home jersey, pitching against the Yankees, the Red Sox, and the Tigers. One day, one day....

His continued correspondence with Connie Mack fueled those aspirations, and his letters to the A's manager may have presented a more optimistic picture than was merited from his condition, though his infections indeed began to seem more contained.

In a letter dated June 18, 1945, on his usual A's stationery, Mack wrote to Brissie at Finney General:

> Dear Cpl. Brissie:
>
> Was pleased to receive your letter and to know that you are making such splendid progress. From what the doctors say it will not be long before you will be able to play baseball again.
>
> One of my pitchers, Phil Marchildon, has reported to our club and will be discharged from the Army July 23rd. As he has not done any pitching for the past three years, it will take sometime to get back his pitching form. Am in hopes he will be ready for next season.
>
> Will be pleased to hear from you whenever it is convenient for you to write.
>
> Sincerely yours,
>
> Connie Mack, president.

But days and weeks passed and Brissie did not receive the call to be reassigned to Northington for the reconstructive surgery he so fervently desired. Brissie was not only getting anxious about the delay in the reconstructive work, he was getting depressed.

"What's wrong with you?" Waters said to him one day. "You seem like you're down."

Brissie told him the story that they were going to send him to Northington but that time was running out. "I want to get started in baseball," Brissie said to Waters, "but it looks like I'm not going to be able to do anything."

The following day Waters came by when Brissie was sitting in bed and said, "C'mon, Brissie. Get in the wheelchair." He rolled Lou to the physical therapy room, went in and, after a little bit, came back with a fifth of liquor.

"Put this under your blanket," he said.

"Waters," I said, "we're not supposed to have this. This is contraband. You're going to get us in some trouble."

"Don't worry. I know what I'm doing."

Waters rolled Brissie up to the office of Col. Samuel N. Brown, the commandant of the hospital.

"Waters had a reputation because he was very outspoken and, when in pain, he would drink," recalled Brissie, "and he was in pain a lot because he had that open shoulder wound that wouldn't heal."

The two of them stopped at the desk of Colonel Brown's secretary.

"We need to see the colonel," said Waters to the secretary. "The corporal here has a problem."

"Waters," she said, "I don't know if he can see you right now."

"Please tell him I'm out here, and that it's really important," said Waters.

She called the colonel and told him. A few minutes later, the secretary was buzzed.

"He'll see you now," she said, with an impatient look.

Waters rolled Brissie into the colonel's office.

"Brissie here has a contract with Connie Mack," Waters began. "And he's got a chance to play baseball and he needs some reconstructive plastic surgery. And they're supposed to transfer him to Northington and he's been waiting weeks and nothing's been happening. And he really needs to get over there."

The colonel turned to Brissie. "Is that true, corporal?"

"Yes, sir. It is."

Brissie reached into his pocket and pulled out the letter from Connie Mack and handed it to Colonel Brown. The commandant looked it over. "Okay," he said, "I'll see what I can do."

"Thank you, colonel," said Brissie.

"Is that all, Waters?" said the colonel.

"Yes, sir." Then Waters looked down at Brissie in the wheelchair and said, "Brissie, give him the bottle."

Brissie then felt under his blanket and pulled out the fifth of liquor and set it on the commandant's desk.

"Colonel," said Waters, "can you get rid of this for us?"

"Waters," said Colonel Brown, "are you trying to bribe me?"

"Colonel!" said Waters in mock shock. "Brissie and me found the bottle and we know it's contraband. Besides, if I was gonna bribe you I would've given it to you before I asked the question."

"We'll try to find some place to put it," the colonel said, unable to suppress a laugh.

"We'd sure appreciate that," said Waters.

They both saluted, and Private Waters rolled Corporal Brissie, liberated from their contraband, out of Col. Brown's office.

Within a week, Corporal Brissie received his orders for the transfer to Northington General Hospital in Tuscaloosa.

But before that, he was going to be reacquainted with the outside world.

4

An Invitation from Connie Mack

1.

In dress khakis, or "sun tans," service decorations pinned on his chest as required, two stripes for his rank on each sleeve, the blue-and-yellow 351st infantry regiment patch on his left shoulder, his left pants leg in a brace to keep the bones from possibly splintering if too much weight were put on them, the tall, slender corporal leaned on his pair of crutches under the hot Southern sun. He stood at a crossroads near the Finney General Hospital in Thomasville, Georgia. A barracks bag, with shoulder sling, carrying toiletries and one change of clothes, lay beside his spit-shined, black shoes. A suitcase, after all, would have been impossible for him to manage when on crutches.

It was July of 1945, and Lou Brissie was taking his first leave from the hospital and going home to Ware Shoals, South Carolina, and his wife and family, and then on to Philadelphia by invitation of Connie Mack. ("It will be a real pleasure to have you come here to Shibe Park whenever convenient to you although would like to have you come while our club is at home for a long stay," Mack wrote in April. "Will take this matter up with you before you decide to make us a visit.")

The war in the Pacific against the Japanese still raged, and transportation in the United States remained difficult. Train travel was onerous to Brissie since the trains were generally packed mostly with servicemen, and there was standing room only, which was impossible for Brissie.

Even if he might have been able to get a ride, the drive from the deep South to Philadelphia was so far that the gas sticker needed would be hard to come by—gas, like butter and nylons and sugar and meat and

45

shoes, was still being rationed and was in short supply. "You would have had to pull off to the side of the road midway to the destination and catch a bus or train, anyway," he said. An "A" sticker was placed on a windshield for "non-essential use of automobiles or non-special cases" while a "B" sticker was for essential travel, which included people such as physicians and industrial war workers, and allowed four gallons of fuel per week. The national maximum speed limit, or "Victory Speed," as the government termed it, was 35 miles an hour. When Brissie's family and wife made the drive from Ware Shoals to Thomasville, they cut down on their driving at home to conserve gas for the trip to visit Lou.

Brissie now saw the bus arrive on time at the dusty crossroads, flagged it down, and managed to climb in.

It was a thrill to leave the hospital, to be sure, but he understood it was only temporary. After his visits, he would be returning to another hospital, Northington General in Tuscaloosa, for the reconstructive surgery that was so needed for his battered leg, and a possible baseball career.

It was a long bus ride to Ware Shoals, taking close to 12 hours, which gave him the solitude to consider where he was going with his life—the "wonderment," as he termed it, of the unfolding of his life, of family, and of career. They dominated his thoughts: "What can we expect from each other, after these changes?" "How long will it take me to get back to pitching?"

He tried to suppress thoughts that he might never pitch again. He peered out the window as the bus rolled through the farmlands of the then mostly nonindustrialized South, though it made a stop in Atlanta. He changed buses in the big city, then rode to Greenville, where a friend picked him up and drove him to Ware Shoals. The factories that he saw on that arduous bus trip were essentially the many textile mills that existed in the South, from the hills of Georgia to the coastal plains of North and South Carolina and Virginia.

It was Brissie's first trip home in nearly two years, and things had hardly changed. On the surface, anyway.

The population of Ware Shoals was still around 1,200, and it was still basically a mill town. There was one stop light, on Greenwood Avenue, where Highway 25 came through town and where the post office and the mostly company-owned stores, such as the grocery and the pharmacy, were located. The adjoining, neatly kept streets contained detached houses with pine and red maple and dogwood trees in the front and back yards. The Brissies lived on Smith Street in a white, three-bedroom clapboard house with peach and pear trees in the backyard. The house was also mill-owned, and rent was $10 a month.

In the morning, Brissie would hear the familiar shriek of the whistle that signaled the start of the workday in the red-brick factory. The locals went to their stations, some running the 70,000-plus spindles and the more than 1,300 looms, others loading and unloading scores of trucks, some, like Brissie's mother and wife, keeping the books.

Brissie also saw an "E" flag fluttering under the Stars and Stripes on a pole in front of the executive office of the Riegel Textile Corporation. The "E" was for "excellence," awarded by the federal government to factories that produced top-quality goods. Workers proudly wore an "E" button, emblematic of their working for an "E" company. During the war, the mill produced clothes almost exclusively for the war effort.

Since most of the people had work in common, they developed deep personal bonds. They took care to look after their neighbors and one another's children, in sickness and in health.

Around the turn of the 20th century, Benjamin Riegel arrived in the area on a horse-drawn wagon and started a textile factory in this relatively desolate part of South Carolina. (The locale was named "Ware" for William Ware, a 19th-century settler there.)

Like many who began such businesses, Riegel was from the North—New York, specifically—and went South to take advantage of a large pool of cheap labor. In short order, it seemed, the town sprang up as a workforce moved to Ware Shoals, as it was named, where virtually everything revolved around the business. Riegel opened a general store, established a dairy with pure-bred Golden Guernsey cows so the Ware Shoals residents would be assured fresh milk to drink, and constructed a five-mile railroad line that connected to the main railroad line at

Shoals Junction in order to pick up freight for Ware Shoals. By the 1920s, Ware Shoals was thriving. Riegel built a YMCA that not only had a swimming pool, it had an entire movie theater inside. He also built the handsome building where Brissie attended school, and it is still in use today.

"Mr. Riegel was really a benevolent owner," said Brissie. "For the most part, it was a happy place." Not all mills were owned by those who were motivated to the same degree with "social salvation," as it was called.

(The simplicity of life in the mill town, wrote Willie Drye in *National Geographic News*, "didn't do away with ambition among textile families, however. Many of the sons and daughters inherited their parents' strict work ethic and went on to brighter futures far from the mill hills." Senator John Edwards, the son of a textile worker in Robbins, North Carolina, said in a statement that "the mill workers shared dreams of better lives, and they shared hard, physical labor under difficult conditions.")

Riegel also constructed a ballpark that, according to Brissie, "was a jewel." The stadium had concrete grandstands that sat 3,500. Riegel put up light towers in the 1930s that resembled those in the major leagues. When Brissie began to play on the mill team, he was immediately impressed with the tile floors and huge showers in the clubhouse.

"Riegel also owned a big store like a Wal-Mart," said Brissie. "It was called The Big Friendly. You could purchase anything—among many other things, Mr. Riegel made the finest shirts you could buy. They were expensive. His store sold furniture and clothing. They had a drug store. They even sold automobiles."

"It was during the Depression, but I never felt poor," Brissie continued. "Like the saying goes, 'No one ever told us we were poor.' Once we got to Ware Shoals, things did get better than they were in Greenville. My dad now had a steady job, and my mother was working, too. I never had the feeling like I was downtrodden. I didn't have many toys, but you can't miss what you never had.

"It was a caring community and they were interested in their young people. They had good teachers at the school. They had a baseball program for the little guys before Little League—they called them the 'Fleas' and the 'Ants.' I was 11 or 12 when I first played with them. My dad would take me out there on a motorcycle at about 7:00 in the morning. I'd go out and sit because I'd been told I couldn't play because I'd had rheumatic fever the year before, when I was 10. So I'd sit there, and one day the community leader for boys' baseball, T.W. McElwee, says to me, 'Boy, what's your name?' I told him.

"He said, 'Don't you want to play ball with these guys?'

"I said, 'They won't let me play ball.'

"'Well, why not?'

"'The doctor says I shouldn't exercise too much.'

"'Well,' he said, 'we're short this morning, so I'll tell you what you're going to do. You go out to right field and stand there and that won't bother anything because nobody ever hits a ball to right field anyway.'

"And that's how I got back to being active again. And my dad didn't know it, nor did my mother, or the doctors. None of them knew it until after the first session of school when they had the first PTA meeting and Mr. McElwee met my father. 'This guy's the best right fielder we got playing,' he said. By then, I had been playing for a few months, and everybody just let it go.

"Of course, from a financial standpoint everybody in my part of the country was in the same boat. And I think that was probably the way it was around the rest of the country. You were either having a hard time or you were one of the few lucky ones that managed. I think it was kind of that way. It wasn't anything that you were disturbed about. You think back about it and say, 'Well, that's how it was.' It was the way life was."

It was harder in Greenville, to be sure, especially after Brissie's father lost his business. There were times his dad came home with a sandwich and said, "Well, I got something to eat on the way home. Why don't you eat the rest of that?" "After a few years you'd think about it and realize that he didn't have anything to eat on the way home," recalled Brissie. His father just wanted to make sure that his son and wife had got enough to eat. He never brought much home to eat, but he'd always say, "I got me somethin' on the way home. I had a bite. I got a hot dog."

And in Ware Shoals, while Brissie still had some minor problems from others relating to his father's views of blacks, it was a calmer time. The mill teams were singularly important to their communities. They were the major leagues of the area and one of the few sources of entertainment in those small towns. Virtually every mill team in every town had superb squads, often filled with former professional players from the lower minor leagues. They drew large crowds. The fans were enthusiastic and loyal to their ball teams. The owners of the mills took great pride in their teams—in some cases, the better your performance on the baseball field, the better, and cushier, the job you might have at the plant.

"We didn't have big-league idols down where I lived," said Brissie. "Our heroes were guys who played textile ball. When I got into textile ball I was 14, and if you were young and threw pretty well or played pretty well there was one rule among the veterans: Don't tell the young guy anything because he's gonna compete for your position." The players were making more money playing for the mills than they had in the minor leagues—$200 and $300 a month, compared to $100 or less in some of the lower minor leagues—and were greatly protective of their situations.

Brissie's high school was too small to field a baseball team, so textile ball was where he learned to play. "I learned without too much instruction," he said. "It was all individual trial-and-error."

But by the time he began to play for the mill team, at age 14— remarkable for someone so young to attain that honor—Brissie was already close to 6'4" and had a whip for an arm. "Brissie," wrote Rich Westcott, a Philadelphia sportswriter, "had become one of the most talked-about players in South Carolina." He drew the considerable attention of big-league scouts as well as that of Chick Galloway, who was coach of the Presbyterian College baseball team, in Clinton, some 35 miles from Ware Shoals.

Galloway had been a shortstop in the 1920s with the Philadelphia A's. He alerted Connie Mack, his former manager and with whom he maintained strong ties, to the young left-hander, Brissie. As soon as Brissie graduated from high school, in June 1941, Galloway, at the invitation of Mack, brought Brissie to Philadelphia to have Mack take a look at the kid.

Brissie, who had never before been outside of South Carolina, left Ware Shoals carrying not only his dreams but his father's as well—and not only to play for Connie Mack but also to comport himself with the dignity of Lou Gehrig. One other thing: his dad hoped that one day his son could throw as hard and as well as another of his icons, Lefty Grove.

When Brissie arrived at Shibe Park, his eyes took in the imposing sight. The exterior was like a cathedral, with a French Renaissance dome on the roof behind home plate that housed Mack's office. Inside the park, he was awed by the double-deck stands—he had never seen a ballpark with double-deck stands—and it all seemed so huge to him. The seating capacity was around 33,000, some ten times greater than the ballpark in Ware Shoals. Shibe Park had another distinction: it was the first fire-proof ballpark, made of concrete and steel, as opposed to wood planks.

Brissie would recall that it was amazing to him to actually be in a big-league clubhouse and to be fitted with an A's uniform. While the A's were a last-place team, and had had mediocre teams for a number of years—finishing in eighth or last place in four of the previous six seasons, with their last championship coming 11 years earlier, in 1930—there still were some very good ballplayers on the team, players Brissie had read about. Now here he was among them—the outfielders Sam Chapman and Wally Moses, the first baseman Dick Siebert, the All-Star catcher Frankie Hayes, and the rookie right-handed pitcher from Canada who appeared to be a star in the making, Phil Marchildon.

Brissie, shy and overwhelmed, came on the field to throw. Earle Brucker handed him a baseball and the lad's hand shook. Connie Mack, in straw hat, black suit, and high collar, watched from a seat in the top row of the grandstands, near his stadium office. Brissie was nervously aware of him as he began to throw to a catcher. As he warmed up, he began to throw harder and harder, his pitches striking the catcher's glove with a resounding smack. Mack, as he later said, was impressed by Brissie's fastball and his free, easy delivery and—despite his height—his athletic grace.

Afterward, Mack called Brissie into his office. The A's owner and president looked just as he did in his photographs, standing straight as a pencil, thin, and with an even, quiet voice.

Even though Mack saw the potential of Brissie pitching for the A's immediately, he said he had thought better of it. The boy's too young, he reasoned, he should go to college. He told Brissie that pitchers, more than anyone else on a ballclub, must think—and that great pitchers were great because they could think: they followed through on hitters' weaknesses, and the best place to develop brains was in college.

He would pay for Brissie's college and upon completion Brissie would join the A's in spring-training camp, probably in three years. "Talk it over with your dad when you get home," said Mack. They did, and Brissie and his father understood the wisdom of Mack's contention and agreed to a deal with Mack.

Brissie wanted to go to college, so Mack gave him three options. He could go to Duke, where his old pitcher, Jack Coombs, was the coach. He could go to Holy Cross, where his old shortstop, Jack Barry, was the coach. Or he could go to Presbyterian College, in Clinton, South Carolina, where Galloway was the coach. He chose Presbyterian because it was closest to home, and that's where Mack sent him. Mack had also wanted to see how Brissie did in the batting cage, and was impressed with his smooth swing and power. And he would decide in time whether it was as a pitcher or an everyday player that Brissie would best fit the needs of the A's.

Brissie went to Presbyterian, with its lovely tree-lined campus. He pitched seven games in his freshman year, winning five—there were a lot of good pitchers there, so he was not called on as much as he had expected. He was amenable because he played first base in more than 90 percent of the games, and there was still some question about whether his future was on the mound or at first base. Brissie batted a healthy .350 for the season.

And then his baseball career was interrupted. Bombs burst in Pearl Harbor, and then in Europe, and not long afterward Brissie paid a visit to his Army enlistment station.

2.

It was good for Brissie to be home, to be seeing family and friends, and knowing the feeling of "being normal," though he was a long way from the normality he remembered before he left Ware Shoals for the icy and dangerous mountains of Italy. It seemed like it had been centuries and worlds apart. Yes, there were some looks by others, including his mother and Dot, looks that seemed to ask, "Are you all right?" and "Why do you seem different—a little distant, pensive?" "Why are you so restless?"

"I'm okay," Brissie would say. He had no desire to go into detail. It was all in his head. "You thought about where you'd been, what you'd done, what you'd seen, what you didn't see. Bodies being torn apart, blown up. The screams of pain. You thought about friends—or guys if you got to know them could become friends—who were in worse shape than you, or who didn't make it. It was all rolled into one. And I'd have nightmares. In those days, no one had ever heard of post-traumatic stress disorder. It was all just something you would rather not put into words. No human being could go through what we went through, saw what we saw, felt what we felt, and come back unchanged."

His father had a sense of it. He said to the others, "He's gone through a lot. We have to understand. It takes time."

It would take time, they imagined, for Lou to make his adjustments. Meanwhile, Brissie limped along the main street, Greenwood Avenue, visiting with old classmates, taking in a game of the Riegel Textile team, enjoying home-cooked meals, and an intimacy that he had missed. Dot and Brissie took pleasure in walks together, but since Lou was on crutches they weren't hand-in-hand, as they had been when courting. And the walks now were considerably shorter due to Lou's disability. They sat on benches and talked, took short rides around the countryside, had a picnic, and then, when the lights were turned off in the house, crawled under the covers. Nine months after Lou's visit, on April 8, 1946, a girl, Susan Victoria, called Vicki, was born to Dot and Lou Brissie.

Following the interlude in Ware Shoals, Brissie went to Greenville to catch a bus to Philadelphia. Before doing so, however, he made a slight detour in Greenville to the home of the parents of Larry Aiken, Brissie's college friend who had also become his platoon leader in Italy. Brissie had great admiration for him.

"Larry was a little older than I was, tall and thin, and he was a remarkable guy," said Brissie. "He was outgoing, positive, confident. He was a lot of things that I wasn't, and would like to have been. I didn't have that kind of confidence. I was more in the background. If there was a pickup basketball game, he'd take charge and no one was offended. He was a natural leader, and people follow leaders like that. He'd perk up people. You'd hear him say, 'Get off your feet, soldiers, and prop 'em up while you have the chance. We'll be moving out in an hour.'

"He ran the mile and the two-mile on the track team at Presbyterian, and I always felt that he could have been the first four-minute miler because he would run and in the last lap he would talk to the guys he was running against and say, 'C'mon, now, fellas, let's give 'em a good race.' And then he'd run off and leave 'em.

"Larry's daughter was born just before he left the States. All he ever talked about was, 'When I get home, they're not gonna be able to get me away from my wife and daughter—never!'

"As our platoon sergeant, he was always out front. You see guys do things that might not appear to be heroic, but they're out there—out front—and doing what they're supposed to be doing, and that's good enough for me."

And that's what Aiken was doing on a gentle September morning in 1944, the leaves of fall changing colors in the mountains. "He was leading the troops, and the Germans evidently knew our position because as we started moving in this area," recalled Brissie, "Larry got hit in the chest 25 or 30 times with an automatic rifle. They picked him out and killed him. I learned that he never knew what hit him because they hit him dead center.

"I didn't see it. I was probably a few hundred yards away. War is chaos. Explosions, shots, ear-piercing screams. Later someone came to me and said, 'Larry got it.' That's all that was said then, all that needed to be said. That's why it was so hard to get too close to your buddies. Because at any moment they could be gone. All of them. Larry and I had gone back aways. We had developed a bond. And so this hurt—this really hurt. And his daughter, the one he said no one would ever be able to get him away from once he returned home after the war, his daughter was only a year old when he was killed."

When Brissie visited Aiken's parents, they were alone. Larry's wife and daughter, who lived with them, had gone to visit her parents in Clinton, South Carolina, not far from the Presbyterian campus, where Larry and his wife had met. Aiken's parents greeted Brissie warmly but somewhat uncomfortably.

Brissie told them of his admiration for Larry, of his leadership and his bravery.

"The first question Mr. Aiken asked," recalled Brissie, "was, 'Did Larry suffer much?' They both looked at me, hanging on my answer.

"'No, not at all,' I said. 'It was in an instant. He didn't have any time to suffer.' And that was the truth.

"I wouldn't say they were relieved, but I think they weren't as tortured." Mr. and Mrs. Aiken had other questions, and Brissie had some answers. The details remained sketchy, too painful for all of them to speak about or hear in full. "But they told me they appreciated my coming by. I wasn't sure they would."

Aiken's wife remarried. Many years later, when Aiken's daughter was grown, Brissie wrote her a letter and told her that he didn't want to interfere in her life, but he knew her dad. He'd been with him at the time he died and he just wanted her to know where he was and, if she'd like, he'd be there for her to talk to him. But Brissie never heard from her. He just figured that since she didn't know him, it was just better left alone.

Another soldier, Bill Jones, had served with Brissie at Camp Croft, and Brissie called his home in Illinois and talked with his mother. She told him that Bill had been killed. "She wouldn't let me speak to his wife," said Brissie. "She said she's not handling it well because everybody's coming home and he is not."

Those were some of the burdens that Lou Brissie bore: the mixed feelings of guilt at having survived while others hadn't made it, and, in contrast, the blessing that he had survived. Also, there was the abiding uncertainty of his well-being and career. Such were the apprehensions weighing on Lou Brissie as he boarded the train in Greenville for Philadelphia, Shibe Park, and Connie Mack.

5

A Bump in the Road

1.

In early July of 1945, a sports columnist and baseball writer for the *Philadelphia Record* named Red Smith (who later became the nationally syndicated columnist for the *New York Herald Tribune* and Pultizer Prize winner for *The New York Times*) wrote that the 21-year-old Lou Brissie "showed up in Shibe Park...a great, big handsome kid in a soldier suit, swinging along on crutches.

"He'd been there before," Smith continued, "in 1941, when he had just turned seventeen. His coach at Presbyterian College, Chick Galloway, brought him up to Connie Mack as a left-handed pitcher. On the advice of his father and Mack, the kid returned to school. He heard a lot of artillery before he got back to Philadelphia.

"Now he visited around with the ballplayers. When they asked questions about his pocketful of decorations he'd brought back, he shrugged and changed the subject to baseball. Seeing the helpless way his left leg hung and hearing him talk about getting rid of his crutches so he could start pitching again, it made you want to cry."

George Kell, a third baseman with the A's in 1945 and a future member of the Baseball Hall of Fame, recalled that "Mack told us, 'Don't mention the war. He doesn't want sympathy from us.'" But a few, unable to tamp down their curiosity, did gently inquire.

Brissie played catch with some of the players. The cast on his leg had been removed in the Greenville hospital and heavy bandages were wrapped around his leg to give him more comfort. But he had to lean on one crutch as he threw and was inhibited from taking a stride.

"I remember that he wanted to take batting practice," recalled Charlie Metro, then an outfielder with the A's. "Well, we said okay." Brissie, a left-handed batter, stood in the batting cage propped up by a crutch and leaning forward on his right leg because he could not put weight on his left.

"And he hit the ball. The batting-practice pitcher served up some soft touches, and Brissie called out, 'Throw it a little harder.' He was a joy to watch, but kinda sad, too. When he was at bat, I saw blood from his leg seeping through his khaki pants."

Brissie and the players, meanwhile, laughed and joked during the pregame rituals. He felt embraced. He told Metro, "I'm going to pitch again."

"He said it with so much conviction," Metro recalled. "He looked you right in the eye and you knew he meant it."

To each other, however, the players shrugged with a certain amount of admiration and, to be sure, sympathy.

"I'll never forget how he looked," Mack recalled to Art Morrow in *The Sporting News*. "I didn't have the heart to tell him how pitiful he appeared. His right leg was broomstick thin. He didn't have the strength to throw. But he kept on trying, balancing himself on one crutch and throwing with his free arm...." When Brissie left after several days, Mack said, "Few [of the players] thought they'd ever see Brissie again."

One of the A's who was particularly friendly was Louis "Bobo" Newsom, the veteran pitcher. He was, like Brissie, from South Carolina, from a town named Hartsville. "I was invited out to dinner with Bobo and his wife a couple of times," said Brissie. "I remember Bobo telling me, 'You gotta watch these people up here, boy.' I think he was saying that there were city slickers in the big leagues, and I'd better be looking in all directions when I get up there.' But I didn't think it was polite to ask what he meant."

Newsom, who made a reputation not only as a fine pitcher who won 211 games for nine teams over a 20-year big-league career but also as a loquacious baseball character, received a quatrain from the popular light-verse poet Ogden Nash, in "Line-up for Yesterday: An ABC of Baseball Immortals." Following in order such poems as "A is for Alexander," "C is for Cobb," and "M is for Mathewson," came:

> N is for Newsom
> Bobo's favorite kin,
> If you ask how he's here
> He talked himself in.

During Brissie's brief visit with the A's, the team played the St. Louis Browns, with their unique outfielder, Pete Gray, the only one-armed ballplayer to ever play in the major leagues. Though he batted .333 with Memphis and was named the Most Valuable Player in the Southern League the season before, the lack of available major league talent had given Gray an opportunity he might not have had otherwise. Lou Brissie watched him from the stands.

"It was just an amazing thing to behold," said Brissie. "Pete Gray caught a fly ball with his left hand, tossed the ball into the air, stuck the fingers of his glove under the nub of his right arm, and threw the ball to the infield. He never wasted a movement or a motion. All of it seemed to take place in a second. It was uncanny, like magic. And then at bat, swinging with his left arm, I saw him pull the ball to right field! Imagine the strength he had."

Gray, who had lost his arm when he slipped while riding on the running board of a truck at age five, played only that one season in the major leagues, batting .218 in 77 games with no home runs but six doubles and two triples, and striking out just 11 times in 234 at-bats. Those are not Hall of Fame statistics, but they were good enough to make a great impression on many, including Brissie.

"Pete Gray obviously learned to compensate some," said Brissie, "but at the same time he had to develop the muscles in that arm to the point that he had the extra power to do what he had to do.

"It was inspirational to see this guy who made this big an adjustment. One of the things that occurred to me was not 'if' but 'how.' Pete Gray was not only inspiring, he was encouraging. Gee, look at this guy. He's doing it with one arm; why not me with my bum leg?"

Brissie returned to Ware Shoals to visit home for a few more days, and then went on to Northington General Hospital in Tuscaloosa, Alabama, for the reconstructive plastic surgery he needed to help tighten and strengthen his left leg—that leg is the one used by a left-handed pitcher to push off from the mound, the leg that would help drive his fastball.

When he arrived at Northington, the first thing Brissie encountered in his ward was other soldiers getting to know him. It was, in its way, a fraternal setting. "Where you from?" they asked. "What are you here for?"

"Well, I got a leg that needs some work." Brissie said. He added, "Look, I need a good doctor. Who's the doctor I should look for?"

One of them said, "Tomorrow they're going to have the rounds. When they come through they'll look at everybody and evaluate each of us. And they'll look at you. But there'll be a short guy with a mustache. That's Major Suraci—Alfred Suraci. If you can get him, there's nobody else can do what he can do. We've seen his work." A staff sergeant named Caldwell was there. He had been in the Eighth Air Force and had flown 25 missions. He was helping a ground crew put out the fire on an aircraft when it exploded. He got burned with flames and gasoline. He had very little nose and no ears, and everything but the top of his head was burned. He had one leg they had to take off. He was one of Suraci's patients. Brissie was told, "Suraci's full up but if you can get him, it's well worth it." One of the guys showed Brissie a procedure that Suraci had done for Caldwell, rolling over some skin to make him an ear.

"So when they came through," recalled Brissie, "I saw Suraci. And when they were about to walk away I said, 'Major Suraci.' He said, 'Yes.' I told him my story, as briefly as I could, that I really needed reconstructive surgery. I told him I had a contract with Mr. Mack and the Philadelphia Athletics. I said, 'The guys in the ward tell me you're the man to do the job.'

"He said, 'I'd like to help you, but I'm really full up.'

"I don't know what I said after that, but I pleaded with him. And he finally said, 'All right. Look, I'm down in D-14. You come down there at 8:00 tomorrow morning and I'll take a look at you. We'll get your records and we'll go through them thoroughly.' He operated but didn't get all of the shell fragments that he wanted to get out. He did cover up the infected part of the left leg by putting a graft of skin taken from my right leg. There would have to be at least one more operation after that, perhaps two."

Frustration for Brissie, however, was mixed with ever-present hope. And Connie Mack provided some of the latter in his periodic letters to Brissie, such as the one Brissie received on September 5, 1945:

> Cpl. L. V. Brissie
> Ward D-5
> Northington Gen. Hosp.
> Tuscaloosa, Ala.
>
> Dear Lefty:
> Was pleased to hear from you and to know that you are doing a little limbering up. No doubt, you will be able to throw that ball by the batters in due time.
> Have heard from quite a few of the boys who are being discharged from the army. Pitchers Marchildon and Fowler* have already joined our club as well as Brancato* whom, no doubt, you have met.
> A number of the boys want to be remembered to you especially Earl Brucker.
> Hope to hear from you often. Please remember me to your father.
> With very best wishes.
>
> Sincerely yours,
>
> Connie Mack, president

---

*Dick Fowler had a 6-11 won-lost record as a rookie pitcher for the A's in 1942 before joining the Canadian armed services. He returned in 1945 to pitch in seven games, starting three, with a 1-2 record; his lone win was a no-hitter against the St. Louis Browns. Al Brancato was the A's regular shortstop in 1941, before enlisting in the United States military—his induction was witnessed by Connie Mack. Brancato, following his discharge, played 10 games for the A's in 1945, batting .118, and never played major league baseball again.

At Northington, Suraci operated on Brissie five more times over the period of eight months, from August 1945 to April 1946. Medical experts looking back at the work Suraci did say that he was "a true artist." Marc Siegel, a professor of internal medicine at New York University in New York City—he did not know Dr. Suraci—said: "Suraci was like a Picasso of surgery. He removed shrapnel that no one else could reach, giving the tibia more of a chance to reunify. If many of those fragments didn't begin to knit together, Brissie would never have had the foundation on which it might be possible for him to throw a 95-mile-an-hour fastball. Through it all the narrow, rod-like fibula, companion to the tibia, had miraculously emerged unscathed. It served as an anchoring rod to Brissie's leg. Without it, he would never have had a chance."

Impatient for the healing to speed up, time crawled by for Brissie. On the other hand, the calendar was flipping by, and it was February, then March, and springtime was nearly upon him. The leg still was not completely at full strength. Some shell fragments remained in Brissie's left leg, despite what was now a total of 17 operations. These operations enabled Brissie to begin to walk, first with crutches, then with a cane, then with another man helping him along, and, finally, unaided.

"The army was closing down the hospital in Tuscaloosa, and Dr. Suraci was being transferred to another army hospital in Michigan and wanted me to go with him," recalled Brissie. "He said that his work on the leg wasn't finished. I said, 'Dr. Suraci, I can't go.' Here it was April of 1946, and I hadn't played any baseball in nearly two years. I felt I had to get to throwing again, and pitching. Suraci said, 'You're going to have trouble if you don't.'" He meant that more surgical procedures were needed before he could feel a greater sense of professional satisfaction regarding Brissie's planned strenuous activities.

But Brissie decided to take his chances, this time without Suraci. The doctor then gave Brissie his phone number and told him to call wherever he was, if he needed him, and he'd also give him a list of surgeons nearby who could help him if necessary.

Brissie remained forever grateful to Dr. Brubaker, who first oper-ated on him in Naples, and Dr. Suraci, who together completely rebuilt Brissie's left leg.

Now Brissie was going home to Ware Shoals, after 16 months in hospitals from Naples, Italy, to Thomasville, Georgia, to Tuscaloosa, Alabama. He had arranged to try to pitch for the Riegel Textile team in hopes of ascending to the A's later that season or the following season. Was this a pipe dream? He had no professional experience. The last time he pitched was for Camp Croft, two years earlier. He had not tested his leg to see if he still could throw hard, or was physically stable enough to throw with control, or could even field his position.

But he still had those letters from Connie Mack urging his recovery and expressing anticipation of his return to form. On April 26, 1946, Mack wrote:

> Note what you say at this time that you are not in the very best of condition that is as far as your running is concerned. Our club will be at home for sometime starting July 1st and am going to suggest that you come up here at that time. Sincerely hope you will be able to join our club at least in another year.

2.

With his wife and, now, a baby daughter, Brissie, who received a medical discharge from the army in April 1946, moved back in with his parents in Ware Shoals. "The birth of Vicki was exciting; you had to marvel at the event," he recalled. "Even though it was a difficult delivery for Dot, when Vicki arrived it gave us the sense that things were moving on, picking up as they would have been had it not been for the war." He was able to support his family with, besides his military severance pay, a salary from the Riegel Company, of $50 a week. Each textile league team was allowed one or two "Outsiders," as they were called, to play for its team. Brissie was the "Outsider" for Riegel.

Brissie woke up early—sometimes earlier than he had anticipated because of the cries from Vicki's crib—and tried to walk. It was slow, it was painful, and it was frustrating. He carried a cane on his walks, but sought not to use it. He had it for insurance, in case of a fall, and occasionally fall he did. But he had his sights set to pitch again. It drove him even in the most desperate moments of agony and uncertainty.

His goal was to walk four miles. He began walking about 300 yards in Ware Shoals right after his release from the army. The bridge over the creek was a couple hundred yards or so from the house, so he'd walk down there and walk back. Then he'd wait a while and walk down again. Then he'd stretch it out and walk a little farther the next day. "I'd have to sit down and stop a while," he recalled. "I never did make the four miles."

He drove out to Riegel Stadium and began to throw on the sidelines with a catcher. He threw easily at first, testing his left leg. He wore a steel brace that covered his left leg from knee to ankle. He had requested one to be fitted for his scarred, fragile leg when he visited the Shriner's hospital in Greenville following his return from Northington. The brace was cumbersome and inhibiting, but he knew he would have to live with it when playing ball and make whatever adjustments he had to make in order to throw hard—to throw on a professional level. "It was trial and error to begin with," Brissie said. "I had to gingerly feel how much pressure and weight I could put on the leg. At first I didn't even take a stride when I threw. Within a few days, I was feeling more and more comfortable, and confident. And I began to throw harder and harder.

"It all came back to 'how?' How? What do I have to do to be more like I was? I kept asking everyone who remembered me—'Am I throwing the way I used to?' And some of the answers were fairly positive. Like, 'You're on the right track.' 'You're coming along.' I was anxious to get it all back, right away."

Brissie, meanwhile, was also aware of others who had come back from the war and tried to resume their playing careers, especially several big leaguers who had been wounded in combat or suffered in POW camps, some succeeding to a degree, some not.

Marchildon, a pilot in the Royal Canadian Air Force who was shot down over the North Sea near Denmark, was one of them, and a player mentioned in several of Mack's letters to Brissie. He was captured by the Germans and suffered malnutrition in a German prisoner of war camp. He was hobbled by a war wound in his groin. While Marchildon was now pitching somewhat effectively for the A's, he was nowhere near his outstanding record with them before he entered service. Broadway Charlie Wagner, a pitcher with the Red Sox, returned from war against the Japanese and said he felt "like a dishrag," and was plagued with dystentery. He was 14–11 in 1942 but foundered when he returned in 1946. Cecil Travis of the Senators, the best all-around shortstop in baseball in 1941 with a .359 average (second only to Ted Williams's .406 in the American League), never regained his prewar skills, having suffered frostbite of the feet in the Battle of the Bulge. He finished with a mediocre .252 batting average in 1946, his lone full season after the war.

One pitcher, Bert Shepard, was fitted with an artificial leg after he was shot down while piloting a plane that crashed in a farm field near Hamburg, Germany. A German doctor pulled him from the wreckage and brought him to a nearby hospital. Shepard woke up several days later with his right leg amputated 11 inches below his knee. He spent the rest of the war in a POW camp. The Senators gave him a chance to pitch in relief against the Red Sox. Striding with a wooden leg, Shepard struck out the first batter to face him, George "Catfish" Metkovich, to get out of the inning. He pitched five more innings, giving up three hits, striking out one more batter, and allowing just one run. As well as it seemed he fared, Shepard never pitched in another big-league game. He pitched for another eight seasons in the minor leagues, with middling success, but was never quite good enough to return to the major leagues.

Brissie took notice of much of this. Where would he fit in?

April and part of May seemed to speed by, but near the end of May he thought he might be ready to pitch for Riegel. He had thrown batting practice, had made his adjustments, had felt the rhythms gradually return in his windup and release. Not the same as it was before the war, but getting better. Since he had little flexibility left in his ankle, he couldn't pivot on the mound's rubber with his left foot, so he used a windup as though starting from a stretch position—his foot parallel to the rubber. He then pushed off to throw. His stride and landing were still shaky, and he never seemed to find his feet in the same place twice as he ended his follow-through (which the most consistent pitchers are able to do). "I had to change my entire delivery," he said. Despite this, his fastball had a sizzle to it as it slammed into the catcher's mitt during warm-ups. And his curve broke beautifully.

In May 1946, Brissie was penciled in to pitch for the Riegel team in a Central Textile League game against Ninety Six, a mill team in the nearby town of that name. "I didn't feel top-notch, but I felt well enough to try," he said.

He was eager, and anxious. Wearing the home team's woolen flannel gray uniform with green lettering, he took the mound against Ninety Six. It was surely an unusual sight for the opposition, this player with the left leg twice as thick as the right, due to the brace under his pants leg.

Unusual sight or not, the Ninety Six team had trouble with him. Brissie pitched reasonably and surprisingly well, throwing a complete game. It was enough to earn a victory, but it wasn't enough to avoid another problem. This was the first time he had pitched seriously in two years, and with a new motion, the result was that he developed a sore arm, the first he'd ever experienced. "Maybe I was overly protective, maybe I didn't throw with enough body, maybe I had been in a state of denial. Whatever it was, I was in pain with my arm," he said. For the next three weeks, he slept with a heating pad on his shoulder, and Dot, encouraging his return to baseball, which she understood to be healthy for his overall mental condition, helped apply a variety of ointments prescribed by his doctors to ease the pain in his pitching arm, as well as the pain in his leg that never seemed to leave him.

Problems around the household persisted, however, regarding the changes in Brissie. Dot and his mother still had difficulty with his seeming distance to them at times. "They'd say: 'You always want to go somewhere, you always want to move.' Every way your conduct would change, they would question. I'd say, 'I'm going up the street for a while.' 'But what are you going to do? Can I go with you?' 'No, no thanks. That's okay. You don't need to go with me.' You know, you just have moments, and you want to be away from everything. You just want to get away by yourself with your thoughts. A lot of times, when you're trying to resolve issues within yourself, the last thing you need is conversation, or some subject that's off the wall, or something like that. That's the difference between being in a hospital ward and being at home. You don't get those things. You just look at each other, not with a critical eye, but with an empathetic and understanding eye. That makes a tremendous difference. It's sort of like the clubhouse. Our house was not the clubhouse."

• • •

In mid-June, with his arm feeling considerably better, Brissie was determined to pitch again—and soon. He spoke with the manager, Red Barbary, who had had a very brief career in the major leagues—one pinch-hit at bat for the Washington Senators in 1943. Brissie asked Barbary to put him back in the lineup. "Are you sure you want to do this?" asked Barbary.

"I sure do," said Brissie.

A week later, in a night game against the Greenwood Textile team in nearby Greenwood, Brissie wound up in his now stiff-legged fashion and let loose the first pitch of the game. Fastball. The hitter swung, and the ball disappeared over the left-field fence. Brissie watched the flight of the ball in dismay. He wound up and threw again, and again, and again. In the first inning, he threw 10 pitches—the home run followed by three doubles, two singles, and another home run. Eight runs in all—and he still hadn't retired a single batter. Manager Barbary, sympathetic to a point, had seen enough. He came out to the mound and put out his hand to take the ball from Brissie.

"Just not your night," Barbary said gently.

Brissie handed over the ball and left the mound, walking with his slight limp back to the dugout bench. He didn't stop there but went straight to the locker room, his cleats clicking on the tile floor. He sat down on the stool in front of his locker and broke down in tears of frustration.

"I thought, 'Is this what I struggled for?'" he recalled. "It was the most disappointing, deflating, discouraging thing to happen to me in baseball," recalled Brissie.

"Barbary came by and patted me on the back and offered some words of encouragement, but most of the other guys just avoided me." One of his teammates, an older man who had once played professional baseball, walked over to Brissie and said sympathetically, "You'd better forget about this, kid, before you kill yourself."

Brissie was "down" for about "a day or two." His parents and Dot continued to be encouraging. He remembers Dot saying, "Lou, follow your heart. Play or don't play according to how you feel about it." She still worried about permanent injury to his leg if he did continue to play, but she also decided that her husband was going to do what he felt he had to do.

Brissie thought, "Yes, I'll just make that game a bump in the road. That's all. Either I was going to be stopped by it, or it would motivate me. I wasn't going to let it stop me. I just knew I had more in me than that."

So he walked some more to try to stay in shape—tried even to run some. But that proved too difficult because of the pain. He began to toss the ball lightly. His arm improved.

In early July, he tried again. This time was different. There was a rhythm that he didn't have in his previous appearance, and a growing confidence. He struck out 14 and won the game. He fanned 16 in the next game and won. He had a couple more successful outings—how good it was to see the batters missing badly on his pitches—and now he wrote Connie Mack and told him that he felt he was "ready" for a visit.

Mack, ever hopeful about the prospect that he had kept in touch with so diligently, told him to "come on up" to Philadelphia. Brissie's father asked if he'd mind company on his trip north, and Brissie said he'd be glad to have him along. Brissie's dad wanted very much to meet "Mr. Mack, the Grand Old Man of Baseball," as he referred to him.

The Brissies traveled to Philadelphia, and Lou, wearing the brace on his left leg, threw batting practice. After two days, his father told him that he had to return to Ware Shoals to take Lou's mother on a vacation.

This was strange, Brissie thought, because the family had never in their lives gone on a vacation.

Brissie said to his father, "Well, this has got to be something new."

To Brissie, his father seemed not quite himself, a little quieter, perhaps, but he thought it just might be the new surroundings. But, as he'd learn, his dad was ill, though he'd never say anything to his son about it. "I guess he just didn't want me to be distracted from my activities with the A's," recalled Brissie.

Pitching batting practice for the A's, Brissie wasn't throwing hard, but trying to establish a "free-flowing rhythm," as he termed it, to continue to work on the coordination of the new pitching delivery that had been forced on him by his disability. Yet he also threw with pain. He tried to ignore the throbbing in his leg. "Felt like I had a toothache in my legs," he said. At one point on the mound, he nearly fell down after delivering a pitch. He waved off help and returned to the pitching rubber and continued to throw.

He also looked thin to the other players, and to Connie Mack. After all, he had been unable to exercise for nearly two years prior to this.

In the trainer's room afterward, the team physician looked at the wound in Brissie's left leg and determined that his bone had become infected with osteomyelitis. "I guess I was trying to do too much," said Brissie, "including trying to run."

On July 8, about a week after he had arrived in Philadelphia, the doctor sent him to Valley Forge Hospital, near Phoenixville, Pennsylvania, some 10 miles from Philadelphia. Roy Mack, one of Connie Mack's sons as well as one of his assistants, visited Brissie at Valley Forge and suggested that instead of returning to Philadelphia—

the A's had planned for him to be there for the two full weeks of their homestand—that he go home to Ware Shoals and rest.

Connie Mack, having observed Brissie and his struggles, later admitted to a reporter that he thought that he'd never "see Lou throw a baseball again."

What Brissie didn't know until about mid-August, when he was released from Valley Forge after the doctors got his osteomyelitis under control, was just how sick his father was.

When his father left Brissie in Philadelphia, he had taken a train to Greenville, where he was met by family friend Charlie Robertson. The train conductor and Robertson helped him off the train, and Robertson essentially carried Brissie's father to Robertson's car for the ride back to Ware Shoals. He was taken to the doctor in Ware Shoals, but was so weak he didn't get out of the car. The doctor came downstairs, looked Mr. Brissie over, and had Robertson drive him back to the hospital in Greenwood, 16 miles away.

When Brissie returned to Ware Shoals from Valley Forge, he learned that his father was dying. He hurried to the hospital and was shocked to see this once sturdy man terribly shrunken, having lost a great deal of weight.

"I was told that it was an abscess of the liver," said Brissie. "An abscess, or inflammation, normally results from a blow, a bad lick. You get hit with something. The liver just never healed from the Klan beating, even ten years later—it seemed unlikely, but the doctors said that they believed that was the cause."

Meanwhile, just as Brissie was not told about his father's condition, he didn't want his father to know about his.

In early September, with Brissie sitting by his father's bedside and holding his bony hand, he thought his dad was just rambling: "I thought Dad was delirious with the things he kept saying—'I know you can do it. I know you won't let your mother down,'" said Lou. "I understood later what he meant. My dad had great faith in me. I shared his dream for me."

Leland Victor Brissie Sr. died on September 8, 1946, in the hospital in Greenwood, South Carolina. He was 44 years old.

"My dad was my hero," Brissie said. "He had such inner strength. I knew I could never get over this loss. And, at that moment when he died, I really didn't know if I wanted to keep trying to be a pitcher, if I had the heart for it anymore, now that the person who had been my biggest supporter in baseball, and in everything else, was gone. But I knew that I had to, that I couldn't let him down."

6

The Savannah Sensation

1.

Written on letterhead of "American Base Ball Club of Philadelphia":

Feb. 13, 1947
Leland V. Brissie, Jr.
48 Smith Street
Ware Shoals, S.C .

Dear Mr. Brissie:

Herewith our check in the amount of $35.00 to cover rail-road and Pullman fares from your home to training camp, West Palm Beach, Florida.

It is Mr. Mack's desire to have you at West Palm Beach the night of February 28th. Reservation will be made for you at the George Washington Hotel.

Very truly yours,

Robert J. Schroeder
(Schroeder was the secretary-treasurer for the A's.)

This note—and the check—was part of a continuing series of cor-respondence between Brissie and the A's—that is, Connie Mack, except in a rare instance such as a club official contacting him in regard to some team business. The previous April, Mack had congratulated Brissie on the birth of his daughter in April 1946 ("...am sure you both must be very proud of your daughter....") and added this hand-written sentiment in a note dated September 26, 1946, with the salutation "Dear Lefty" (Mack switched from the formal greeting to the informal for no apparent reason): "Was pleased to hear from you, thou (sic) sorry to hear that you lost your dear Father. You will get the contract at close of next season. Will be pleased to let you have same." The contract called for a salary of $200 a month.

On Feb. 6, 1947, Mack wrote:

Dear Leland: Have been thinking of you and would like to know how your leg feels after the winter. Would like you to answer just as soon as you receive this short letter. Also, how is the family? The weather here the past ten days makes one feel that they would like the baseball season to start. Hope you are in the best of health.

Sincerely yours, Connie Mack.

Brissie responded immediately. "I told Mr. Mack that I felt I'd be ready for spring training in 1947," said Brissie. "I just wanted to let him know I was okay."

In a note dated February 12, six days after his previous note, Mack wrote back: "Dear Leland: Pleased to hear from you—and to know you are in such good shape. Will see you in West Palm shortly. Best wishes, CM."

While Mack had been saddened by how weak Brissie appeared when the young man had visited the team in Shibe Park the previous summer, he was still going to give him a chance.

And Brissie, preparing for what would surely be his chance of a lifetime, had been arduously working out with weights over the winter and walking greater distances. He even did a modicum of painful jogging. The muscles that had been atrophying in his 16 months of hospital stays were considerably strengthened. He began loosening up by throwing a ball to a neighbor in Ware Shoals, two weeks before he was to report to West Palm Beach at the end of February, reasoning that he needed more time than others to get into pitching condition. He also worked on his pitching mechanics to get more power into his pitches even though he could no longer push off the mound as he did before the war.

When Brissie arrived in West Palm Beach, after an eight-hour train ride from Greenville—the $35 sent from the A's indeed covered the trip—the players, wrote Art Morrow in *The Sporting News*, "hardly recognized in the powerfully-built southpaw the anemic invalid they had seen at Shibe Park the previous fall." Brissie was impressive on the ballfield, as well. "And," added Morrow, "he was throwing with plenty of speed."

Out of necessity, Brissie's throwing motion was, as he described it, "stiff-legged." He was able to throw straight overhand, however, and that contributed to the speed on his fastball because he was able to get more of his body into the throw.

Brissie, meanwhile, also experienced soreness in the index finger of his pitching hand because of shrapnel that doctors had been unable to remove completely. "But in the scheme of things," said Brissie, "that was just a minor annoyance. When the finger got tender I'd just have to throw fewer curveballs."

It was obvious that Mack cared about Brissie as well as the several other veterans returning from war to his team. Particularly, however, for Brissie. Some of the A's getting into shape on the playing field bordered by palm trees—from second baseman Pete Suder and outfielder Elmer Valo to pitchers Bob Savage and Phil Marchildon and Dick Fowler—were all players who came back from the war with various disabilities. The wounds were either physically apparent or, because of the bestiality of combat, psychological. On observing Brissie, however, Mack told beat writer reporter Art Morrow of *The Philadelphia Inquirer* that he had never "seen anything like his pluck and faith."

Morrow wrote, "Out of sentiment and pity, the A's invited Brissie to West Palm Beach for spring training in 1947, and miraculously he fooled them."

Brissie was not unaware of the sentiment that Mack may have had for him. "I knew he was someone who was willing to take chances,"

Brissie recalled. "One of the chances he took that he was proud of and spoke about and all the players knew about it was the story of Howard Ehmke." Ehmke, unlike Brissie, was not a wounded veteran who tried to make a comeback, but was simply a 35-year-old pitcher who had seen better days. In a surprising move, Mack picked Ehmke to be the starting pitcher against the Chicago Cubs in the 1929 World Series. Ehmke, a big right-hander at the end of a 15-year major league career—he had once been a 20-game winner—had appeared in only 11 games during the season.

As Mack told the story—Brissie had heard him tell it more than once—he called Ehmke into his office near the end of the season. "Howard," he said, "do you have one great game left in your arm?"

Ehmke said, "I think I do."

Mack said, "Okay. I'm going to start you in the World Series. What I want you to do is scout the Cubs. You'll leave the team and follow the Cubs for their last games of the season. Don't say anything to anybody."

The A's had some outstanding pitchers that season, including Robert Moses "Lefty" Grove, who had led the league in earned-run average, George Earnshaw, who led the league with 24 wins, and Rube Walberg, who had an 18-11 record.

"When Ehmke came out to start the game, I guess everybody fell out of their chairs," said Brissie. "Ehmke not only won the game, 3-1, but he broke the World Series strikeout record." Ehmke struck out 13 batters, a record that stood until Carl Erskine struck out 14 Yankees in the 1953 World Series. Ehmke set the tone for the A's to win the Series in five games. A year later, Ehmke retired from baseball. Now, Mack was taking a chance on Brissie.

For spring-training exercises, necessity made an inventor of Brissie. He whittled a regular catcher's shin guard down and taped sponge rubber underneath it to make a protector for his lower left leg. "He was hit in the leg with a line drive," wrote Morrow, in an account from West Palm Beach, "and shouted proudly from the mound, 'Look, I hardly felt it at all.'"

Every day Brissie had to undergo an involved and delicate process in order to protect the weakened appendage. He put olive oil on the leg, wrapped it in an Ace bandage, and then covered it with a sanitary sock before finally putting a magnesium plate that had holes in it so the leg could "breathe." He also discovered that he could compensate for his left leg being three-quarters of an inch shorter than his right, due to the loss of bone in the leg, by adding rubber padding to the inside heel (in-soles did not then exist). His right foot also caused him periodic pain, since the mortar shell had broken that foot and the metatarsal bone in the instep would flare up. He has never been able to totally flatten out his foot and has always needed a special right shoe to ease the problem.

There also remained the uncertainty of whether his leg would allow him to field his position, and whether, added Morrow, "it would stand up when the opposing team started to bunt and drag and force Brissie to cover first."

"When I first saw Brissie in 1945, when he came to Shibe Park on crutches," said George Kell, then the A's third baseman, "I thought, 'Boy, if he makes the club one day we'll have to help him. I'll have to play closer to guard against bunts.' We thought he was crippled." Kell was traded from the A's to the Tigers early in the 1946 season, but saw Brissie pitch in spring training, 1947, against the Tigers' Triple A team. "He came out like General Eisenhower. As if nothing was wrong. I don't remember anyone ever saying he fell down. He astounded people at the way he handled himself."

He learned to have an answer for the bunt tactic, however. When a leadoff hitter on a team he was about to pitch against threatened to bunt, Brissie yelled, "You bunt on me and I'll stick it in your ear." It was important for Brissie, as he said, to "let it be known right away—let the word get out—that if you tried to bunt on me I'd knock you down. It's called retaliation. I loosened them up. I kept them on their toes." The brush-back pitch would be a necessity in Brissie's pitching arsenal—in most pitchers' arsenals, in fact. That was a harsh reality of professional baseball.

Bob Savage, the A's relief pitcher who had been wounded three times while serving in the infantry in Europe, had this vision of Brissie in spring training: "We saw his leg in the showers. We were all quite amazed when you looked at his leg. It was half a leg. You could see all the veins working. He never discussed it. But then, none of us really talked much about what we did in the war."

It was Brissie's belief that veterans avoided talk about the war because they were simply glad to be alive, glad to be back home, and glad to be playing baseball again, and what they had seen, what they experienced, was sometimes too painful for them to wish to recall.

On the mound, said Savage, Brissie "looked powerful, even with the bulge in his left leg from the protector. And he had excellent control, a real strength after going through what he did."

Charlie Harris, another A's relief pitcher, said, "I marveled. Brissie could get around on one leg as well as some guys could with two legs. And even with his disability he threw the ball at, I'd say, close to 100 miles an hour. He had guts."

Eddie Joost, the star shortstop and field leader of the A's—and another player whom Mack took a chance on when no other team showed interest in him—recalled: "He was supposed to not play baseball again. But he could throw like anybody else, absolutely—but not as agile. We all were surprised at how well he performed. I thought, 'Holy mackerel, how the hell does he do this?' I don't know how he walked on it, let alone played baseball. Bones broken to pieces. We knew he was in pain, but he didn't say anything, wouldn't give in."

Connie Mack pitched Brissie exclusively against Triple A teams. Competing against major league players, Mack reasoned, might not have been beneficial to Brissie's confidence. But when the team broke camp, Brissie discovered that he had made the cut, so far. The A's boarded a train from West Palm Beach to play an exhibition game in Savannah, the site of their Class A minor league team. On the train, while Brissie was in the club car watching a card game of hearts played by Dick Fowler and Joe Coleman, one of the A's coaches, Dave Keefe, came by.

"Mr. Mack wants to see you," Keefe said to Brissie.

Brissie made his way back through the train and knocked on Mack's compartment door. He was uncertain why he had been summoned.

"Come in," Mack said to Brissie. "Sit down."

Brissie sat down. Mack was in shirt sleeves, unusual for a man who was usually seen in more formal attire.

"You've had a good spring, you've done well," said Mack. "And you've got a decision to make."

Brissie listened.

"Do you want to be a spot pitcher, or do you want to find out if you can pitch a full season?" asked Mack.

"I want to find out if I can pitch a full season," replied Brissie.

Mack said, "Then I can do one of two things. I can leave you in Savannah—I control the Savannah ballclub, and I can guarantee you that you will find out if you can pitch right now—or I can send you to Buffalo in the International League with Paul Richards, the manager, and see how it goes there. You've done well against Triple A teams. They will decide if and when you will pitch. Which do you want?"

Buffalo was a Triple A team, which meant in most cases just one step from the major leagues, while Savannah was a Class A team in the South Atlantic League (commonly known as the Sally League), but it was a fast league, with many former major leaguers and up-and-coming players.

"I prefer Savannah," said Brissie.

Mack most surely was aware of an earlier conversation that Brissie had with Earle Brucker, the A's pitching coach. "Earle," said Brissie, "wherever I go, let me go someplace where I can pitch. With this thing on my leg, if I'm not working, people are going to start saying, 'The war's over now. Why carry a guy like him?'"

Mack told Brissie that they would send him to Savannah "on option, so we can get you at any time."

When the A's departed from Savannah, they left Lou Brissie there. Brissie called Dot and told her the news, and she packed her bags and, along with their one-year-old daughter, Vicki, took the train to Savannah to join her husband.

For six weeks, however, his combat injuries wouldn't permit him to work. His leg became infected again, draining and bleeding. The Savannah Indians team doctor, E.J. Whelan, attended to him almost daily, with consultations on the phone with Dr. Brubaker, now in Cleveland, and Dr. Suraci, now in Washington, D.C.

But in time he was ready to take the mound in the old red-brick stadium, which was situated in a pleasant city park at the end of Victory Drive. Brissie drove to the ballpark in the two-door, black 1934 Chevy coupe that he had purchased for $150. Victory Drive was lined with mansions and bordered by azaleas and great oak trees that formed a tunnel over the street. It was a long way up from the cramped quarters he and his family moved into in Savannah. There, as well as across the country, was a housing shortage due to the return of so many veterans, many of whom had brought back wives from Europe and Japan.

At Grayson Stadium, he'd look around and see the shirt-sleeved crowd sitting under the roof that overhung the entire grandstand. There were no seats down the third-base line, though they were intended to be there. After a devastating hurricane had blown through the coastal Georgia city, workers were rebuilding the park in December 1941 when the Japanese struck Pearl Harbor. The workers essentially dropped their tools and stopped work to enlist. All that remained was a jagged brick wall showing where they quit.

Brissie's start with the Savannah Indians turned out to be less than auspicious. He lost his first game, when he entered in relief and balked with the bases loaded, allowing the winning run to score. He was mortified. He was also booed. He later was able to joke, "The booing didn't bother me much. After all, I had lost a lot of hearing in my left ear from the concussion in the mortar attack, and I had only about 60 percent hearing left in my right ear."

And there was a lot to learn about the craft of pitching, a craft in which young Brissie had had little actual training. It might seem easy on the surface. It's a small, relatively easy ball to hold, about five ounces in weight. Inside the cowhide of an official baseball is a core of rubber-encased cork, which is then surrounded by 1,100 feet of tightly wound yarn. But there were the mechanics to learn, the rhythm of the windup, the hiding the ball from the batter until the last possible moment, the whip of the arm release, the various spins on the ball for the various pitches, the stride, the follow-through, the locations, the study of the weaknesses of the batters, the fielding of the position, covering bunts and covering first base, backing up third base and home plate, the staying in shape to last through the later innings, and the pacing to maintain stamina throughout the game. All of it had to be learned and relearned. It could be onerous. Especially when done on one shattered leg. He also couldn't get as much back and legs into his delivery as pitchers with two good legs. "I was blessed with good coordination and a good arm," Brissie said, "and that in many ways made up for what I lacked in other areas."

Brissie started in his next outing and lost, 3–0. While the leg bothered him to an extent, he pitched reasonably well, but without much support from his teammates' bats.

At about that time, he received a letter from his friend Morgan Waters. "Still here," Waters wrote from Finney Hospital. "We're all pulling for you, Lou."

"That meant a lot," recalled Brissie. "Really did."

He started another game and lost, 1–0. After that defeat, in the hotel lobby in Charleston, the Savannah manager, Tom Oliver, called Brissie over to him. "I'm making out the game report to go to Philadelphia," he said, "and I'm putting this game in the win column for you. You should've won it. We didn't give you the support." Brissie said that had boosted his confidence, despite hearing whispers of another kind: "I know some people were saying, 'Tough luck. What a great pitcher he would have been if he hadn't been shot in the war.'"

Not only was Brissie experiencing problems on the ballfield, there was also trouble at home, or what passed for home.

2.

When Dot and Vicki came to Savannah, the Brissies moved into a single-room converted garage, behind the landlord's house. Dot, while hardly spoiled, had nonetheless grown up in more comfortable surroundings. Her father, a department manager in the textile mill in Spartanburg, had provided a solid, spacious wood-frame house for her mother, sister, and her. When she moved in with the Brissies in Ware Shoals, when Lou was away at war and in hospitals in the States, it was again a life of uncomplicated surroundings.

In Savannah, however, the kitchen was about 30 inches wide and had nothing more than a hot stove; the toilet area was bricked off; and a bedroom—with a double bed as well as Vicki's bed—was separated from the rest of the room by a six-foot-high wooden divider. In addition, there was one window, a small portal that was at the front door of the garage, and Dot had covered it almost pathetically with a dainty curtain.

Torn between Lou's aspirations and her desire for better living conditions for the family, Dot grew increasingly frustrated. As the weather grew warmer—Savannah could get stiflingly hot and miserably humid even in late spring—it compounded the displeasure. The Brissies had no air conditioner and no cross-ventilation to cool them. Dot was not only uncomfortable, she was embarrassed. And while the Spanish moss trees in the yard alongside the garage were pretty, they could hardly make up for the conditions of their "home."

When friends wanted to come for a visit, she insisted they meet downtown. When a few of Lou's teammates came by to say hello, they were asked to sit on chairs on the sidewalk in front of the garage. It was a miserable, embarrassing existence for the Brissies.

Then Vicki came down with a chronic kidney infection that required constant attention.

And while Dot commiserated with what Lou was going through in his tough playing days in Savannah, she sometimes felt she couldn't take much more. They had words. She talked about packing her bags and taking Vicki with her back to Ware Shoals.

"Who do you know that lives in a place like this?" she complained. "Who lives in a place like this, period!"

"I'm trying to get by, trying my best," he replied. "This won't be forever. I promise you. It can't be forever."

But Dot, Brissie would recall, understood. "She had her moments," he said. "It was understandable, given the circumstances."

After each game Brissie pitched, Dot nursed his leg. The strain from pitching made the leg cramp and swell. Brissie was in agony. Their conflicts put aside, Dot applied hot towels to his leg and ran the hot water in the tub for him to soak his aching body. And always in the back of Dot's mind, Brissie understood, was the concern that "I'd do something on the ballfield that would cripple me up for life." In 1947, with antibiotics in their infancy and with the disabling possibilities of osteomyelitis, Dot's fears then had a strong basis in reality.

Brissie also suffered fevers. But he refused to tell anyone on the club about them because he was afraid that people "would write me off right quick."

Meanwhile, Brissie sought to master the art of fielding bunts, hobbling from the mound encased in his cumbersome brace. Some of his teammates worked with him to get the play down. Some teammates, however, resented him. Brissie, they believed, had no realistic future as a player and so was taking a position away from an able-bodied player. In their estimation, he was also hurting the team's chances for a championship, which would mean extra money in their wallets and possibly swifter advancement in baseball for them.

Brissie also had to run the bases, since pitchers batted in all leagues in those days. His heavy leg protector gave an odd appearance to his base running. "Just call me Speedy," he joked to a reporter. "But if I can keep the opposition from getting on base, it won't make much difference what I do when I get on."

He was a good hitter, even without the ability to put much weight on his left foot—the back foot for a left-handed batter such as Brissie, which provides the drive to the swing by pulling the rest of the body into the pitch.

Then, despite all the setbacks, he began to get his rhythm on the mound, and his confidence. His arm was powerful. The strength in his shoulder, his back, his arm, even his legs, felt stronger than ever. The work with weights during the off-season was paying off. And, naturally, time helps to heal. He pitched and won a complete game against Macon. He did the same in his next outing, against Charleston.

At this point, Walt Campbell, the general manager of Savannah, called Brissie into his office and gave him an additional $150 a month. "That extra money helped our financial situation, and that plus seeing positive results gave Dot more comfort than she'd had about my baseball career," said Brissie. "And she became friends with some of the other players' wives, especially Regina Nance." She was the wife of Hilliard Nance, the Savannah shortstop. "Dot began to understand that all of us players, and their wives, were all going through a lot of the same things regarding baseball and salaries—and dreams."

Joe Astroth recalled that Brissie had run into some trouble on the mound at about this time. "I thought he was losing it," said Astroth. "I went to our manager, Tom Oliver, and said that stamina could be a problem with Lou. I told him, 'If we don't get a fungo bat and start him running for the ball in the outfield, we might lose him.' Lou didn't want to run—it hurt too much. We took him to dinner and explained what we thought was needed, that he had to work through his aches and pains to stay in shape. We tried to get him to see it our way—sort of like an alcoholic, they try to make you see it their way. I wanted to see Lou succeed, and I felt this was important. And he did start running in the outfield. We forced him to, even though when he ran he had tears in his eyes."

And obviously, it helped. In June *The Sporting News* noted: "Lou Brissie, Savannah right-hander (sic), ran his strikeout string to 78 in 60 innings when he whiffed 16 Columbus Cardinals, to win, 3-2, in ten innings in the first game of a twin-bill, May 23."

A week later, however, Brissie jumped into the headlines when he tied a modern Sally League record by striking out 17 while defeating the Macon Peaches, 4-1, May 29. And on June 7 he won his seventh straight, defeating Columbia, 4-1, allowing five hits and fanning seven to run his strikeout string to 109.

Feeling a rhythm and a power that he had only dreamed about in his hospital stays, Brissie ran his string to 12 straight victories before Columbus on July 7 defeated him 3-0, despite his striking out 10 batters.

"He had 12 victories in Savannah before they knew what hit 'em," recalled Astroth. "If you got one run for Lou, you could win. He was that kind of pitcher. He could throw that ball by guys. Great fastball and curveball."

Brissie was picked to play in the midseason Sally League All-Star Game.

"On our ballclub, Lou quickly became the best pitcher," said Astroth, "We treated him like every other human. He was touted as the next Lefty Grove. So there was a lot of pressure on him. And he had to do it with a leg that was nearly blown away."

Brissie gave much of the credit for his success in Savannah to Astroth. "I really had had very little coaching for pitching," Brissie said. "Since I had never before played professional ball, the chance for me to get that coaching was in college. And in college I mostly played first base. But it was Astroth who really taught me about pitching. Joe made all the difference in the world."

Astroth, short and stout as a beer keg, had played a handful of games for the A's in 1944 and '45. "Joe had the knack of making you think anything's possible, that whatever it was, we could do it," said Brissie. "He had a way of never talking down to me. He had a lot of experience in catching and he never said anything about my inexperience. But he evidently knew by watching me, and he'd come out to the mound and say, 'You know, we've got so-and-so coming up and we can't give him any curveballs because he hits the curve pretty good.' Just like I knew that! It was always 'we.' He always put it in a way where I never felt like he was telling me what to do, or I didn't know what I was doing, although he knew that I didn't. He never imparted that, and I think that's a gift. I owe Joe Astroth a great debt."

As Brissie's star rose, so did fan interest in him. He became not only a drawing card for his pitching ability, but also, to be sure, as a comeback kid of, as it was written in The Sporting News, "heroic proportions."

"Brissie could not only pitch, but he also packed Savannah's Grayson Stadium like it had never been packed before or since," recalled Timothy Daiss, a Savannah journalist and author. "Savannah had a tremendous turnout that year, nearly 200,000. On a Brissie night, you had to go out early to get a seat."

Tom Coffey, who covered the Indians for the *Savannah Morning News and Evening Express*, said, "1947 was the premiere, honest-to-God best season we ever had." Before Brissie was able to play, the team floundered in last place. When he came back, their fortunes turned. "The team took off," said Coffey, "and did everything right."

Coffey added that attendance for a game that Brissie started could "easily fill" the 8,000 seats at Grayson Stadium, "with several thousand more spilling out onto the grass between the grandstand and the left-field bleachers." In one game, 11,000 fans jammed the park.

Among those in the stands on a regular basis were Dot and Vicki Brissie. "They cheered me on," said Brissie. "Dot was taking heart in my success. It helped everything. And Vicki came to know everyone in the park."

Every club in the eight-team Sally League had outstanding players, players who went on to excellent careers in the major leagues: Columbia had Ted Kluszewski and Frankie Baumholtz (both later with the Cincinnati Reds); Jacksonville had Don Mueller (later with the New York Giants); Charleston's star was Roy Hartsfield (who went up to the Boston Braves); Lymie Linde pitched for Greenville (and later the Indians); Bobo Holloman was at Macon (the St. Louis Browns); Tom Poholsky (Browns and Cubs) and Don Bollweg (Yankees and two other teams) were with Columbus. Four of Brissie's teammates went up to the majors, as well—Astroth, and pitchers Harry Byrd (A's) and Ed Burtschy (A's), and Bill Connelly (White Sox). But Brissie, despite these superb players, suddenly became one of the league's prominent stars.

"When Savannah played around the league, big crowds came to see Lou," said Joe Anders, who played third base for Greenville against Brissie and Savannah, and who was a friend of Brissie's from Greenville. "And he rarely failed to give the fans their money's worth. He was tough."

During his winning streak, there was a moment when he was booed in, of all places, his hometown ballpark. "There was a left-handed batter for Macon named Milt Tico, who came to the plate against me one night," recalled Brissie. "He was crowding the plate, so I threw a side-arm fastball to move him back. I threw it too high and it hit him square in the head. No one wore a batting helmet in those days, and you could hear the ball crack against his head. It was a sickening sound. Tico went down as if he was shot. He lay there motionless on the ground. Players and coaches and umpires hurried around him. I couldn't walk up to see him. I was afraid I had killed him. I just stood there on the mound, almost paralyzed. And I heard some boos, people thinking that it was hard-hearted of me not to see how Tico was. I was thinking that if I had killed him, I could never pitch again. It would have been too much to bear."

After several minutes, Tico rose on his own power, and was taken to the hospital where, the following day, Brissie visited him. Tico recovered and continued playing.

Brissie returned to the mound and continued winning. Meanwhile, a sportswriter in Charleston was critical in print of his local team for losing to Brissie and not bunting on him. "And we challenged Charleston to bunt," said Brissie. "Our manager, Tom Oliver, said 'Go ahead and try. He's not that easy. This guy throws pretty good.'" Charleston tried, and Charleston failed to take advantage of Brissie. "I had difficulty getting off the mound for bunts, but I managed okay," he said, "but also we had a third baseman named Bill Hockenberry who had a tremendous arm. The only thing I had to make sure I did was get out of the line of fire if they bunted the ball to third base."

Pepper Martin, the former star third baseman for the world champion "Gashouse Gang" Cardinals of the 1930s, took over as manager of Greenville for a brief period. He became incensed that his batters were such frequent strikeout victims of Brissie. He was known as a world-class competitor in his playing days, called "The Wild Horse of the Osage." He nearly invented the headfirst slide on steals and taking extra bases. Now, at age 43, and three years out of the major leagues,

Martin decided to pinch-hit against Brissie, to show his players how it was done.

"The count went to 3–2," recalled Brissie. "And he fouled off—he must have ticked off about six or seven pitches in a row. I then threw him a change-up. He swung and missed, and the bat flew out of his hands. The next night, he saw me before the game and said, 'You knew you couldn't get the fastball by me.'" Brissie laughed. "He was still the old warhorse."

While he was enjoying this success, Brissie would come back from a game in agony. On the road, he would draw a bath of hot water and soak for hours. "I had a roommate, our shortstop, Hilliard Nance, and I'd be in the tub after a night game I'd pitched, all stiff and sore," recalled Brissie. "He'd come over and draw up a chair and sit down. He'd say, 'I'm not sleeping tonight, so I might as well keep you company.' And we talked until I was feeling better. We didn't go to bed until 3:00 or 4:00 in the morning. Some guys were good friends."

Brissie gained his 22nd victory, August 27, at Savannah. Four days later he fanned 14 to run his strikeout string to 278, but he did not get credit for the victory. Starting six weeks after the season began, he finished the regular schedule with 23 victories and five defeats (four of those losses came when his team was shut out), a sensational 1.91 earned-run average, 278 strikeouts in 254 innings, and he gave up only 100 walks and just 167 hits. "If you got a hit off Brissie," said Astroth, "it made your day, your week. It was a feat, like getting a hit off Bob Feller." Feller, with the Cleveland Indians, was considered the best pitcher in baseball.

Brissie led the South Atlantic League in wins, ERA, and strikeouts. He was the only unanimous selection for the All-Star team.

"That season was phenomenal," Brissie recalled. "They gave me my schedule up front, at the start of the season, and told me that I would pitch every fourth day, regardless, and that on some third days I might be used in relief. That was my real advantage. I knew how to prepare myself, and I knew my schedule. That way, I stayed in shape. I couldn't run a whole lot on off days because of my leg, but pitching that much I didn't need to run."

Brissie led the Indians to a second-place finish, just a half game behind Columbus. The Sally League semifinals began in the home park of the first- and second-place teams, with the first-place team playing the fourth-place team and the second-place team playing the third-place team. Savannah played Charleston, and it went to a seventh game, in Charleston. Brissie was called upon in relief and saved the game to clinch the series.

They next played Augusta, which had beaten Columbus. Savannah won the series, 4 games to 1, with Brissie winning one of those games with a shutout. Savannah, with Brissie winning three games and losing one, was the Sally League champion.

The New York Giants promptly offered $50,000 for Brissie's release, but Connie Mack, Art Morrow wrote, "merely smiled and shook his head. He had other plans."

And the day after the Indians won the pennant, their ace pitcher, Lou Brissie, received a call from the A's. Mr. Mack wanted him to come to New York to pitch against the Yankees in the last game of the season.

"This was unbelievable," said Brissie. "The last time I had been in New York was when I was flown to Mitchel Field from Naples. It had only been a little over two years before. I was on a stretcher then, both legs in casts, not knowing if I'd ever walk again, or walk normally, let alone be playing on a ballfield. And in Yankee Stadium! My God, it was unbelievable."

He called Dot with the news and they were both so excited they could hardly contain themselves. But Lou didn't want to go to New York alone. Having Dot there wasn't feasible, because of her taking care of Vicki and the added expense, which would be burdensome. No, he wanted Joe Astroth to come with him.

"You know me, Joe," Brissie told him. "You know how to catch me."

Recalling this years later, Astroth said, "I told him, 'Lou, the A's are a big-league team with big-league catchers—Rosar and Guerra. They know what they're doing. I've taken you so far. You'll be in good hands with those guys. You know the old saying, *They put their pants on one leg at a time like you do.* Just make 'em hit you. You'll do fine.'"

On September 26, Brissie boarded a train for New York and the fulfillment of a dream.

A large crowd was expected in Yankee Stadium for the last game of the 1947 regular season for both the A's and the Yankees. After all, the advance promotion had been great: It was Old Timers' Day, but in actuality it was a Tribute to Babe Ruth Day, honoring the old great ballplayer ravaged with illness.

Lou Brissie, in a sport jacket and tie and dark hair trimmed short, was naturally filled with expectation and excitement as, just arrived from Savannah by train, he came out of Penn Station in Manhattan carrying his suitcase and stepped into a crowded and noisy and very tall city. He hailed a cab for the ballpark.

He was 23 years old.

7

Ted Williams' Line Shot

1.

It was a chilly, cloudy, somewhat windy Sunday afternoon, top-coat weather in Yankee Stadium. The temperature on this day, September 28, 1947, hovered around 55 degrees. It was the last game of the season for both the Yankees, who had clinched first place in the American League—they would meet the Dodgers in the World Series two days later in the stadium—and the visiting Philadelphia A's, who had clinched fifth place. Despite the less than summertime conditions, a good-sized crowd was on hand.

"All Savannah was tuned in on a special radio broadcast," wrote Art Morrow, covering the A's for *The Philadelphia Inquirer*, "and 25,000 were scattered about Yankee Stadium."

Few in the stadium were there to see the debut of the tall left-handed pitcher of the A's, Lou Brissie, who stood on the mound with an odd-shaped left leg, looking twice the size of the right one. (Under his pants leg, of course, was the aluminum-and-steel brace that extended from knee to ankle.) And few surely had come specifically to watch the Yankees' rookie catcher, who that day had been named to start in the World Series—a stubby, odd-talking player referred to in the press as "Larry 'Yogi' Berra."

Appearing at the preceding Old Timers' Day game was a galaxy of former baseball stars, from Ty Cobb to Tris Speaker to Home Run Baker to Charlie Gehringer and Lefty Grove. They were paying homage to the sickly Ruth, suffering from throat cancer (he had less than a year to live), and receipts for the game would go to the Babe Ruth Foundation for youth baseball. And it was fitting, since the ballpark was called "The House That Ruth Built," when the Babe began drawing great crowds with his home-run-hitting prowess from the time the stadium opened in 1923.

When Brissie was warming up, he glanced up and saw Babe Ruth come down an aisle in the stands and onto the field. He wore a camel's hair coat and newsboy's cap, and he appeared very thin and weak. He held onto another man as he walked. His face looked drawn. Nothing like the heavy-set guy with the round face Brissie had seen in pictures. He looked Brissie's way and gave a little wave to him. The great Babe Ruth! "I just sort of, well, nodded back," recalled Brissie. "My first day in Yankee Stadium, and pitching my first major league game, and Babe Ruth and all these great stars were there. It was a jaw-dropper. It was like a dream world. But I also had to do a job, to prove to Mr. Mack and everyone else that this is where I belonged, in the big leagues."

When he stood on the mound in the bottom half of the first inning in gray uniform and blue cap to face the first Yankee batter, second baseman Lonnie Frey, in the imposing triple-decked stadium, he tried not to think of the surroundings, tried only to consider the batter in pinstripes 60 feet away. The famous façade that hung from the roof like an upside-down picket fence, the monuments of former Yankee manager Miller Huggins and the late Lou Gehrig in center field, the fact that Yankee greats like Red Ruffing and Lefty Gomez and Waite Hoyt pitched from this mound—each of them in attendance and watching him—and that the Babe had played right field here, and Gehrig first base, and Bob Meusel in left field, and Tony Lazzeri at second base had to be dismissed from his mind.

He also had to deal with a current legend in the lineup playing center field and batting fourth that day: Joe DiMaggio.

Brissie asked Al Simmons, the A's coach, how to pitch to DiMaggio. "Don't let anybody in front of him get on base," said Simmons. "And if he hits one, it won't hurt you too bad." Brissie nodded. That wasn't much help.

There were other things going on of greater global significance than the game in Yankee Stadium that fall afternoon. *The New York Herald Tribune's* front-page headline read "Truman Plan of Half a

Billion Dollars to Aid Europe"; another front-page story dealt with "Eastern European Exiles" asking the United Nations "to End Red Rule of Their Lands"; "Jews Will Seek to Set up State if British Leave: Ben Gurion Hints Palestinians Will Use Arms if Arabs Fail to Agree"; there was a "$5 Million Fire" that "Wrecks Pier on Hudson," and a feature on "Why Meat Prices Are So High."

For Lou Brissie, however, the mound in Yankee Stadium at that moment was, understandably, the center of his universe. "I was nervous," recalled Brissie. "I had read where someone asked Warren Spahn when he came back after having fought in the Battle of the Bulge if he was nervous, and he said, 'No! There was no one in the stands pointing a gun at me.' True, there was no one in Yankee Stadium pointing a gun at me, but it was a different kind of nervousness. You want to do well. You want to win—you always want to win. It wasn't fear that I felt, it was an anxiety."

He also felt a responsibility to succeed, an obligation to "Mr. Mack," who had shown such faith in him; to Dot and his mother—especially to the memory of his father; and not least of all, as he said, "to the wounded guys in the hospitals who were rooting for me, looking at me as a kind of symbol, as someone who could overcome obstacles, and give them hope. I had heard that at the hospitals I'd been to, and I was getting letters to that effect. I also had my own dreams that I wanted to fulfill for myself."

Lou Brissie's first big-league pitch, his first pitch to the leadoff hitter Lonnie Frey, was a fastball. It didn't go over the heart of the plate as he had aimed. It sailed over Frey's head, over the outstretched glove of the catcher, and banged against the backstop.

Upon seeing this, Simmons, the A's third-base coach who was in the dugout, later told Brissie, "The guys in the Yankee dugout were falling off the bench. They said, 'We've just won the pennant, and here they got some guy who's trying to kill us!'"

Brissie battled his nerves and got Frey on a fastball to ground out to the shortstop. The A's gave him a two-run lead in the third when Austin Knickerbocker tripled. Billy Johnson threw wildly on Sam Chapman's bouncer to third, and Dick Adams slammed a three-base hit to right center. But New York immediately tied the score on a single by Berra, a double by DiMaggio—"it was literally frightening to face DiMaggio, that long stance of his, the bat waggling"—and an infield hit by George McQuinn. Oh, if only he could have acted upon Simmons' advice not to let anyone get on ahead of DiMaggio!

In the fourth inning the Yankees scored again, with a home run by Johnny Lindell into the left-field seats. Four hits, including a triple by Tommy Henrich, gave the Yankees two more runs in the seventh. And that was all for Brissie.

Morrow's game story read: "Leland (Lou) Brissie, the fire-balling left-hander who burnt up the South Atlantic League....received his major league baptism at Yankee Stadium today, and no one can say the Athletics picked a soft spot for him...the 23-year-old war hero lost his maiden effort to the Yankees, 5–3." The Yankees rapped nine hits in his seven innings.

He noted that Brissie had allowed five walks, made a couple of wild pitches, and struck out four. "But his jitters were natural and even the Yankees found him by no means a soft touch. With better luck, indeed, he might have gotten by." DiMaggio had that one hit in three at-bats against Brissie, and rookie Berra managed a single in four tries. Good, yes, but Brissie had hoped to do better. He had hoped to win the game. He was disappointed.

Morrow reported, "There were tears in Brissie's eyes as he went into the shower after the game, but Connie Mack quickly dried them with a smile."

Morrow continued, and in reference to Lefty Grove, who had been a long-time ace of the A's and had been inducted into the Hall of Fame earlier that year, he quoted Mack saying to Brissie, "Bob Grove didn't go that far his first start." Brissie knew why his dad had said that Mr. Mack was the kindest man in the world.

• • •

"It was a long winter," recalled Brissie. "The game against the Yankees was a tough loss for me. You're thinking that you can do it, and when you don't, it's kind of crushing. I know the Yankees were a great ballclub—the world champions it turned out because they beat the Dodgers in the Series—but sometimes your heart doesn't listen to your head." The game was an ever-present reminder for Brissie of how far he had come, how much he had accomplished, and how far he had yet to go. It was not enough to play one game in the major leagues. His goals were to make a permanent place for himself on the A's roster and to help the A's and Mack win a championship.

All winter, back in Ware Shoals he watched his diet with a reliance on fruits and vegetables, he worked with weights, he walked longer and longer distances, despite the difficulty at times from an ever-aching leg, and he dreamed his dreams. He also attended fall and winter classes at Erskine College, located in nearby Due West, taking courses in education. He pursued this for the next couple of off-seasons and amassed three years of college credits.

What helped the Brissies' modest financial standing was a letter from Mack, dated January 8, to "Mr. Leland V. Brissie, Jr. 48 Smith Street, Ware Shoals, South Carolina." Brissie and his family were still living with his mother.

> Dear Mr. Brissie (no more "Lefty," no more "Leland; perhaps Brissie had truly arrived in the eyes of Mack):
>
> Am enclosing 1948 contract at a salary of $5,000. (Some $3,000 more than his 1947 salary.) Please sign and return to me at Shibe Park as soon as possible.
>
> It is my intention to have all players report for training at West Palm Beach, Florida, ready to work out the morning of March 1st.
>
> Our headquarters will be the George Washington Hotel. As the number of reservations at the hotel are limited, we will be unable to secure accommodations for players' wives; the hotel insists that two players be assigned to each room.
>
> With kind regards, I am
>
> Sincerely yours, Connie Mack.

Brissie was happy with the raise, as well as the invitation to spring training, but this meant that he couldn't afford to bring his family to Florida because of the added expense to find living accommodations. The Brissies, again, would make their adjustments. And it might be just as well, given that they had a three-year-old daughter. It might have been a distraction for Brissie, who was trying to earn a place on the team.

The A's were known for being as tight with the dollar as any team in baseball. Mack was often criticized for paying players a lower wage than they might otherwise have received with another club. In his long career, he twice made what were termed "clearance sales" of some of his best players, most notably selling off the famed "$100,000 infield" of the 1914 A's, who had been upset in the World Series by the Boston Braves. And if there was a promotion to draw more fans into Shibe Park, Mack rarely missed the opportunity. One such promotion was related in *Baseball Goes to War*, by William B. Mead:

Pitcher Phil Marchildon, who had been a gunner in the Royal Canadian Air Force, had his plane shot down in the North Sea. While most of his crew drowned, Marchildon was rescued by Danish fishermen, only to be captured by the Germans when he got to shore. He spent nine months in a Nazi prisoner-of-war concentration camp and lost 40 pounds. In June of 1945, following war's end in Europe, he returned home to Penetanguishene, Ontario, Canada.

"He was too weak to pitch," wrote Mead, in regard to September of 1945, "but Connie Mack coaxed him into one appearance. The Athletics were drawing about 3,000 per game, and Mack knew that his returned hero would help roll in dollars at the box office. Mack staged a 'Marchildon Night.' About 35,000 fans turned out. Marchildon pitched three innings and was awarded a $1,000 War Bond for his heroism. Mack kept the rest of the night's profits. In 1946, Marchildon regained his skills." Marchildon, who before entering service had been 17–14 in 1942, was 13–16 in 1946 and 19–9 in 1947, winning his 19th game the day before Brissie made his big-league debut.

Marchildon had earned the nickname "Fidgety Phil" because he seemed never able to relax. "He wasn't that way before the war," said

Brissie. "And you just don't know what's going on in someone's mind who had gone through what Phil went through. But he was an amazing pitcher. He was like Bob Lemon. He couldn't pick up and throw a ball that didn't jump and move one way or the other. His ball was very alive. Even if he threw easy the ball was always moving."

While Mack surely had a special feeling for the returning veterans, like Marchildon and Brissie, he also was a businessman—a baseball businessman, one of the few major league team owners not to have another business (such as the previous and present Yankee owners, who made their money in real estate and a brewery). Mack might use a player's background to draw a crowd, as he did with Marchildon, but the player, to remain employed, also had to produce on the ballfield.

And Mack had great expectations for Brissie, which were expressed to the surprise of many at the annual Philadelphia Baseball Writers' Dinner in late January 1948. Brissie, after all, was still a prospect, and a handicapped one at that.

"Connie Mack stunned a group of baseball writers a few weeks ago when he declared that he had a pitcher who would be greater than Lefty Grove, better than Rube Waddell and more durable than Eddie Plank," wrote Stan Baumgartner, a *Philadelphia Inquirer* baseball writer whose article appeared in *The Sporting News*. Grove, Waddell, and Plank were three of the best pitchers in A's history. "The writers gasped, looked at each other, then again at Connie. Greater than Grove, the southpaw whom Mack had named as the greatest of all time? Was Connie finally losing his touch? No, he looked as keen as ever. At 85 he looks 65.

"Don Donaghey, columnist of the *Philadelphia Evening Bulletin*, faced Connie with what was a challenge: 'Did you say, Mr. Mack, that this fellow will be better than Grove?'

"Connie nodded. But Donaghey refused to be convinced. 'Is he as fast as Grove?' asked Donaghey, incredulously.

"Mack smiled like a father being patient with an inquisitive son. 'Not yet,' he replies. 'But he will be soon, when he gets a little more confidence.'

"They asked about his curveball, his control. Both got high marks from Mack.

"'Does he have a change of pace?' Donaghey asked.

"'With his stuff,' said Mack, 'he doesn't need a change of pace.'

"'Okay,' said Donaghey, 'who is he?'

"'Lou Brissie,' said Mack, and added, about the Yankee game, 'He got beat but only because that fellow Guerra (Mike Guerra, the catcher) didn't do a good job of catching him. I could have done better myself.' (Mack, in fact, had been a catcher in his playing days, which ended in 1896.) 'Brissie had great stuff, a beautiful fastball and a fine curve, but he was a bit nervous and wild. A good catcher could have held him up. You watch—he'll be the greatest left-hander in baseball in two years.'"

While Mack had said and written sentiments along those lines to him, Brissie thought this still amounted to a startling elevation. "It was something to try to live up to," said Brissie. "And I sure was going to try. But it wasn't any more pressure than I was already dealing with, or anyone else to make the club, or keep their jobs." He also had kind words for Guerra: "I had no problem with him in that game. I thought he was fine. He didn't give up those hits and walks—I did. I understand that Mike had wanted to play that winter in Cuba, where he's from, and Mr. Mack had just refused him permission to do so. Mr. Mack thought he should rest over the winter and be ready for the big-league season. Mike pouted about that."

At the Baseball Writers' Dinner, Brissie was introduced and received "The Most Courageous Athlete" award, a co-winner along with James E. "Sonny" Fraser, who had been stricken with Hodgkin's disease seven years earlier, was paralyzed from the waist down, but overcame the disability and won a national amateur golf tournament.

Brissie also received another surprise at the banquet. Joe DiMaggio, who was another honoree, met Brissie after the dinner and told him he thought he had an outstanding future. "But try to keep your curveball breaking at the shoe tops to right-handed batters," said DiMaggio. Brissie had kept the curveball higher to DiMaggio. "I was grateful for the advice," said Brissie, "but there wasn't much a pitcher could do to get DiMaggio out. The advice might help with other right-handed batters, though."

• • •

On March 1, 1948, Red Smith, now a nationally acclaimed sports columnist for the *New York Herald Tribune* and who had formerly covered
the A's with the *Philadelphia Record*, wrote his column from West Palm
Beach with the heading: "Sometimes It Was Discouraging":

"The Americans were moving up against German positions in the
Apennines when an advance echelon got into trouble. The infantry outfit
that included Leland Victor Brissie, Jr., out of the agreeable metropolis
of Ware Shoals, South Carolina, went up to see what assistance it could
offer." And then Smith related Brissie's story, from the hospitals in Italy
to those in America, including when he got blood poisoning when he
threw batting practice for the A's in 1946, and told Smith, "Seemed like
I wasn't having any good luck. Sometimes it was discouraging."

Smith wrote that his "luck" seemed to change, and extolled
Brissie's success in Savannah. "If there was ever a man with two legs
who made a more remarkable record in his first year in any league, the
name doesn't come to mind.... He gets around astonishingly well with
a cast that makes his lower leg as thick as a fence post."

And Smith quoted Connie Mack in the same vein as at the
Philadelphia Writers' dinner about a month earlier.

"He should be a great pitcher," said Mack. "Maybe he won't be
ready this year, but he should be as good as Rube Waddell."

Smith wrote, "Connie took a breath. 'Better than Waddell,' he
said."

2.

By the end of a very good spring in 1948, pitching against major league
teams now instead of the Triple A ballclubs he faced the previous
spring, Brissie was "ready," as Mack had put it.

He was also being accepted by the rest of the team, particularly the
guys he spent the most time with, the pitchers. "We got along real well,
and I knew I was in pretty good standing when they started to needle
me," said Brissie. "I was given No. 19. It was also Bob Feller's number

99

with Cleveland. "Hmm, wonder what the other No. 19 feels about that?" jibed Dick Fowler. "Twenty-five wins ought to be easy for you."

The A's played the National League Philadelphia Phillies in the final game of their annual weekend city series on Sunday, April 18. Instead of going to the ballpark in Philadelphia, Marchildon and Brissie were told to take a train that day to Boston to rest for the next day's pitching chores, since neither would be called on to pitch against the Phillies.

"Hubtown is more than a little excited over the prospect of a return to 1946 American League glory and a crowd of 34,000 is expected...," wrote Morrow in *The Philadelphia Inquirer* of Monday, April 19, the day f the A's 1948 opening games of the season, in Boston. It was Patriots Day in Boston and a doubleheader, an annual Opening Day ritual, was scheduled. Mack had named his "1947 ace pitcher" Marchildon to start the first game and, Morrow noted, "the left-handed mainstay of the spring corps, Lou Brissie, to hurl against the Red Sox" in the second game.

"Hubtown" may have been excited, but hardly more exhilarated than Brissie. He had gone to Shibe Park with the team for the last game of the city series when Earle Brucker, the pitching coach, approached him and Marchildon. "Mr. Mack wants you two guys to catch a train and go up to Boston tonight, late this afternoon, and check into a hotel," Brucker said, "because you're both pitching tomorrow."

It came as a surprise to Brissie, but one that was met with confidence, as well as butterflies. In Boston on Sunday afternoon, the two pitchers checked into the Copley Plaza Hotel. The rest of the team came up to Boston on the sleeper train, getting in early Monday morning.

"Phil and I went down to have breakfast, and the team came in and Brucker says, 'Well, you know, we're going to be leaving for the park, so Brissie, there's no need for you to go. You can take a rest and come out about 1:00. Your game is gonna start about 2:30.'

"So I waited 30 or 40 minutes, maybe an hour. But I was anxious to get to the park. I thought, 'Well, I'm going.' I called a cab and rode to Fenway Park.

"I got there and the guy at the players' gate wouldn't let me in. He said, 'The players are already here.' I said, 'Yeah, but I'm pitching the second game.'"

The gatekeeper looked at Brissie, in street clothes, and may have noticed the slight limp as he approached the gate, and wasn't convinced he was a player. "Call Benny McFarlane," said Brissie. McFarlane was the A's traveling secretary. McFarlane came down and "identified me," said Brissie.

"About the time we finished our discussion there at the gate, I heard a roar and it seemed as though the stands were going to collapse. They were vibrating. I got about halfway to the clubhouse and it happened again. I walked into the clubhouse and it happened a third time. I couldn't imagine what was going on because I couldn't see the field. I was in the runway under the stands. One of the kids that worked for the clubhouse man walked in the door and said, 'The Red Sox just hit three consecutive home runs off of Marchildon.' It was in the second inning, and Stan Spence, Vern Stephens, and Bobby Doerr hit back-to-back-to-back homers. I was sitting in front of my locker, and I can't tell you the things that went through my mind. Here's a guy, Marchildon, who's a great pitcher, highly thought of before the war, who's back now and all he lived through, and now he's getting battered out there. And the Red Sox had some great hitters besides those guys who hit the homers—Johnny Pesky and Dom DiMaggio and of course Ted Williams. And I thought 'Well, I got myself in a big mess now.'

"But Marchildon settled down and won the game, 5-4.

"Funny thing is, when I came into the dugout and looked around the ballpark before I was going to warm up for the second game, the first thing I compared it to is the ballfield back home in Ware Shoals. In Fenway Park you had that great big wall in left field. That impressed me. The Green Monster, that 37-foot-high green-painted wall in left field. It's 315 feet down the line to left. In Ware Shoals, it was about 440 feet to left field. And then it was a small fence. In Fenway, with that thing at your back, you're walking on egg shells when you're pitching. This was new territory for me, a new experience."

Brissie moved around those egg shells with dexterity until the sixth inning. The A's were leading, 4-1, when Ted Williams came to bat. There was no more powerful batter in baseball than the Splendid Splinter. He stood at the plate pumping his bat with customary intensity. It was a sight that most pitchers could do without. But Brissie was challenged, having gotten Williams out on both previous at-bats. Brissie wound up and threw.

In Williams' autobiography, *My Turn at Bat: The Story of My Life*, he relates what happened next: "I will never forget the day I hit Lou Brissie with a line drive...He had come out of the service a great war hero with part of his leg blown off. He had to wear an aluminum plate. We opened the season in Boston and gee, Brissie looked good. A fine arm, sneaky fast. He was beating us (4-1 in the sixth inning) when I hit a ball back to the box, a real shot, whack, like a rifle clap off the aluminum leg. Down he goes, and everybody rushes out there, and I go over from first base with this awful feeling I've really hurt him. Here's this war hero, pitching a great game, and they don't know if the rest of the leg's been knocked off or what.

"I'll never forget Brissie. He sees me in the crowd, looking down at him, my face like a haunt, and he says, 'For Chrissakes, Williams, pull the damn ball!' Well, he was all right and I remember the next time we played he threw me everything inside, making sure I did pull, and I hit one out of the park. As I was trotting around he yelled, 'You don't have to pull it that far, Williams.' Brissie was a great guy."

When Brissie got hit by Williams' line drive he thought that it might have broken his leg. "I lay there and my first thought was, 'I'm back where I started. I'm back in that creek bed in Italy—all that work and it ends here?' But then I didn't feel anything grinding, didn't feel anything shifting in my leg. It hurt, but I thought maybe it's going to be okay."

Earle Brucker came running out to the mound from the A's dugout. He asked Brissie if he was all right. "I'll see," said Brissie. He recalled: "I lay there for a few minutes, letting the pain subside, and when I finally got up I told them I felt okay. I said, 'Let me throw a couple.' The first one I threw, I fell down. Brucker helped me up. 'Lou, we'll have to take you out.' I said, 'Earle, I'm okay, really. I just didn't stride right. I had a twinge and it bothered me a little.'" He threw a few more warm-up pitches and didn't fall down. "I'm okay," Brissie announced. And he remained in the game.

While the day had begun in bright sunshine, the weather changed. Clouds blocked out the sun, and a light drizzle began to fall. In the ninth inning, with the score 4-2, a man on base, and one out, Ted Williams came to bat again. Waggling that menacing bat and glaring at Brissie, Williams, the consummate slugger, wasn't giving in to any emotions. (Williams was also a war veteran, having served as a fighter pilot in World War II. He was one of many major league stars who enlisted in the military, such as Bob Feller, Joe DiMaggio, Hank Greenberg, and Stan Musial.)

Brissie now kept his pitches inside to Williams—if he was going to hit it, he'd have *have* to pull it—and ran the count to 3-2. Then Brissie threw what he believed was one of his best curveballs. It cut low and outside over the plate. Williams swung and missed. "That was satisfying," recalled Brissie, "and a relief." He got the next batter to pop out—and Lou Brissie had won the first game of his major league career, giving up just four hits, striking out seven, walking just one batter, and throwing one wild pitch.

After Brissie got the last batter, Dave Keefe, an A's coach, came running out from the dugout to Brissie. "Mr. Mack wants to see you," he said.

"So I went over to the dugout," recalled Brissie, "and Mr. Mack was standing on the step and he said, 'You just pitched a great game and I'm proud of you. You did a fine job. Now take care of yourself and go let 'em take care of your leg.'"

Johnny Pesky, the Red Sox third baseman, who had gone hitless in four at-bats, recalled many years later, "I couldn't hit the guy with a tennis racket." And Doerr, hitless in three at-bats, was asked years later why he hadn't tried to bunt on Brissie: "He threw too hard to bunt on him," said Doerr.

Brissie remembers the A's joy after the game. "That clubhouse," he said, "was in an uproar. That was a great experience and a great day."

It wasn't over for Brissie, however. He was taken to a nearby hospital. X-rays were taken, and they were negative. "I was told, 'You got a bad lick and we can see it.'" They kept him overnight for further observation. He returned to the Copley Plaza Hotel the next morning, but the leg ached and he saw that a red line had developed. This meant that an infection might be setting in.

Brissie called Dr. Brubaker, with whom he was regularly in touch, and Brubaker prescribed penicillin. He told Brissie, "The osteomyelitis will come and go if you're on your leg too much." Not great news for a pitcher, to be sure, but Brissie sought to walk and run as little as possible, and he would virtually limit his time on his feet to when he was pitching.

And pitch he did. The A's had an excellent ballclub that season, built carefully by Mack. The young Ferris Fain was at first base; he would go on to win two American League batting titles. The reliable Pete Suder was at second, the All-Star Eddie Joost at shortstop, and hard-hitting Hank Majeski, a Yankees and Braves castoff, at third. Majeski would drive in 120 runs, among the league leaders in that category. The outfield was one of the best in baseball. As Bob Considine wrote in *Life* magazine in July 1948, Mack "inspired a phlegmatic young Czech named Elmer Valo with the energies of a human dynamo and breathed new life into a Detroit outfielder named Barney McCosky. In the other outfield position he placed Sam Chapman, a muscular former All-American gridman." The catcher was a standout, pudgy Buddy Rosar, in his tenth big-league season. The starting pitching staff of Marchildon, Coleman, Fowler, Carl Scheib, and Brissie was formidable. In the bullpen were Bob Savage, the first big-leaguer wounded in World War II, and Charlie Harris; that season they would go 5–1 and 5–2 respectively. The 1948 pennant race was one of the most dramatic in history. Five teams—the Yankees, the Red Sox, the Indians, the Tigers, and the A's—battled for the American League lead deep into the season. At nearly any time during the season, if one of those teams lost a doubleheader, it might drop from first place to fifth place. It was that tight a race. (In his book, *Epic Season: The 1948 American League Pennant Race*, David Kaiser, a professor of history at the Naval War College, wrote that this "historic season" was "unfolding at a time when baseball truly was America's 'national pastime.'")

And Lou Brissie, the astonishing 24-year-old rookie left-hander, found himself in the thick of it.

8

Pennant Race Heats Up

1.

"Marked by record-breaking attendance throughout the majors and minors, 1948 produced many other outstanding developments which made the season one of the greatest in the history of the game," wrote Clifford Kachline, in the *Baseball Guide's* "The Year 1948 in Review," "[and included] one of the bitterest pennant races in the history of the American League." And distinguishing themselves in that rugged pennant race were the Philadelphia A's, and their rookie left-hander Leland Victor (Lou) Brissie.

The A's remained at or close to the top of the American League standings from Opening Day, when they took the Patriots Day doubleheader from the Red Sox, 5-4, behind Marchildon, and 4-2, behind Brissie. Not only did Brissie pitch splendidly, but, as the Associated Press reported, he wielded a potent bat. With the score tied 1-1 in the fourth, the A's loaded the bases when the Red Sox walked Pete Suder intentionally to get to Brissie, "but Brissie crossed up the Sox strategy by banging a hit into right field on the first pitch," the story read. "The blow scored Chapman and Rosar...." It gave the A's a lead that Brissie didn't relinquish.

Johnny Pesky, the Red Sox's longtime shortstop and third baseman, remembered Brissie's quick delivery, which was "over the top." And many years later he said, "Brissie threw as hard as Roger Clemens or Nolan Ryan or Bob Turley."

On the mound, part of Brissie's left foot was numb from his injury. The sole of his foot had feeling, but not the top of his foot. And then there was the inevitable throbbing of the whole left leg. Because of the pain, Brissie rarely slept through the night. From his exertion during a ballgame, his sores would invariably open. He would wake in the night and either soak in a tub or cover the sores with salve, often doing both.

"I wouldn't say anything to anybody about it," he said, "because I figured that if I said anything they'd put me in a hospital and make me quit. So what I would do is I wouldn't do anything. I called Brubaker or Suraci and got a prescription, mostly for penicillin. I'd take it and try to stay off my feet. And I'd get up and go to the ballpark, but then during batting practice I'd stand there and wouldn't do anything. I was just lucky enough to where I got by with that."

John Chandler Griffin, a freelance writer and English professor at the University of South Carolina–Lancaster, took particular interest in Brissie. He traveled to Philadelphia when Brissie was scheduled to pitch.

Griffin wrote: "Pain was a constant companion. In the late innings, fans would become hushed as they watched him limp about the mound, his face contorted with pain as he pushed off on that shattered left leg. To those who knew his story, he was more than a great pitcher; he was a living symbol of man's will to win against all odds."

Brissie endured some hardships against opposing batters, as well. On April 25 he was belted for five runs in 6⅓ innings by the Senators, and the A's, taking a 7–3 loss, dropped to third place behind the Indians and Senators.

A little more than a week after Brissie had beaten the Red Sox on Opening Day, he faced the Red Sox again, in Shibe Park. This time he lost 11–5, including giving up a towering home run to right field by Williams.

But the A's were back in first place within days and the phrase "surprising A's" began to be used with regularity. On May 13, the headline in The New York Times read, "Athletics Overcome Browns with Aid of Brissie's Brilliant Relief Pitching/Athletics Annex 10th Straight, 8–4."

Writing in The Times before a series between the Yankees and A's, Louis Effrat noted, "Not since the glorious pennant-winning years of

1929, 1930 and 1931, has the 85-year-old (Mack) enjoyed so much continued success as that of the moment. Thanks to the best and certainly the most consistent pitching staff in the majors, right up to now, the Philadelphians are in first place. That's four notches higher than they were generally rated at the start of the season."

"The surprising Athletics," as David Kaiser wrote in his book on the 1948 pennant race, "swept a three-game weekend series from the Senators in Washington, putting them among the league leaders." Philadelphia took two games and first place from the Indians on May 4 and 6. The A's and the Indians were the two top teams at this time, and the Indians knocked the A's out of first and took a half-game lead on May 19, with Gene Bearden, a knuckle-balling rookie left-hander, beating Brissie 6–1 in Cleveland.

The A's came back and on May 26 moved into first place. The A's truly "got the baseball world's attention," wrote Kaiser, by taking a series from the Yankees in New York. After losing on Friday, the A's came back and "shocked 69,416 enthusiastic New Yorkers the next day," sweeping a doubleheader 8–6 and 3–1.

The Sunday game was rained out, but, to emphasize that the A's were legitimate, Mack declared that his infield of Fain, Suder, Joost, and Majeski was even better than his famous 1914 $100,000 infield of Stuffy McGinnis, Eddie Collins, Jack Barry, and Home Run Baker. (Rather an exaggeration, since Collins and Baker are in the Hall of Fame, while none of the '48 infield, though very good, was ever chosen for the baseball shrine.)

Of more immediate significance, it seemed, was that Mack purchased the contract of 36-year-old Nelson Potter from the Browns. The right-handed Potter had pitched capably for Mack and the A's in the late 1930s, and was a star for the pennant-winning St. Louis Browns in 1944, winning 19 games. By 1947, he had slipped to 4–10, with the lowly Browns, though his ERA was a relatively hopeful 4.04. He was 1–1 in early May when Mack, believing Potter still had enough left to help his staff, paid the then handsome sum, especially for the parsimonious Mack, of $20,000.

On Memorial Day, the A's and Boston hooked up once more, with Brissie once again on the mound. Brissie, against the now struggling seventh-place Red Sox went down to defeat, 7–0, with Williams banging a two-run homer. Despite this, the A's still found themselves on top of the standings, one game ahead of Cleveland, four ahead of New York, and 7½ ahead of Detroit.

Nelson Potter, meanwhile, had appeared in seven games for the A's and had a 2–1 record when, on Sunday, June 13, he relieved Brissie in the eighth inning, with the A's holding a 5–1 lead over the Indians.

Potter proceeded to give up six runs and lost the game. Mack was steaming. He waived Potter to the bench. "Were you doing your best out there?" Mack demanded of Potter.

Before Potter could answer, Mack said, "I paid $20,000 for you and that was my mistake. I don't care how good any player ever was, has been, or could be. All I care about is how much good he is now." Mack believed that Potter was giving only partial effort and gave him his release that night.

"Mr. Mack just got excited about losing a ballgame and flew off the handle," Potter told reporters. "It isn't true, as Mr. Mack inferred, that I wasn't trying my best. I told him I was doing the best I could, but otherwise, I kept quiet. I have respect for his age. That's the only time anything like that happened. I won two games for him in the New York series and I saved one in Detroit. He thought I was doing all right then." (Potter was signed by the Boston Braves and contributed to their winning the 1948 National League pennant, winning five games, losing two, and finishing with an overall 2.86 ERA.)

Potter had been brought in as a veteran, steadying influence on the A's. "I think that Potter's leaving us deflated a few fellas," said Brissie. "I think it discouraged them. It didn't affect me. I had other things to be concerned with. I thought we had a good pitching staff, and I thought we would be able to make it. But we did run into some tough breaks."

Bill McCahan, who had pitched a no-hitter in 1947, and whom the A's were counting on, ended up with a shoulder problem and contributed little. Dick Fowler suffered with bursitis in his pitching arm but still managed to do well, though not as well as he might have. (McCahan finished the season with a 4–7 record; Fowler was 15–8, the most wins on the club.)

Another veteran player picked up by Mack was Rudy York, the onetime slugging first-baseman, who had starred with pennant-winning Tigers and Red Sox teams. This was his 13th year in the big leagues and, at age 35, it would be his last; he played in just 31 games and hit .157 with no homers. "Rudy took an interest in me," said Brissie, "and if I had a bad outing he'd say, 'Don't worry, kid, you're gonna do okay.' During the season he'd say, 'You goin' to the bullpen today?' And I'd say, 'No, I pitched yesterday, so I won't go out there 'til later in the game.' He'd say, 'C'mon over here and sit with me.' And we'd talk about the pitcher.

"York would say, 'If you watch this guy, any time you see the white of the ball when he puts his hand in his glove, he's gonna be throwing a curveball.' And he started up talking about things like that. Helped me both as a pitcher—I became more careful of tipping off my pitches—and as a hitter. I remember one time we were playing the Yankees and there was somebody on base. I was going up and I got my bat and York took me by the arm. I turned to see what he wanted. He said, 'The first pitch to you will be a curveball.' It was and I got a base hit. He had studied the pitcher's habits. The pitcher was Red Embree, a right-hander.

"York was always talking about things like that. He was good at that. I'm sure a lot of it came from Hank Greenberg, when York was with Detroit, and Williams, when York was with Boston. So Rudy had been around, and he was passing some of that knowledge on to me, and it was highly appreciated. He got me looking at things that I'd never looked at before and didn't know a whole lot about. Eventually you reach a point where the coordination and the reflexes are not there, and you know what you ought to be doing but you just can't do it. And he was gone from baseball after that season, didn't really help us much. But he was very kind to me."

June was a good month for both Brissie and the A's. *The New York Times* noted: "Brissie stars in relief in a win"; "Brissie matches Hal

Newhouser virtually pitch-for-pitch but loses 2-1"; Brissie, turning in an "artistic six-hitter beats the Red Sox 4-2." The A's are in first; the A's drop out of first and go back into first again.

While some ballplayers say that they don't watch the scoreboard to see how other teams they are contending with are doing, Brissie wasn't one of them. "You always take a glance to see who was doing what—how they're coming along," he said. "But pressure affects you in one of two ways. It either makes you a better pitcher, or it has a negative effect." At this point, the pressures of the pennant race were having a salutary effect on Brissie and the A's.

To a large extent, Brissie had learned to handle bunts, but he still was vulnerable, especially later in the game when his leg began to tire. "A lot of it had to do with which foot I had to put forward first. If it was the left foot I had a hard time getting started because that one was bad. If it was the right one, I had to shift my weight and do my pushing off. But I managed okay most of the time.

"But I'll never forget an incident in a game against the Browns in Philadelphia. I had Fain push me out of the way to get a bunt on the third-base side and throw the runner out at third," Brissie recalled. "He knocked me down doing that. He said, 'I'm sorry, big fella, but I knew I could get him.'

"Sometimes, though, Fain was a bit too ambitious on bunts. We were playing the Red Sox, and Dom DiMaggio was the hitter and the bunt was in order. Fain would get to hoppin' and he'd keep creepin' in from first base as he hopped. He couldn't have been more than 20 feet from the plate and at the last minute Dom took a full swing at that ball and hit it square, and Fain went down in a heap hollering, 'No! No!' The ball sailed foul over the first-base dugout. Ferris sure didn't charge in on him as far as he did the next time."

Fain, who batted and threw left-handed, grew up in poverty in a tough section of Oakland, California. At 5'11" and 180 pounds, he was relatively small for a first baseman but proud of his defensive skills, though, as Brissie observed, he could tend toward the reckless. And while he frequently led the league in errors, he also led in assists, because of the chances he took. His aggressiveness made him a fan favorite. Fain's nickname was "Burrhead," for the severe hair style he sported. It may also have been indicative of a hard-headedness. A heavy drinker, Fain was prone to barroom brawls (he fractured a finger in one in 1953 and for his effort was fined $600) and temper outbursts. A slashing rather than a power hitter, he twice led the league in hitting, in 1951 and '52. In '51, he batted .344, despite missing several weeks with a broken bone in his foot after kicking the first-base bag in frustration at making an out.

(Retired, and living in California in 1986, Fain was arrested for growing a small quantity of marijuana in his backyard, and served 18 months in prison. He remained feisty until his death in 2001. He once said of the current players, "Most of them belong in the bushes." He believed he could hit better than many of them, if he could just "convince the commissioner to let me get my wheelchair on the field." Coincidentally, his teammate, the soft-spoken second baseman Pete Suder, also served in prison, but in another capacity than inmate. In retirement, Suder was warden of the Beaver [Pennsylvania] County Jail for 13 years.)

Now, in 1948, his second year in the big leagues, Fain was a more-or-less steady presence in the lineup and wound up with a .281 batting average and 10 stolen bases, tying Elmer Valo for high on the club.

• • •

By July 4, the A's had won 14 of their games by one run, with Brissie the winning pitcher in one of those games (he won three one-run games overall that season). Mack called the 1948 A's "the fightingest team I've ever had." While still capable of being an astute manager, at 85, Mack was increasingly forgetful. His coaches were taking over more and more of his duties and helping him with decisions. And he retained his idiosyncrasies. For one thing, to bring in pitchers he ignored the use of a telephone line from dugout to bullpen and used a hand-and-arm signaling system that had gone out of style many years earlier. Mack, born Cornelius Alexander McGillicuddy in 1862, was already a teenager and working in a shoe factory when Alexander

Graham Bell invented the telephone in 1876. Perhaps Mack, in 1948, 72 years later, was still suspicious of the newfangled instrument. Regardless, to get Joe Coleman from the bullpen, Mack had one of his coaches stand in front of the dugout and mimic shoveling coal. To get Dick Fowler, he had the coach imitate someone picking flowers, because with unfailing courtliness he always addressed Dick Fowler as "Mr. Flowers." It was even simpler with Brissie. To summon him, the coach just raised his left arm. Brissie was the lone left-hander on the A's staff for most of the season. (In 1949, the left-handers Alex Kellner and Bobby Shantz became starting pitchers but at times did relief work as well, and the signals for them were the same as for Brissie—except for the 5'6" Shantz the coach waved his arm at the knees; for the 6' Kellner it was at the shoulders, and for the 6'4½" Brissie it was over his head.)

In another historical oddity, just before the 1948 season began, another handicapped pitcher who developed into a star died on Valentine's Day, at the age of 71. This was Mordecai "Three-Finger" Brown. In his hometown of Terre Haute, Indiana, Brown worked as a miner until his baseball skills surfaced. Brown actually had four fingers on his pitching hand. At the age of seven he lost his index finger above the knuckle on his right hand in a farm accident that also left his pinkie useless. He also had a mangled middle finger. Brown believed the impairment was a significant aid to his pitching. "It gives me a bigger dip," Brown once said. In 14 seasons, most with the Chicago Cubs, from 1903–1916, Brown won 239 games and lost 129 and had the third best earned-run average of all time, 2.06, including six seasons under 2.00. That, plus five World Series wins, put him in the Baseball Hall of Fame.

While Brissie also had a problem with the index finger of his pitching hand, because of the imbedded piece of shrapnel, it did not help his pitches "dip." Rather, when it shifted just a little under the skin, and with the pressure applied to throwing a ball, it hurt.

2.

In early July, the A's whipped Boston two out of three games. Brissie gave up just six hits to win the series opener, 4–2, and got a little revenge against Williams, who went 1-for-4 and dropped his average to a paltry .399.

Shortly after, Brissie received a note from John Larner, an executive with the Boston Metropolitan Chapter of the American Red Cross:

Dear Lou:

This is just a brief note to thank you for helping us out at the Red Cross blood center in Boston. It was really good of you to give up some of your time to visit the place.

Incidentally, I had a pretty good seat at the game Friday night and you pitched a sweetheart of a game. It isn't often I've seen Ted Williams strike out, but you must have had plenty of hop when you got him twice!

Thanks again, and I hope you get your record into double figures in the win column.

• • •

On Monday, July 5, Cleveland led New York and Philadelphia by a game and a half. Boston had moved up to fourth, eight games out.

On July 7, Cleveland owner Bill Veeck signed Leroy "Satchel" Paige, the lanky, legendary, longtime Negro Leagues pitching great. It was also Paige's birthday—he was reportedly 42 years old—and became the oldest rookie in major league history. The conservative *The Sporting News* called Paige's signing "a travesty on baseball."

Paige made his big-league pitching debut two nights later, against the St. Louis Browns, relieving Bob Lemon in the fifth inning at Municipal Stadium in Cleveland. He thus became the seventh black major leaguer and the first black pitcher in American League history (the National League had broken that barrier with Dan Bankhead of the Dodgers, who pitched four games in 1947). Paige yielded a single to the first batter he faced, Chuck Stevens, but settled down to allow only one more hit and no runs before Larry Doby pinch-hit for him in the sixth inning.

Paige, who was so quotable that he is represented in *Bartlett's Book of Familiar Quotations*, said, when asked about being such an elderly rookie, "Age is a question of mind over matter. If you don't mind, age don't matter." In *Bartlett's*, one of Paige's bits of advice for keeping young is included: "Don't look back. Something might be gaining on you."

Brissie, in the A's dugout, saw Paige for the first time six days later, when the A's played a twi-night doubleheader against the Indians. In the second game, Paige came out of the bullpen in the sixth inning with the Indians ahead, 5–3, and two runners on. He retired the side, then gave up a two-run homer to Majeski in the seventh. Ken Keltner homered in the eighth, Doby cracked a two-run homer in the ninth, and the Indians won. Paige retired Philadelphia in the final two innings for his first major league win. Cleveland now had a 2½-game lead.

"Satchel must have been phenomenal in his day, and he had tremendous control, even in his old age," recalled Brissie. "He could thread a needle with that ball. He had a hesitation delivery—he'd stride out to the plate and he'd throw out that big foot and his arm would come through just a little bit later, throwing the hitter off his timing. There were a lot of complaints about that move, but the umpires simply couldn't see that what he was doing was illegal."

(Paige continued to excel and was drawing packed houses whenever it was announced he was scheduled to pitch, such as on August 13, against the White Sox in Chicago. A crowd of 50,013 packed Comiskey Park, and another 15,000 were turned away. Paige responded with a five-hitter, beating Chicago 5–0, with his first complete game and fourth straight win.)

On July 16, the night after Paige pitched against the A's, it was Brissie's turn to shine. He beat the Indians 10–5. Coleman beat them the following night. And the A's were a half-game behind the league leaders.

Brissie's won-lost record at that point was 10–8, he was among the league's strikeout leaders, and baseball fans were appreciative. Brissie began receiving letters like the following, from an 11-year-old boy in Las Vegas named Terry Jones (whose story had appeared in the *Las Vegas Review-Journal* in late July):

July 26, 1948:

Dear Lou: I was surprised and happy to receive your auto-graphed picture. Thanks so much, it was swell of you to send it. I'm not sure who told you about me, but I think it must have been Warren Williamson, the sports announcer here in Las Vegas. On his radio program he often tells an interesting story about some famous baseball player. The night he told about you, he said, 'Did you hear that Terry?' I called and told him I heard the broadcast and maybe I'd be a ball-player yet.

Philadelphia is in first place, but no wonder for they have a swell fellow like you on their team. My dad wants me to be a pitcher like you, but there are a lot of people who want me to be an umpire. But to me it doesn't make any difference, just as long as it is connected with baseball.

Things were a little rough last fall when I was having a series of operations. I told Mother, 'I sometimes have doubts about God—maybe it is just another glorified story like the one about Washington never telling a lie. For if the world was distroyed (sic) by water and only Noah and his family were saved—how do we know there is a God or the story is true? If He is a just and merciful God—then why does he make me and others crippled?—we didn't do anything wrong.' I'll never forget what she told me. She said, 'Terry, you nor anyone else is being punished. We all have a certain set of problems and circumstances facing us. Some are tested occa-sionally and others every single day. The greater the test, the greater are the potentialities of the person who is being tested. Christ was the greatest man spiritually, and he received the greatest test. You are receiving a very great test and there

115

you are undoubtedly capable of corresponding greatness of soul....

I am sending a clipping out of the paper here. May I say thank you again for your picture and I want to wish you the best of everything always.

Your Pal and Friend; Terry.

The clipping noted that Terry Jones was a victim of poliomyelitis. The accompanying photo showed a small boy holding a cane.

"I wrote back and tried to answer some of his concerns," Brissie recalled. "I tried to encourage him, as I did with other letters like his that I received. I told Terry that some things happen in life that can't be explained. I know it's frustrating, sometimes to the point of tears—and I've surely shed some out of frustration—that when you want to do something very much, and know how to do it, but can't, it can really get you down. I said that it's my belief that God doesn't control everything, and that when roadblocks are placed in our way, we have a choice. Try to do better every day, or not. You hate what you can't do, but when you have a serious injury you just have to try to take one step at a time. Sometimes you wonder: Will I ever get better? I've been on this walker so long, will I ever be able to throw it away? I guess it's a cliché but it was true for me: you try to do a little more today than you did yesterday. If I had a philosophy, that was it. That was my philosophy to try to get back into baseball."

It was also Brissie's philosophy that he couldn't, or wouldn't, allow himself to feel sorry for his situation. "When I came back to baseball, I knew I had to earn my way and I'm going to pitch whenever I was asked," said Brissie. "I was never going to say my leg's bothering me or I feel bad. I couldn't do that. I think that helped me in a way and it hurt me in a way. A fellow who kept track of my pitching sent me a letter and told me, 'Do you realize that although you were only in 35 or 40 games that you warmed up and were ready to go in close to 70 ballgames, where they would get you up and get you warm and not use you? I wonder what kind of toll this takes.'" Brissie added: "There were times when Mr. Mack called on me a lot to get warm and I did. I'm not using that as an excuse because that's the way I wanted it. I wanted to make sure that I earned my way on that team, and that I didn't get any kind of free ride. I started and relieved every year I was in the big leagues. Some of the other pitchers did some of both, but I think not as much."

Brissie, meanwhile, found himself continually having to make adjustments that other pitchers would never even have to consider, such as trying to hold a runner on first base.

"When there was a runner on first, I had a problem," he said. "Once I kicked up my right leg in my delivery, I didn't have the mobility in my left leg like other guys to turn to throw to first base. I couldn't change, and had to throw to the plate. So I had to decide before I got set to pitch whether to throw to first or not. I had to make the commitment up front. Bill Wight, another lefty, who played with the White Sox and Red Sox when I was in the league, had the best pickoff motion I've ever seen. He told me once, 'Make sure the guy has stopped.' You see, someone like Rizzuto would not take much of a leadoff at first, but he'd start to walk slowly toward second, which would give him a very good jump on a steal when you threw to the plate. So I'd hold my stretch position, hands in front of me, until the runner stopped moving. Wight was so good, so adept at changing in midmotion and throwing to first instead of home, that I saw him pick a guy off who was nearly standing on the bag. I could never do that, but I compensated well enough that I didn't have an excess amount of guys stealing off me."

• • •

On July 18, White Sox outfielder Pat Seerey, in his sixth season in the big leagues, and known around the league as "Fat Pat," hit four home runs in an 11-inning game against the A's. He knocked in seven runs in the 12–11 Chicago victory, becoming the fifth player with four homers in a game, thereby joining modern players Lou Gehrig and Chuck Klein in the record book. Lou Brissie took the loss, entering the game in the eighth and giving up Seery's fourth home run. But pitchers would have little trouble with Seery from that point forward.

Seery, thickly built at 5'10", 200-plus pounds, would lead the league in strikeouts (for the fourth time) despite hitting 19 homers, and was gone from the game the next season, suffering from a surfeit of beer and cheeseburgers. For Brissie, however, Seery's home-run flurry seemed but a momentary hurdle; the A's suffered an even more serious setback a few weeks later.

On August 3, four clubs, Cleveland, Philadelphia, New York, and Boston, were in a virtual deadlock for first place, separated by just six percentage points. That day, the season for the A's, in Brissie's estimation—and an opinion shared by others, as well—changed the good fortune of the team. Eddie Joost, the A's standout shortstop, jammed his thumb while sliding into third base in a game at Chicago. He was out of the lineup for about two weeks. During that period, the A's, while maintaining a presence in the pennant race, were without their field leader for the crucial stretch run, and it would take its toll.

On Monday, August 9, the standings read: Cleveland ahead of Philadelphia by a half-game, 2½ in front of New York, and three ahead of Boston. Later in the week the A's took two of three from the Senators and, on Friday, August 13, were in first place by a half game.

David Kaiser wrote: "The (A's) were a team of good average hitters with fine on-base percentages, including Elmer Valo (.322), Barney McCosky (.327), and Joost and Fain (who were both hitting around .250 but drawing a lot of walks). Hank Majeski, meanwhile, had more than 80 RBIs, rivaling the Indians' Ken Keltner as the league's most productive third baseman. Fowler and Coleman had been excellent of late, and Brissie had pitched well as a starter and reliever.

"The Athletics were a fine club, but they lacked the power to compete with the three teams over whom they enjoyed a momentary ascendancy. More than half of the remaining games pitted them against the other three contenders, including nine straight over the next 10 days against the Yankees and the Red Sox. Few people really believed they would be on top in September, and such in fact was not destined to be the case. Yet we must pay tribute to this remarkable aggregation of gutsy pitchers, fine fielders, and line-drive hitters, which, on the morning of August 13, 108 games into the season, led the most remarkable pennant race in the history of major league baseball."

As for the manager, Kaiser wrote that Mack, "could no longer remember his players' names or maintain his concentration over the full length of a game, and coach Al Simmons, a veteran of Mack's great 1928-1932 teams, frequently had to disregard his signs and give the team instructions on his own. ('You used better judgment than I did, Al,' Connie would sometimes admit.)"

By the second weekend in August, the A's, having lost their hold on first place, beat the Yankees twice on Sunday, August 15, before 72,468 fans in Yankee Stadium. "Brissie stopped yet another Yankee rally after Joe D had tripled," wrote Kaiser.

On August 16, Babe Ruth died, at age 53, after a two-year battle with throat cancer. The day before he passed away, Connie Mack visited him and Mack said that Ruth told him, "The termites have got me." The following day, Ruth's body was on display at Yankee Stadium, and an estimated 100,000 people passed by to pay their respects. The flag on Main Street in Cooperstown was flown at half-mast and the lights in all ballparks were dimmed in tribute. The Ruth family received condolences from, among others, President Harry Truman and former President Herbert Hoover. It was remembered that, in 1930, during the Depression, the story went that Ruth, who had signed an $80,000 a year contract, was told he was making more than the president (Hoover). "Why not?" responded Ruth, "I had a better year than he did." *

On August 19, Francis Cardinal Spellman celebrated a funeral mass for Ruth at St. Patrick's Cathedral in New York. Some 6,000 mourners were on hand. Two of the pallbearers, infielder Joe Dugan

---

* For the record, Ruth hit .345 in 1929 and added to his incredible dominance as a power hitter: he led the league that year in both slugging percentage with .697 (the 11th time in 12 years he had done so) and home runs with 46, the 10th time in 12 years. At his death, Ruth held, among numerous records, the highest career slugging percentage (.691), most career homers (714), and most lifetime walks (2,056). Also, from his first four years in the major leagues as a pitcher, he held the record for having pitched the most scoreless innings (29⅔) in World Series play.

and pitcher Waite Hoyt, had been Ruth's teammates. It was a very hot day that afternoon and as they helped carry the casket out of the church, Dugan said to Hoyt, "I'd give a hundred dollars for a cold beer." Hoyt responded, "Joe, so would the Babe." According to the *1949 Baseball Guide* detailing news of the previous season, "the story is told with some variations, but sources agree on the basics."

Brissie recalled seeing Ruth when he warmed up for his first major league game, against the Yankees in Yankee Stadium on the last day of the regular season, some 11 months earlier. He remembered seeing a wan and frail Ruth. "Seeing him then," recalled Brissie, "he looked like the most unlikely person to be a great home-run hitter. But when he died, we were all saddened. At the ballpark, we all stood for a moment of silence. He meant so much to baseball, and I'd say, to America, too. Years later, when I'd travel out of the country, and mention baseball, in many cases the only baseball player anyone ever heard of was Babe Ruth. Except for maybe George Washington and Abraham Lincoln, it seemed he might have been the most famous American."

Meanwhile, the pennant race continued. And on the day that Ruth died, the A's fortunes took a blow. The Associated Press reported that "Eddie Joost, shortstop of the amazing A's, was forced to leave the (Red Sox) game in the third inning when he aggravated an injury to his right hand." While Fowler, with Brissie in relief, beat the Red Sox without Joost—Majeski moved over to shortstop, and rookie utility man Don White went in at third—and regained second place in the pennant race, the team simply was not the force it had been.

"We lost Eddie for much of the rest of the season," recalled Brissie. "Eddie was our leader, and that took some of the starch out of us. Eddie had a lot of home runs for a leadoff hitter, so he always had an early affect on our games. Losing him made a tremendous difference. It was like losing Rizzuto or Derek Jeter—especially up the middle. It lessened our double plays, where Eddie had great range. We battled and battled and then, 'Gee, you lose the guy you need the most.'"

On August 28, Brissie went the distance in beating the Browns in 10 innings, 5–4, for his 13th win of the season, but two days later working in relief against the White Sox, he failed to hold a ninth-inning lead.

"Brissie was greatly responsible for the A's being in the pennant race late in the season," Bobby Doerr, the star second baseman for the Red Sox, recalled years later. "His ball was alive. Very remarkable."

Buddy Rosar, the A's starting catcher, said that Brissie had "the hardest curveball I've ever caught."

Time, however, was running out for the A's. On September 1, McCahan started against the Indians in Philadelphia, walked three straight batters in the first inning, and Mack immediately replaced him with Brissie, who pitched the rest of the game. But the left-hander struggled and the Athletics lost 8–1 to Bob Feller.

Following that loss, the fourth-place A's were still in contention, 5½ games behind league-leading Boston. By Wednesday, September 8, the Athletics had fallen 9½ games behind Boston. New York, in second place, was 1½ games behind the leader, with Cleveland in third, 4½ behind.

Throughout the season newspaper stories around the country followed Brissie's success with the A's, invariably using the phrase "war hero" to underscore the courage of the young pitcher with the brace to protect his shattered leg. "Writers call me a hero, but I wasn't a hero," said Brissie. "So many guys did so much more than I did—even on my own team, like Marchildon and Savage and Joe Coleman, who was a fighter pilot. Each of them played in the major leagues before giving up baseball to go to war for three years.

"As for me, I left a lot of guys in hospitals, guys fighting bigger battles without anyone cheering for them. I thought just by showing I could do it, I could help them."

Meanwhile, as he had throughout the season, Brissie felt obliged to visit veterans' hospitals as he made his travels around the league. One of those visits was to the Veterans Administration Hospital in Perry Point, Maryland. The A's were playing the Senators, and before a night game, Brissie took the train to Maryland in the morning and returned early enough to suit up with the team. The director of the hospital, A.H. Hughes, wrote a thank-you note to Brissie, dated September 10, 1948:

> *Dear Lou:*
>
> *Our patients are still remarking about your visit to the hospital Thursday. All the boys who received your autographed balls and the others who had an opportunity to talk with you were greatly benefited by your presence. One as yourself, who in spite of physical handicaps, has shown the determination and courage to fulfill an ambition serves as an ideal example for the men who are hospitalized here. You made a deep impression on them.*
>
> *The personnel and patients of this hospital are most grateful to you for taking your valuable time to be with us. We sincerely hope that your career in the major leagues will be as successful as your freshman record indicates it will be....*

Brissie also lent his name to any cause he felt worthwhile, and there were a number, including the United States National Guard.

> *Dear Mr. Brissie, began a letter from Major General Kenneth F. Cramer, Chief, National Guard Bureau, Washington, D.C. Inclosed is a proof of an advertisement which the National Guard Bureau will run in the October issues of* Boys' Life *and* Open Road. *This is one of a series of such ads which have been run in boys' magazines.*
>
> *As you may know, the National Guard is an integral part of the Nation's military establishment and the Secretary of the Army recently announced that six of its divisions will be included with 12 Regular Army divisions in a striking force to be organized by the end of the present fiscal year....*
>
> *We would appreciate it greatly if you would give us permission to use your picture and an appropriate quotation in a similar advertisement....*

Approval granted and quotation supplied.

• • •

On Monday afternoon, September 20, Boston was ahead of Cleveland by a half game with 10 games to go, followed by New York one game out, and Philadelphia 7½ behind.

By the time the Indians took the field Monday night, before another big crowd of 44,492, they knew they needed another win just to stay in second place. Bearden, facing Lou Brissie, had another shaky start, but double plays bailed him out of jams in the second, fourth, and sixth innings. The Indians, meanwhile, got a run in the first and two in the fourth, and Joe Gordon doubled home Lou Boudreau in the fifth for a 4-0 lead. The A's came back with three in the seventh, but wound up losing, 6-3.

On September 24, with seven games left in the season, the Red Sox, Yankees, and Indians were in a three-way tie for first at 91-56. The A's were fourth, where they found themselves at season's end.

Brissie also read that Potter had won another game for the Braves (his fifth against two losses). "If Mr. Mack hadn't lost his temper," said Brissie, "I think Potter could have helped us during the season."

Out of contention, the A's could only watch the three other teams in a mad scramble for the pennant. On October 2, the next-to-last day of the season, Gene Bearden shut out the Tigers 8-0, and eliminated the Yankees, who lost to the Red Sox 5-1.

On October 3, the last day of the season, the Indians held "Bill Veeck Day," drawing 74,181 fans. The hometown fans saw the Tigers beat the Indians 7-1, on Hal Newhouser's five-hitter. Bob Feller was the losing pitcher. With that crowd, the Indians set a one-season major league attendance record of 2,620,627, and Cleveland owner Veeck, with ingenious promotions and management moves—not the least of which was the signing of Satchel Paige, and his subsequently success-ful season—solidified the nickname ascribed to him by Indians general manager Hank Greenberg, "The Pied Piper."

Meanwhile, at Fenway Park, the Red Sox again whipped the Yankees, to set up a one-game playoff between the Indians and Red Sox, both with 96-58 records. At Fenway Park on October 4, in the first pennant playoff in American League history, Bearden, in his only truly standout season of seven in the major leagues, beat the Red Sox, 8–3, for his 20th win; he was supported by two homers and two singles from player/manager Lou Boudreau, named the Most Valuable Player in the league. The game ended one of the most stirring pennant races of all time.

Almost as an anticlimax, the Indians went on to beat the Boston Braves in the World Series, four games to two.

Braves shortstop Alvin Dark, who batted .322 for the season, received the Rookie of the Year award (at that time, only one award was given for the two leagues). Satchel Paige said, "I declined the honor. I wasn't sure which year those gentlemen had in mind." Brissie placed third in the voting behind Bearden, and beat out Paige, who was fourth.

Brissie was, however, named to the Major League Rookie All-Star team. He finished the season with a 14–10 record and a respectable 4.13 earned-run average in 194 innings. He started 25 games and was 4–2 in relief, with five saves. Compiling 127 strikeouts, he ranked fourth in the league behind Bob Feller, Bob Lemon, and Hal Newhouser—all future Hall of Famers—and just ahead of the Yankees' Vic Raschi, "the Springfield Rifle." Brissie led the league in strikeouts per nine innings, averaging 5.89, ahead of Feller's 5.27.

Despite his inability to plant his left leg and drive off it, as do all left-handed batters, Brissie still managed to bat .237, with 18 hits—one of which was a double—and had 10 runs batted in 83 plate appearances.

Even before the season was over, the AP reported that "Lefty Lou Brissie, rookie southpaw of the Athletics, was hospitalized for infection of his war-shattered left leg."

In October, he was honored by the Christian Athletes Foundation as a "most wholesome influence on youth." In early November, the Clemson (South Carolina) American Legion Post awarded Brissie a plaque for "distinguished service as a soldier and courageous achievement as a citizen which are an inspiration to all men everywhere."

In late November, he went into the hospital for a surgical procedure to remove bone chips and shell fragments that had remained lodged in his leg and had caused soreness and irritation, with always the possibility of infection. About a week later, accompanying a photograph in *The New York Times* of a smiling, bald Mack and a smiling, thick-haired Brissie together holding a contract, a caption read: "The young southpaw of the Athletics, just out of the hospital after another operation on his leg injured in the war, comes to terms with Connie Mack in the latter's office in Philadelphia."

"The Lou Brissie story was widely publicized around the world," wrote Dr. Wilbur K. Brubaker, who had saved his leg with surgery in the Naples hospital, "and was said to have a tremendous inspirational effect on youngsters everywhere. The true significance of the Lou Brissie story does not pertain to the miracle drug called penicillin or the brilliant execution of surgical skill, but rather to the remarkable recuperative resources of the human body and the indomitable raw courage of a most determined young man, Lou Brissie."

On April 10, 1945, Dr. Brubaker was called to the office of Commander Col. George Reyer, and was presented with a citation of distinguished service from the Surgeon General of the United States in recognition of his management of the Lou Brissie case.

9

All-Star Lefty

1.

Before a spring-training outing in 1949, in West Palm Beach, Florida, Brissie received a message that Gen. George Marshall, then Secretary of State, wanted to meet him. General Marshall was revered as one of the great military geniuses of the Second World War—he was the one, after all, that chose General Eisenhower to lead the D-Day invasion. And it was his Marshall Plan, giving aid to countries in Europe, that helped rebuild Europe after the war had torn the continent apart. "I was thrilled that he wanted to meet me," said Brissie. "Well, I pitched my three innings—I was having a pretty good spring—and had a shower and went over to where he was sitting in a box behind the home-plate screen." Brissie took two baseballs along and signed one for the general and then asked if Marshall would sign one for him. "We had a nice little visit. He said, 'Your leg's doing all right?' I said, 'Yes it is, Mr. Secretary.' He said, 'You seem to be doing well.' And he asked which hospitals I'd had my work done. It was more of a formal thing. And of course I excused myself because he was there on vacation."

The Associated Press took pictures of the pair, of the general and the former corporal, and it ran in newspapers across the country. It was an indication that, though the war had been over for four years, it was still paramount in Americans' minds, and some of its particularly visible participants were still respectfully and gratefully recalled.

• • •

Off their relatively strong 1948 season the "surprising" or "amazing" or maybe just fortunate A's, who had finished fourth, some experts,

127

or so-called experts, picked Philadelphia to win the American League pennant, for the first time since 1931. It was also the first time since 1933 that they had finished first in the division (in the then eight-team league). Their record also included nine last-place finishes in those 14 years. There was no chance that the owner would fire the manger for this abysmal performance. After all, the owner *was* the manager.

And, though he was 86 during the 1949 season, he was being hailed in some quarters as not just "the Grand Old Man" of baseball, but as a resurrected genius, a title that he had sometimes laid claim to in his great championship seasons, the first coming in 1902, followed by '05, '10, '11, '13, '14, and '29 to '31. When Mack first became manager of the A's, in 1901—two years before the Wright brothers' first flight at Kitty Hawk—he was 38 years old. "Old," it was said, "for a freshman manager." "Old" would be an adjective forever applied to Mack. He seldom saw his players after a game, unless there was something exceptional to relate in regard to the game, good or bad. If his ballclub had won a particularly tough game, as Bob Considine wrote in *Life* magazine in 1948, he would "poke his head" into the locker room, pat "his long, knuckly hands together in polite applause, looking around the room and say, 'This is for you,' with quiet warmth."

Before every game, in warm weather, a fresh bath towel was placed behind his back by one of the coaches, clubhouse personnel, or players. "He makes impatient sounds like 'Stop babying me,' when minor homages are paid to him," wrote Considine, "but it is the belief of those very close to him that the Old Man would feel hurt if he were not thus pampered."

Mack had the nucleus of his 1948 team back and he was counting on, among others, the solid second-year pitcher Lou Brissie, honored as the starting pitcher for the home opener, on April 19, against the Red Sox in Shibe Park. (Dick Fowler had pitched the season opener the day before in Washington, the site where the season traditionally began—and lost 3-2.)

Brissie began the season "just as he had last year—beating the Red Sox 3-2," read the Associated Press report. He gave up seven hits, two to Williams. Joost homered in the seventh for the deciding run.

All-Star Box Score

AMERICAN LEAGUE

	ab.	r.	h.	po.	a.	e.
D. DiMaggio, Bos, rf-cf	5	2	2	2	0	0
Raschi, N. Y., p........	1	0	0	0	1	0
Kell, Detroit, 3b........	3	2	2	0	1	0
Dillinger, St. L., 3b....	1	2	1	0	2	0
Williams, Boston, lf....	2	1	0	1	0	0
Mitchell, Cleve., lf.....	1	0	1	1	0	1
J. DiMaggio N. Y., cf.	4	1	2	0	0	0
Doby, Cleve., rf-cf.....	1	0	0	2	0	0
Joost, Phila., ss........	2	1	1	2	2	0
Stephens, Boston, ss...	2	0	0	2	0	0
E. Robinson, Wash.. 1b	5	1	1	8	0	0
Goodman, Boston, 1b..	0	0	0	1	1	0
Michaels, Chicago, 2b..	2	0	0	1	3	0
J. Gordon, Cleve., 2b..	2	1	1	3	3	0
Tebbetts, Boston, c....	2	0	2	2	0	0
Berra, N. Y., c.........	3	0	0	2	1	0
Parnell, Boston, p......	1	0	0	1	0	0
Trucks, Detroit p......	1	0	0	0	0	0
Brissie, Phila., p......	1	0	0	0	0	0
Wertz, Detroit, rf.....	2	0	0	0	0	0
Total	41	11	13	27	15	1

NATIONAL LEAGUE

	ab.	r.	h.	po.	a.	e.
Reese, Brooklyn, ss....	5	0	0	3	3	1
J. Robinson, B'klyn, 2b	4	3	1	1	1	0
Musial, St. L., cf-rf..	4	1	3	2	0	0
Kiner, Pittsburgh, lf...	5	1	1	3	0	0
Mize, N. Y., 1b........	2	0	1	1	0	0
Hodges, B'klyn, 1b.....	3	1	1	8	2	0
Marshall, N. Y., rf.....	1	1	0	1	0	1
Bickford, Boston, p.....	0	0	0	0	0	0
bThomson, N. Y.......	1	0	0	0	0	0
Pollet, St. Louis, p.....	0	0	1	0	0	0
Blackwell, Cinc'nati, p.	0	0	0	0	0	0
Slaughter, St. L., rf...	1	0	0	0	0	0
Roe, Brooklyn, p.......	0	0	0	0	0	0
Kazak, St. Louis, 3b...	2	0	2	0	0	1
S. Gordon, N. Y., 3b...	2	0	1	0	4	0
Seminick, Phila., c.....	1	0	0	3	0	1
Campanella, B'klyn, c.	2	0	0	2	0	1
Spahn, Boston, p.......	0	0	0	0	0	0
Newcombe, B'klyn, p..	1	0	0	0	0	0
aSchoendienst, St. L...	1	0	1	0	0	0
Munger, St. Louis, p...	0	0	0	0	0	0
Pafko, Chicago, cf.....	2	0	1	2	0	0
Total	37	7	12	27	10	5

aSingled to center for Newcombe in fourth.

bFlied out for Bickford in Sixth.

Amer. League...4 0 0 2 0 2 3 0 0—11
Nat'l League....2 1 2 0 0 2 0 0 0— 7

Earned runs—American League 7, National League 7.

Runs batted in—J. DiMaggio 3, E. Robinson, Tebbetts, Musial 2, Newcombe, Kazak, Joost 2, Kiner 2, D. DiMaggio, Dillinger, Mitchell.

Two-base hits—J. Robinson, Tebbetts, Gordon, D. DiMaggio, J. DiMaggio, J. Gordon, Mitchell. Home runs—Musial, Kiner. Stolen base—Kell. Double plays—Michaels, Joost and E. Robinson; Joost, Michaels and E. Robinson; J. Robinson, Reese and Hodges. Left on bases—American League 8, National League 12. Bases on balls—Off Spahn 2 (Joost, Williams), Parnell (Marshall), Newcombe (Williams), Trucks 2 (J. Robinson, Marshall), Munger (Michaels), Bickford (Kell), Brissie 2 (Campanella, Reese), Raschi 3 (S. Gordon, Pafko, Musial). Struck out—By Spahn 3 (D. DiMaggio, Williams, Parnell), Parnell (Mize), Brissie (Pafko), Blackwell 2 (J. Gordon, Stephens), Raschi (Campanella).

Pitching summary—Off Spahn 4 hits and 4 runs in 1 1/3 innings, Parnell 3 and 3 in 1 (none out in 2d), Newcombe 3 and 2 in 2 2/3, Trucks 3 and 2 in 2, Munger 0 and 0 in 1, Bickford 2 and 2 in 1, Brissie 5 and 2 in 3, Pollet 4 and 3 in 1, Blackwell 0 and 0 in 1, Roe 0 and 0 in 1, Raschi 1 and 0 in 3. Hit by pitcher—By Parnell (Seminick). Winner—Trucks. Loser —Newcombe.

Umpires—Barlick (N) plate, Hubbard (A) 1B, Gore (N) 2B, Summers (A) 3B, Ballanfant (N) LF, Grieve (A) RF. Time of game—3:04. Attendance—32,577 (paid). Receipts— $79,225.02.

Lou Brissie was featured on baseball cards each year of his professional career. This is the 1948 card from Leaf.

With the folding of competitor Leaf, Bowman was the primary publisher of baseball cards in 1950. This is their Lou Brissie card from that year.

The box score for the 1949 All-Star Game in Ebbets Field, Brooklyn.

Lou Brissie writes,
"Schoolmates Earl and
Doris Elledge (left), Dot
and I. February 1944."

Lou (standing left) visiting
with friends Red Riddle and
Milton Roberts from his
Presbyterian College days.

This hospital (foreground) in Naples, Italy, served as the U.S. Army 300th General Hospital during World War II. Nestled in the shadow of Mount Vesuvius, it was here that persistence, penicillin, and skilled surgeons saved Brissie's shattered left leg.

On a sunny day in April 1944, the first day the cast was removed from his broken right leg, Dot and Lou Brissie enjoyed the lawn at Finney General Hospital in Thomasville, Georgia.

"Mr. Mack shows us how," writes Lou Brissie. This image was taken in 1947 at the A's spring-training camp in West Palm Beach, Florida. Brissie stands second from the left.

Lou Brissie,
demonstrating
his pitch form
for the
Philadelphia A's.

Lou Brissie and Gen. George Marshall, then Secretary of State, exchange auto-graphed baseballs before a 1949 spring-training game in West Palm Beach, Florida.

Mr. Mack congratulates Lou Brissie, Eddie Joust, and Alex Kellner on their selection to the 1949 American League All-Star team.

Ron, Rob, Vicki, Dot, and Lou Brissie in 1951, the year Lou was traded to the
Cleveland Indians.

The 1951 Cleveland Indians pitching staff (left to right): Lou Brissie, Steve Gromek,
Early Wynn, Bob Lemon, Mike Garcia, and Bob Feller.

Mickey Mantle signs autographs for American Legion player of the year, Pete Fox, at the 1956 World Series. "Mickey was always available for us," commented Brissie.

In a good will effort, the State Department sent Brissie to Australia to run baseball clinics. During his two-month stay in 1959, he visited children in a Sydney hospital and enjoyed sharing the finer points of the game with his eager audience.

Lou Brissie greets President Bush on the tarmac of Dobbins Air Reserve Base near Atlanta, Georgia, on July 22, 2008. The 84-year-old Brissie's efforts mentoring wounded veterans at the Department of Veterans Affairs Medical Center in Augusta, Georgia, earned praise from the president.

Sam Chapman made a superb running catch in the eighth off Bobby Doerr's long drive to center with two on to help seal the win. It was hardly unusual for Chapman to make an outstanding play.

"Sam was a wonderful athlete," said Brissie. "He could hit, hit for power, had a strong arm, could cover a lot of ground in center field—he led the league in putouts for four seasons—and he could run, and not just on the baseball field." Besides being an All-American center fielder for the University of California, Samuel Blake Chapman, with dark, matinee-idol good looks, was an All-American halfback, too, and led the Golden Bears to a national championship in 1937 and a Rose Bowl win in 1938. Born and raised in Tiburon, California, across the Golden Gate Bridge from San Francisco, he was nicknamed "The Tiburon Terror." He was also a basketball and track star in high school. Shortly after graduation from Cal, Chapman, at a well-knit 6' 180 pounds, turned down a pro football career after being drafted by the Washington Redskins, and made his debut with the A's on May 16, 1938.

"Sam told me about the first time he came to the major leagues, and thought it might be a mistake," recalled Brissie. "The A's were playing a series against Cleveland, and Sam batted against three outstanding pitchers, Mel Harder, Bob Feller, and Johnny Allen. They knocked him down a lot. When he faced Feller, it appeared that Feller was looking at third base in his windup, and all at once the umpire called, 'Strike one.' He hardly got his bat on the ball against those guys. He told me, 'After those three games, I thought, I made a bad decision. I'm not sure I belong in the big leagues.'"

Chapman got himself together nicely, immediately becoming the starting center fielder and batting .259 with 17 homers the rest of the season. He got better and better. In 1941, he batted .322, then joined the Navy, and served as a pilot and flight instructor in Corpus Christi, Texas. He returned to baseball in late 1945, and while he never reached .300 as a batter again, he remained a formidable player on a formidable team and made the 1946 All-Star team.

Now, shortly after the 1949 season was under way, the A's looked as if they might recapture some of the magic of the previous season, even when encountering trouble. The May 22 doubleheader was a prime example. The A's won both ends, with Brissie winning the second game, 7–3, despite bouts of wildness, walking nine batters, including forcing one run home with the bases loaded. The A's moved within two games of the idle league-leading Yankees. But they began to slowly sink after that.

"We ran into some rough going," recalled Brissie, "and we never seemed to regain traction." Unlike 1948, the A's rarely saw the light of first place, or second or third, for that matter. The Red Sox, the Indians, the Yankees, and the Tigers were all superior to the A's. By June 3, the A's were in sixth place, 8½ behind the Yankees. "We just had a hard time scoring runs," said Brissie. And while they showed the grit of '48—they moved into second place, five games behind the Yankees as late as midway through the season, on July 7—a six-game losing streak sank their chances for good.

Not one of the starting eight players hit .300, with Elmer Valo the leader at .283. Sam Chapman, with 24 homers and 108 runs batted in, and Eddie Joost, with 23 homers and 81 RBIs, provided what power the A's could generate. The defense tried to make up for the light hitting; the infield of Fain, Suder, Joost, and Majeski helped the team turn 217 double plays, still a major league record, but it hardly offset the offensive deficiency.

And they had pitching problems. Joe Coleman came down with a sore arm, and Phil Marchildon was out the entire season, pitching in only seven games, while Carl Scheib, who won 14 games in 1948, won just nine. However, Alex Kellner, a rookie, came through with 20 wins.

Charlie Harris, the A's relief pitcher, recalled that Earle Brucker, the pitching coach, watched Brissie warm up in the bullpen before a start in Chicago. He noted the sound Brissie's pitch made when it popped loudly into the catcher's mitt. "Man, he must have his stuff today," said Brucker. "They'll be lucky to get a hit off him."

Harris said that, in the major leagues, "if you don't throw it right, if you get the pitch in the wrong place by even just a little bit, you'll be in trouble." And, unfortunately, that was what happened to Brissie that day.

"Lou was not a high-ball pitcher," continued Harris, "and his ball was high that day. Not a good day for Lou. I don't think he lasted three innings. But when he was right, he was amazing. He could throw the ball somewhere around 100 miles an hour."

So far this season, the losing game against the White Sox was a relative aberration for Brissie. By June 14, after beating the Tigers 7–3 on eight hits in a complete game ("Brissie hurled one-hit ball the last five innings," reported the AP), his record stood at 6–3. And one month later, on Independence Day, having won three more games in a row and improving his record to 9–3, he received the news that he had been selected to play in the All-Star Game. Lou Boudreau, the manager of the American League team that year (the manager who won the league pennant the season before is traditionally named for the honor the following July), chose both Brissie and Kellner from the A's. The other American League pitchers were Vic Raschi and Allie Reynolds of the Yankees, Bob Lemon of the Indians, Mel Parnell of the Red Sox, and Virgil Trucks of the Tigers. Ted Williams led the poll of all players with more than 2 million fan votes. The game also had a particular historic element: Jackie Robinson, voted onto the National League starting team at second base, became the first black player to play in a major league All-Star Game (three other black players, pitcher Don Newcombe and catcher Roy Campanella of the Dodgers, and outfielder Larry Doby of the Indians, also later appeared in the game).

"The first time I saw Jackie Robinson was in the spring of 1947," recalled Brissie. "We were playing the Dodgers in Vero Beach and Jackie was trying to make the team, as I was. During batting practice, we crossed paths on the field. I thought he and I shared something in common, that we were both trying to overcome obstacles. He had to be having a tough time. You're alone with the struggle, and you have to fight a lot of battles internally. There were so many unknowns—Will I be accepted? What's it going to be like?

"I said to him, 'Good luck,' and he nodded but kept going. It didn't upset me. I figured he didn't think it was such a good idea to be talking to the opposition. He was certainly in a different position than

I was, with all eyes on him. And I respected that. Just as I did at the All-Star Game."

The only other A's player on the team was Joost, whom the fans voted to start at shortstop. Joost acknowledged that he owed a lot to Connie Mack for reviving his baseball career. Joost had a reputation for being outspoken and contrary. Most of that came from his first big-league manager, Charlie Dressen of the Cincinnati Reds. In 1936 the Reds purchased Joost, then 19, from the San Francisco Missions of the Pacific Coast League. Joost recalled: "I took some infield and a few batting practice swings and Dressen called me over. 'Kid,' he said, 'you look pretty good. You've got ability, but you'll never be a major league player.' I asked why he had said that. 'I can tell,' said Dressen, 'by your mannerisms, how you do things, you'll never progress.' I said, 'I understand what you're saying, but I don't like it.'"

Dressen sent him to the minors the next day. Dressen's label followed Joost every place he went. Every manager he played for had heard about and seemed to accept Dressen's views. And yes, he was outspoken. Joost recalled playing for another manager and "one day I'm playing third and I booted a ball," he said. "The manager said, 'You played that ball wrong. When I played third base, I knew how to make that play. Here's how you should have done it.' So I looked up his record and he wasn't so great. The next time he tried to tell me how to play third, I said, 'Don't you tell me how to play. I looked up your record. You stunk.'"

Although Joost started for the Reds in the 1940 World Series, and in 1941 and '42, and for the Braves in '43, he retained the bad reputation. He was out of baseball in 1944 and most of '45, working in a meatpacking plant in San Francisco that was considered critical to the war effort. In 1946 he signed with the Rochester Red Wings, who needed a shortstop, and his life began to change dramatically. Almost overnight he went from a singles hitter to a hitter with power.

"Two things made the difference," he said. "One, I started wearing glasses. The wire frame got in my line of vision, so to pick up the ball I had to open my stance more. Second, for years I worked winters for that meatpacker in San Francisco. I had previously cut meat and the drivers loaded it on the trucks. In 1944, I worked as a driver. Now I'm loading the stuff on the trucks. I got stronger lifting whole lambs and sides of beef."

Joost hit 19 homers at Rochester, a good sum for a shortstop. He also led the International League in fielding. Connie Mack took notice. Mack called Joost to come to Philadelphia. As Joost recalled, the 84-year-old manager spoke to him by phone and said, "Boy, I know that you've had a lot of problems."

"Yes, Mr. Mack," said Joost, "and a lot of them have been created by myself. I'm a different person now."

"I know all about it," Mack said. "You can play. That's all I care about."

Mack said, "You're my shortstop." And Joost thrived in Philadelphia, as did Brissie.

The 1949 All-Star Game was played in Ebbets Field, Brooklyn, that quirky old park where "Howling" Hilda Chester rang a cowbell incessantly in the stands, the Dodger Sym-Phony struck up something resembling music in Section 8, the overhang of the center-field upper deck extended out over the field, and the outfield walls were covered with a profusion of commercial signs, ranging from Esquire Shoe Polish to Bulova Watches to the Abe Stark sign that offered a free suit at 1514 Pitkin Avenue to any batter hitting the 3' x 30' sign—and which was made famous by a *New Yorker* cartoon drawn by George Price showing a short man in suit and hat wearing a baseball glove and crouched in front of his sign.

"When I came into the clubhouse in Ebbets Field and sat down, I looked around and could hardly believe that I had done this, that I could have come this far," said Brissie. "I mean, there was Joe DiMaggio, and over there Ted Williams and Dom DiMaggio, and Joe Gordon and Lou Boudreau, and Raschi and Reynolds and Trucks. My mind wandered back to that creek where I lay virtually bleeding to death in the snows of Italy, just four and a half years earlier, and now I'm here, in this dream, this dream world, with all these great ballplayers. And I'm on the team. I was moved to—well, I wasn't about to sit there and break down sobbing, but I sure could have."

In the bottom of the fourth inning, before a capacity crowd of 32,577, with the American League ahead 6–5, Lou Brissie entered the game, having succeeded starter Mel Parnell and reliever Trucks.

A 10-year-old boy named George Vecsey, later the nonpareil sports columnist for *The New York Times,* was in the stands with his father, also George Vecsey. At the time, the elder Vecsey was working for the Associated Press and part-time for the *New York Daily News.* "I have no idea how my dad got such good seats, but we were behind home plate," recalled Vecsey in an email. "I remember the day. I think it might have rained earlier, and I remember it as muggy but with a hot sun through the clouds by game time. I can still see the view of our Dodgers and Stan Musial and the rest coming up to bat, straight on.

"I cannot envision Brissie going to the mound, but I remember seeing him on the mound, not necessarily him pitching but just him being out there. And I can remember the applause at some point. I couldn't tell you if people stood and cheered—that would be a little too theatrical for those days—but I'm sure my dad had told me about Brissie in the car coming in on the Interborough Parkway (now the Jackie Robinson Parkway) from our home in Queens, or told me a shorter version as Brissie was warming up. But I remember the applause, and the idea that a guy had gotten whacked during the war, and now he was pitching in the All-Star Game.

"I don't remember anything about what he did in the game, or when he left the game, but I remember my identification that he had been hurt in the war. I attribute it to my dad knowing all this stuff, and always telling me stories that journalists know.

"The war was personal to us by then. My mother, who was also a journalist, had lost two cousins, Florrie Duchene in Bergen-Belsen, after the whole Irish-Belgian family in Brussels had shielded Scottish troops in their home. The other cousin, Florrie's brother Leopold, got out of a German prison after the war but soon died, from either tuberculosis or just emaciation, judging from a postwar photo of him. So we had respect for people who had given something in the war. Did that add to our identification with Brissie? I can't say. Only that we were aware people, and that I knew about Brissie, and so did the crowd."

Brissie pitched two scoreless innings, striking out Andy Pafko of the Cubs, pinch-hitting in the fifth. In the top of the sixth, the American League batters provided Brissie with a greater cushion when they scored two more runs in the top of the inning. Brissie, however, ran into trouble in the bottom of the sixth. He walked Pee Wee Reese, the Dodgers' shortstop, got Jackie Robinson to hit into a force-out and Stan Musial to ground out, and then faced Ralph Kiner, the Pirates' slugger.

"I threw him a fastball over the plate, too much over the plate and up," recalled Brissie, "but not far enough up." Kiner swung and made contact. "It didn't look like he hit the ball that well, but it carried and carried." The ball landed in the lower stands in left, scoring Robinson ahead of him, and cutting the A.L. lead to one, 8–7. "My only consolation was that Ebbets Field was not a bad ballpark to hit in, kind of compact. And later other pitchers told me that Kiner had a swing in which the ball carried."

That was evident by the record. Kiner had led the National League in home runs every season since he was a rookie in 1946, and would again in 1949, and led the major leagues in homers for the three years after that—credentials impressive enough to be elected to the Baseball Hall of Fame.

Vic Raschi followed Brissie to the mound for the American League in the seventh inning of the '49 All- Star Game, and held the National League scoreless. The A.L. scored three more runs to win 11–7.

About Brissie, Kiner recalled: "Left hander, good stuff. I wasn't even conscious of the brace on his leg. I was concentrating on what he was throwing me." His home run was not necessarily an insult to Brissie's talents, he made clear. "I homered in the next two All-Star Games, too, in Comiskey Park in Chicago and in Detroit," Kiner recalled in an interview years later.

"Didn't feel he was handicapped," Kiner added, of Brissie. "He could get off the mound pretty quick. Strange thing is that I also faced Monty Stratton. I may be the only ballplayer who ever batted against both those pitchers. But they bunted Stratton out of the league."

Stratton, an All-Star pitcher for the White Sox in the 1930s, shot himself in the leg with a pistol in a postseason hunting accident in 1938, at age 26, and underwent amputation of the limb below the knee. Stratton, who was 36–23 in four seasons with second-division White Sox teams (15–5 and 15–9 the last two seasons), tried a comeback with the White Sox the following year but was unable to field his position. A well-received movie, *The Stratton Story* (it won the Oscar for Best Original Screenplay) starring Jimmy Stewart as Stratton and June Allyson as his wife, was released in June of 1949. Stratton hung on in baseball with the White Sox as a coach and scout, but in 1946 he tried again to make the major leagues, again with the White Sox. Both the White Sox and Pirates trained in California, and the rookie Kiner batted against Stratton (though, some seven decades later, he didn't remember how he fared against him in that exhibition game).

"The difference between Brissie and Stratton was huge," said Kiner. "Despite Brissie's leg problem, he could do it. Stratton no longer could."

Stratton pitched in the minor leagues for a few seasons after that but was unable to make it back to the big leagues.

"I remember seeing *The Stratton Story*," said Brissie, "and I had read about Monty Stratton's experiences playing in the minor leagues in Texas. And, sure, you relate to it. The same way I related to watching Pete Gray play with one arm. You relate to anybody who's trying to overcome a difficulty. You wonder, 'What was their battle like? Was it the same as mine?' Lot of curiosity. But I always admired Stratton for trying so hard. I never met him, but there was one moment in the movie that has stuck with me. It was when he fell down running to first base. He said, 'I think I started my slide too early.' Now, I don't know if he really said it, or if that was a line written for Jimmy Stewart, but I related to his trying to use humor to downplay things that really concern you, or embarrass you. I'd joke about being speedy on the base paths. It made it just a little easier for me to deal with, and for my teammates to deal with. We didn't have to walk on egg shells."

Brissie's ability to "do it," in Kiner's phrase, was exemplified in a May 28 game against the Yankees in which he pitched 14 innings against New York hurlers Vic Raschi and Joe Page, but lost 2-1. (He completed a remarkable 18 games of his 29 starts. He also relieved in five other games, posting three saves).

However, running the bases on offense was an adventure for Brissie. "I had an awkward style because of the brace," he recalled. "But I learned to compensate. Like a tennis player who doesn't have a good backhand, he tries to run around the ball to hit the forehand. I think most athletes do that with a weakness, or try to.

"And I didn't do much running, like a lot of pitchers do. I could run 10-12 minutes, at most. And then only rarely because it would irritate my leg. So I tried not to run as much as possible. In fact, I tried to stay off my feet as much as possible." He added, with a laugh, "I didn't steal any bases."

In the record book, however, there is a particularly eye-catching statistic for the 1949 season. It reads that Brissie hit a triple.

"Must be a mistake," Brissie said when it was pointed out to him years later. "Maybe somebody hit a wrong button in putting in a double for me, and it came up with a triple."

When it was mentioned to Al Rosen that Brissie may have hit a triple in a game, and he was asked if he remembered seeing it or hearing about it, the former Indians' star third baseman said, with a chuckle, "No—but if it happened, all the outfielders must have fallen down."

(Author's Note: A call to the Baseball Hall of Fame Library in Cooperstown, New York, during the writing of this book sent library director Jim Gates to the records file. He returned the following: The box score of a game on August 10 in which the Senators beat the A's, 8-7 reads, alongside "3b," "Suder, Brissie." That translates to each player having hit a triple. Brissie, who finished the game having come in in relief of Alex Kellner, Charlie Harris, and Bobby Shantz, also was mentioned in the 19th and last paragraph of the game story by Jack Walsh of the *Washington Post*: "The A's made it 8-7 when Lou Brissie tripled to start the seventh and came home on Joost's long fly to center." So, not only did Brissie pitch shutout ball in the final 2 2/3 innings of the game in which he was on the mound, but he also contributed with that mysterious, but undeniable, triple.)

Like most pitchers, Brissie felt a responsibility to "protect" his players, as it were. It is understood, and appreciated, sometimes even by opponents as well as teammates. In a game against the Yankees, for example, outfielder Johnny Lindell tried to break up a double play by coming in spikes high to A's second baseman Nellie Fox. The next time Lindell came to bat, Brissie plunked him in the ribs with a fastball. During batting practice the following day, Brissie crossed paths with Lindell. "I earned that one," Lindell told Brissie.

Brissie won three more times in September and finished the season with a respectable 16–11 record, and an earned-run average of 4.28. He again was among the league leaders in strikeouts, with 118 in 229⅓ innings, and was seventh in the league in most strikeouts per nine innings, with 4.63.

The A's, despite a winning record of 81–73, finished fifth, 16 games behind the pennant-winning Yankees.

And while the A's were not one of the teams fighting for the pennant in the deciding last week of the season, they were involved. The Yankees, with their first-year manager Casey Stengel, maintained a hold on first place for the entire season up to the last few days. They lost three straight to the Red Sox in Fenway Park and fell to second place. The A's then came to Yankee Stadium for three games, with a chance, if the Red Sox could win their next three over Washington, to knock the Bronx Bombers out of the championship. The A's lost two of three; the Red Sox lost one of three; and the Red Sox came into Yankee Stadium one game up on the Yankees, to play the final two games of the season.

The Red Sox needed to win just one of the two games to win the pennant. They lost both, and Casey Stengel had his first pennant as a manager, a position he first held in 1934 with the Brooklyn Dodgers. He managed the Yankees to five straight World Series wins, from 1949 to 1953, and 10 pennants in 12 years, before he was fired after the Yankees lost the seventh game of the 1960 World Series to the Pirates. Stengel was then 70 years old. He was philosophical about the firing.

"I'll never make the mistake of turning 70 again," he said.

In Stengel's three years managing the Dodgers, his team never finished higher than fifth. Nor did his teams do any better in his next managerial job, with the Boston Braves, from 1938 to 1943. He then managed in the minor leagues. He was known as a kind of character to many—sometimes employing an inscrutable but humorous use of words and sentences termed "Stengelese"—but to others he was an astute baseball mind. When he was first named to manage the pin-striped Yankees (Red Smith once wrote that "Rooting for the Yankees was like rooting for U.S. Steel") there was skepticism. Not the least of those questioning the move was the Yankees icon, Joe DiMaggio. Early in spring training of 1949, DiMaggio "was agreeing" with sports columnist Arthur Daley of *The New York Times* that "the manager appeared bewildered...and saying that 'the rest of the fellows' had the same impression," as told in Robert Creamer's biography, *Stengel: His Life and Times*. Daley printed the assertion, and Stengel just shrugged when he read it.

However, Red Smith saw it differently from those Yankees players. "It is erroneous and unjust to conceive of Casey Stengel merely as a clown. He is something else entirely—a competitor who has always had fun competing, a fighter with the gift of laughter.... There is wisdom in comedy." Brissie came to view Stengel's clowning as "an act" that covered up brilliance for his own purposes. "No one accomplishes what he accomplished by being a fool," said Brissie.

Stengel, it turned out, knew more than DiMaggio and those other players could have imagined.

When Stengel left the Yankees, he became manager of the Mets, an expansion team that, not surprisingly, finished last in each of Stengel's four seasons as their manager.

Warren Spahn, the Hall of Fame left-handed pitcher, broke in as a rookie under Stengel in 1942 with the Braves, and in his last season in the major leagues, 1965, pitched for Stengel's Mets. He once said, "I played for Casey before and after he was a genius."

While Stengel was still managing the Mets, Brissie, now retired, ran into him and his wife, Edna, who were with the former Senators pitcher and a professional comic, Al Schacht, in a hotel in New York. "Casey began telling us this story," said Brissie. "He said, 'Well, you know I'm on the board of that bank in Glendale (California), and every now and then they have a big get-together. They were having one, one night, and Edna didn't want to go because she knew it was going to run late, so I went and it was late when I got home. So I thought I'd help the old girl out. I take off my shoes so I won't wake her when I go up the stairs. I started up the stairs and I got right to the top and I drop the shoes and each shoe hit every step all the way to the bottom. So Edna called out, 'Casey, is that you?' And I said, 'By God, it better be!'"

Another Hall of Fame manager that Brissie played against was Joe McCarthy, when he was with the Red Sox in the late 1940s, after having managed the Yankees. When Joe McCarthy was inducted into the Baseball Hall of Fame in Cooperstown, in 1957, Brissie was in attendance (he had become director of the American Legion junior baseball and he annually brought that season's best player with him to the induction ceremonies.) When Buddy Rosar, the A's first-string catcher for most of the time Brissie pitched in Philadelphia, was traded from the Yankees, he told Brissie that his previous manger, McCarthy, would sit on the bench during a game and carry on a running dialogue of analysis of the opposition, on their strengths and weaknesses. "He had a lot of respect for McCarthy," said Brissie. "At the Hall of Fame festivities, McCarthy said he wanted to thank all the players and all the owners who had given him a chance to spend all those years in baseball. He said, 'We had some great players and some great clubs. And while I'm thankin' everybody there's one little lady I wanna thank that's here. She's been with me all the way and she supported me all the way and I don't think I'd be here without her.' And then he turned around and said, 'Babe, stand up and take a bow—while you still can!'

"Everyone sitting there nearly fell off their chairs with laughter."

2.

In regard to families, the Brissies expanded in August of 1949. About seven months into Dot's new pregnancy, she and Lou were told by her gynecologist that they could expect twins. They were boys, Robbie and Ronnie. Brissie and the A's were in Washington and had played a night game against the Senators when he was awakened in his hotel room at 1:00 AM. It was the doctor. He was a father again. "We had one more game in Washington the next day and then we were going home," recalled Brissie. "I couldn't wait." Dot had made friends with the wives of some of the A's players, but was closest to the wives of pitchers Charlie Harris and Dick Fowler. It was Doris Harris who had been at home in Philadelphia with Dot and had taken her to the hospital to give birth.

When the team came back from Washington, Doris Harris picked up her husband and "Bris," as she called him, from the train station.

"Where's Dot?" asked Brissie.

"Don't you know?!" said Doris.

"And then," Doris Harris recalled years later, "he and Charlie broke into this big grin from ear to ear."

The day after the birth of the boys, Brissie, as was customary, handed out cigars to his teammates. "One of them, I don't remember who, said, 'Don't I get two?'" Brissie recalled with a laugh.

"Dot and I were the best of friends," said Doris Harris. "When the team was on the road, I always stayed at their house. Charlie and I didn't have any children then. I helped Dot with the kids. When the twins were born, I took Vicki home with me. I said to her, 'Guess what—you have two little boy brothers.' She looked disappointed. She said, 'I wanted a sister.'"

Ballplayer husbands on extended road trips left the wives to virtually care for the children alone. But a community feeling that took place between Dot Brissie and Doris Harris and Joyce Fowler helped greatly. "They were like kindred spirits," recalled Brissie. "And when I was on the road, I tried to stay in touch as much as possible. That didn't help much with changing the diapers, but it was what I could do."

When the team was home, the wives generally sat together, a few rows up from behind the A's dugout. "I'd buy a scorecard—it was ten cents in those days—and I'd keep score," said Doris. "I don't know if Dot knew how to keep score, but she'd help me along. And she worried about Lou. She didn't talk about it much, but she worried about him and how he was doing with his leg. If you ever saw his leg, it would certainly give you cause for concern."

Throughout the seasons—and off-seasons—of his major league career, Brissie visited veterans' hospitals, hospitals for children, and the homes of some of the soldiers, alive and dead, whom he had served with. It wasn't simply that he was doing a good deed for others, which, to be sure, was part of it, but it was important for him, as well. He needed the support. The war still was ever-present in his mind, the fighting, the chaos, and the dying.

"I had my A-team all around the circuit," Brissie recalled. "Almost every town we played in, I had a friend who I visited with, guys I had served with either in America or Italy, and my doctors. There was Joe Brien, in New York, and Capt. Tom Sears, who'd come up to Chicago from his home in Urbana, and Joe Kane who lived in Chicago, and Francis Silva in Boston, and Shorty Williamson in St. Louis, and of course Dr. Brubaker in Cleveland and Dr. Suraci in Washington.

"Joe Brien was from Long Island, New York. He was in the hotel-management business—but there wasn't a day when I came to New York that he didn't spend with me. He was the first sergeant that I ever had, in Camp Croft. He was a bonafide, 100 percent hero. He fought in Italy with the 3rd Division. He got the Silver Star and a Bronze Star. He cross-trained guys at Camp Croft, from combat instruction to logistics. Nobody was doing cross-training at that time—it was all about 'team' with him. We simulated battle conditions, like being in a village when an army was taking over a territory. He was tough, but we sure learned. We became very close.

"When I pitched my first game in Boston in 1948, he wired me and said he was looking forward to seeing me when I got to New York. In New York I'd always have breakfast or lunch or dinner with Joe, and it was always so good to see him. He especially helped get me through being able to live as best I could with that incident in Italy, when I told that young recruit not to go out past the house if there was a noise. And the kid did, and was shot and killed by a German sniper. And I dragged his bleeding body back to the house in the snow. And he died in my arms. I had visualized and repeated this story in my head for years. I had a hard time putting it to bed. Sometimes even on the mound it would come to me. I'd be staring down at the catcher to get a sign, and then, out of the blue, I'd see this kid's face in the snow, bleeding, pleading for help. I'd have to try to shake off the image and get back to the ballgame. I'd have to give myself a talking-to: 'C'mon, now, get yourself together here. You have a ballgame to play.' Other guys have told me several stories, of their minds wandering like that. We all kind of lectured ourselves.

"But Joe Brien helped me gain perspective. He said, 'It's wartime. You try to do the right thing, and if someone doesn't follow what's to be done, it's not your fault. You can only control what you can control.' I knew all this, and yet I still had continued to feel some blame, some responsibility for that young private's death. Couldn't get it out of my mind. But you just needed someone to talk to, someone who had been through it, someone who you felt truly understood what was going on in your head and heart. Not a psychiatrist, but a friend, a buddy, a guy who might have shared your foxhole. And Joe made a lot of sense to me. He said, 'You have to snap out of this, otherwise it's going to spoil your whole life for you.' And he never brought it up again. But when we'd meet, he'd say, 'Is everything okay?' And if I needed to, we'd talk about what was troubling me. And because of Joe, that incident in Italy with that kid didn't bother me quite as much. I'm grateful to him for that. Joe died in 2004 and he's buried in Arlington Cemetery, in a hero's grave."

Joe Kane was in the hospital in Naples with Brissie, and came to see him every time the A's were in Chicago, along with Tom Sears. "Joe owned a bar on Cicero Avenue on the south side," said Brissie. "He had a walking cast in the hospital, with shell fragments in his foot. He eventually healed and was sent back to the front after I had returned home.

"But one day I was lying on a gurney and he said, 'I'm taking you to church.' I said, 'But I'm not Catholic.' He said, 'Today you are.' And he rolled me off to church.

"We talked in the hospital and he said his ambition was to open a bar. And he did. This first time he came to see me, I said, 'Joe, how can you take time off from your business?'

"He said, 'I don't close down. I have someone run it for me.'

"I said, 'Don't you go by and check?'

"He said, 'Don't have to. I can look at the liquor and see how much money they took in.'"

Tom Sears owned a food market in Urbana, and he and Kane would get box seats behind the A's bullpen in Comiskey Park, which were located beside right field. And Kane and Sears, from their nearby seats, would chat with Brissie whenever, as he said, "there was a break in the action."

The war, its memory, and what Brissie's struggles meant to people, were kept alive in numerous ways, to be sure, not least of which were the letters that continued to arrive for him.

One such correspondence came on the stationery of the Mount Carmel Playground Association in Pennsylvania, sponsors of Mount Carmel Little League Baseball:

> Dear Lou: On Wednesday, Oct. 26, 1949...we will have our annual banquet for the Little League.... As a physically handicapped person myself, I suffered a crushed knee in a mine accident and underwent 23 operations to save the leg, I can appreciate the splendid fight you are putting up with your leg. It is very gratifying to see that you are winning the fight. I am also the father of an 8-year-old son Billy Schultz who was born with two club feet yet tries to play ball with the other boys. I know it takes a special brand of courage to do this under such handicaps. My reason for writing you is this: One of the boys, 10-year-old Wm. Urbanowicz of the Maurers Dairy team, played the season as an outfielder even though he has a withered right arm which is useless to him. I think he displays remarkable courage in attempting to play under such a handicap. Strangely enough he is a fine bunter with his good arm, his left, and gets on base often. Will you please consider sending me some sort of trophy from you to William to be presented to him at the banquet in tribute to

his courage, perhaps an autographed ball or photograph or anything else you might think will be appropriate.

Thank you very much for anything you will do to make this boy happy.

Sincerely yours,

Elmer Schultz
341 East Seventh St.
Mt. Carmel, Pa.

Brissie sent both an autographed ball along with an autographed picture inscribed to Bill Urbanowicz and a short note of encouragement.

10

Falling Behind

1.

In June 1950, the United States suddenly found itself engaged in another war, less than five years after the conclusion of World War II. North Korean armies invaded South Korea, and America sent in forces to combat what President Truman and the United States government viewed as an increasing attempt by America's foes to spread Communism. Within a few weeks, the U.S. Army and Marines were in combat on the ground as the crisis heightened.

In Philadelphia, in their home about a mile from the ballpark, Dot Brissie had concerns as she read newspaper accounts of the situation in Korea.

"Lou," she said, "do you think you'll have to go?"

"No," he replied, "I don't think so."

Considering the physical problems Brissie endured—to the point that there were days he could barely get out of bed when not going to the ballpark and Dot even brought him his meals in bed—it might seem that Dot's worries were baseless. Not so, Brissie recalled: "You never know. Things happen. You'd think that with my disability, I'd never be recalled. But others might say, 'If he can play ball, why can't he serve again?'"

In fact, some ballplayers who had served in the Second World War would be talked about in regard to a recall, including two Marine fighter pilots, Ted Williams and Yankees second baseman Jerry Coleman.

One day in the off-season Brissie received a letter to report to the Veterans Administration hospital in Columbia, South Carolina, for a physical examination. "I didn't know what it was about until I got there," said Brissie. "I had been given a medical discharge and received disability payments and, now, since I was earning a decent living, I was handling my medical problems personally and not going to a VA hospital. Well, the doctor who examined me said, 'Some politicians wanted you to have a checkup because they can't believe you're doing what you're doing and being disabled.' And after the two-day checkup, the doctor said, 'Son, with all your problems, I don't know how you can do what you're doing. It's a miracle you can get around on that leg, and more power to you.' And the next month I received my disability check—and there was a 10 percent raise in it!"

Carl Scheib might also have been called to testify as a witness for Brissie. Scheib, a right-handed pitcher who joined the A's off a farm in Gratz, Pennsylvania, in 1943 when he was 16 years old, roomed with Brissie on the road.

"At night the thing would crack and ooze," recalled Scheib, about the injury to Brissie's left leg. "There was no shin bone. He'd put salve on it. It was terrible to look at." Scheib said that Brissie's dedication to his job was impressive. Not only did Brissie minister to his leg, but he made a point of carefully observing the batters. Scheib said he regularly sat in the bullpen with Brissie who "was always studying hitters. He'd really concentrate, whether he was apt to pitch that day or not."

The Korean War was disturbing to Brissie on another level. "So many of us who fought in the Second World War felt we were solving the problem, that we were going to have peace from then on, but here we were starting all over again," he said. "It was terrible."

He added, "And a lot of the country didn't want to hear about it. We'd gone through an awful time just a short while ago. So people just wanted to keep it on the back burner."

While ground fighting continued in Korea, there was a need to add tactical air support. As Michael Seidel wrote in *Ted Williams: A Baseball Life*, "Plans were drawn to activate reserve forces in highly skilled areas. Ted Williams, at nearly 32 years of age, was a highly skilled pilot. He had no idea at this time, but his days as a civilian were numbered."

Both Williams and Coleman were activated. Williams complained that the government was picking out people like him and Coleman because they were well known. "In my heart I was bitter," Williams wrote in his autobiography, My Turn at Bat, "but I made up my mind I wasn't going to bellyache. I kept thinking one of those gutless politicians someplace along the line would see that it wasn't right and do something. I knew that winter my number had come up, that it would just be a matter of time."

Brissie recalled: "A lot of us agreed with Ted and Jerry and were upset about their being activated. I mean, there were Navy pilots on the street looking for a job. But Williams and Coleman went."

Seidel wrote, "The very nature of the draft was controversial, precisely because of the wholesale recall of veterans from the last war while a generation of college students was exempted under provisions of the draft code formulated in March of the previous year. Last spring, Congress refused to grant President Truman his request for a universal draft.... One thing was clear though: aerial support and strategic aerial combat missions were essential to the war effort, and the United States did not have enough pilots to fly fighter jets. It became necessary to dip into the fighter-pilot reserve from World War II."

In April 1952 both Williams and Coleman passed their physical examinations for military service.

At his induction, Williams, wrote Seidel, "was good-natured about it." Williams said, "I'm praying for an early truce." Coleman, too, expressed no complaint about being recalled. He said that if the country needed him, he was willing and happy to serve again. Williams, meanwhile, played in just six games in 1952 and was hitting .400 when he went off to join the Third Marine Air Wing, 223rd Squadron. The Red Sox had been looking to make another run at the pennant, when their star player was lost to them. The Yankees, who had won three straight pennants with Coleman as their regular second baseman, made do with Coleman's able substitute, Billy Martin, and won again, and again, making it five straight pennant and World Series wins for Casey Stengel's teams.

Lieutenant Colonel Coleman, who had flown 57 missions during World War II, would fly 63 in Korea before his discharge in August 1953. Captain Williams, who began his 17-month hitch in May, flew

39 combat missions in Korea. When Williams was mustered out of the service, in the summer of the following year, he began taking batting practice in Fenway Park on July 29, coincidentally the day that a truce was formally enacted in Korea. Williams played in 37 games at the tail end of the season and took up where he left off, hitting .407, for the fourth-place Red Sox.

One of the lesser-known major leaguers drafted for service in Korea was Frank Saucier, an outfielder who had played in only 18 games for the St. Louis Browns in 1951, his rookie season. He was a World War II veteran, and while in the Browns' spring-training camp in Burbank, California, in 1952, he received a collect telegram from the Department of the Navy—he had to shell out $1.86 to take it—ordering Lieutenant Saucier to report to the Pensacola (Florida) Naval Station. Of the handful of games he played for the Browns in '51 (his lone major league season), one would be historic. It was the game against Detroit in Sportsman's Park, St. Louis, on August 19, in which the midget Eddie Gaedel pinch-hit. Bill Veeck, who became the owner of the Browns three months earlier, had planned another of his ingenious promotions in an attempt to make a bad team interesting, and inserted the midget into the lineup. The player he pinch-hit for was Frank Saucier. Gaedel, who had popped out of a huge cake and wearing number ⅛ on the back of his uniform, walked on four pitches, naturally, since he was crouching and displayed virtually no strike zone to the pitcher, Bob Cain. Veeck had told Gaedel that he must not swing, and he warned Gaedel that he would be in the stands with a rifle and would use it if he disobeyed orders. "For a minute, I felt like Babe Ruth," Gaedel later said about his at-bat. He left the game for a pinch-runner, Jim Delsing. Gaedel trotted back to the bench—his baseball career over since American League president Will Harridge outlawed "midgets" in Major League Baseball games following Gaedel's performance. On the Browns' bench, he took a seat beside Saucier and the two chatted.

The following year, when Saucier had been called up and was at the naval base in Pensacola, he noticed in the newspaper that the Ringling Brothers Barnum & Bailey circus was coming to town, and one of its attractions was Eddie Gaedel. Saucier decided to go to the circus and say hello to Gaedel. He did, and Gaedel was happy to see him.

"How's life in the circus?" Saucier asked him.

"It's a living," replied Gaedel, "but it ain't baseball."

An addendum to Gaedel's banishment from baseball: Bill Veeck took pleasure in a note he wrote to Harridge: "Fine. Let's establish what a midget is in fact. Is it 3 feet 6 inches? Eddie's height. Is it 4 feet 6 inches? If it's 5 feet 6 inches, that's great. We can get rid of Rizzuto." (Rizzuto, of course, was the Yankees' star shortstop.)

Brissie became friendly with Zach Taylor, who had been the manger of the Browns in 1951, and recalled the Gaedel incident with laughter to Brissie. Taylor also liked telling the story of a pitcher with the Browns named Tex Shirley. In one game, Taylor went out to the mound in Sportsmen's Park to remove Shirley. The pitcher was so upset about this that instead of giving the ball to Taylor he threw it as far as he could, the ball landing in the left-field seats. Taylor told Shirley, "Be at the ballpark tomorrow at 2:00." Shirley had no idea why, but he arrived at 2:00. Taylor then had a groundskeeper measure the distance of the throw by Shirley the day before. "And I fined him one dollar for every foot that ball traveled," said Taylor.

• • •

As the drumbeat of the Korean War continued, Dot had thoughts not only of her husband being drafted into another war but that he was the sole bread-winner of an increasingly larger family. The twins were a year old and, of course, Vicki was growing up, now age three. While sleep could at times be a luxury in a house with three small children, Brissie could look back just a few years when sleep in a foxhole was even more difficult. He could handle this.

On the baseball diamond, the 1950 season started poorly for Brissie and the A's—despite expectations of a better season than their fifth-place finish in 1949. Connie Mack was celebrating his 50th year as manager of the A's. During the winter before the 1950 season, Mack acquired All-Star third baseman Bob Dillinger and outfielder Paul Lehner from the Browns for the considerable sum of $100,000 and four players. Mack now believed he had an outside chance to win that "one more pennant."

Brissie, coming off his 16–11 All-Star season, lost his first six games—and he suddenly found himself, by mid-May, pitching for an eighth-place team. There were still days in this period when, because of the pain in his leg, he was unable to get out of bed until it was time to go to the ballpark. He had been the home Opening Day pitcher and lost to the Red Sox, 8–2, but gave up just three earned runs in eight innings. In his next outing, another eight-inning stint, the Yankees beat him 6–3, on five earned runs, with the diminuitive shortstop Phil Rizzuto, who would be named Major League Player of the Year, sparking the attack with four hits.

Brissie got battered in his third game as Detroit knocked him out of the box in the second inning, giving up three runs on five hits.

On May 7, he pitched his first complete game and lost to the White Sox, 7–3, all the runs earned, and he walked seven batters. Brissie was staggering from the bombardment of losses. But he persevered. And on May 12, in Yankee Stadium, he *almost* won a game. He pitched his second complete game in five days and lost 3–2, with one run unearned. Six days later, in Cleveland Stadium, he suffered another one-run loss, 4–3, to the Indians.

On May 21, his second straight day in relief, he entered the game with the A's ahead in the ninth inning against St. Louis and retired the side in order to get the save.

But his record still stood at no wins and six losses.

"I wasn't pitching well at all," recalled Brissie. "And when I did pitch well, the other guy pitched just a little bit better. It was frustrating; it was difficult. And we weren't hitting. You just keep walking out there every time, thinking something positive will happen."

He would not use his shattered leg as an excuse for his disappointments on the mound. "I didn't have any more trouble with my leg in 1950 than I did in '48 or '49," he said. "And when I did, I'd call Dr. Brubaker or Dr. Suraci and they'd prescribe more antibiotics, and rest, if I could. So when I could I'd spend all day in bed, and get up only to go to the ballpark. If my leg did influence my performance, I wasn't aware of it. It may have, in regard to stamina, to my leg tiring and then something came off my pitches, but I really didn't notice it."

One particular at-bat against Brissie sticks out in the memory of Dom DiMaggio, the relatively slight, bespectacled Red Sox center fielder. It occurred on June 28, 1950. "The hit-and-run was on and the runner broke for second," DiMaggio told me, "and Brissie threw a fastball high that knocked me on my fanny and the catcher had a perfect throw to second to get the runner. On the next pitch I hit a high fastball, at the letters, onto the roof of Shibe Park. I could just feel the bat bend. I hit the bejeezus out of the ball. The ball hit the sloping roof and fell back onto the field. God, I don't ever remember hitting a ball harder. Well, so much for knocking me down."

Years later, Brissie was asked about that and said he didn't recall Dom DiMaggio hitting a home run off him, but he did remember Joe "beating me with a homer in the last inning." The blow, with the bases empty, came on August 18 of that year. It was "an electrifying shot," as John Drebinger of *The New York Times* described it, that landed deep in the left-field upper deck in Shibe Park, giving the Yankees and Vic Raschi a 3-2 win over Brissie, who had otherwise pitched a fine ballgame, going the distance and allowing just six hits.

Brissie's appearance in that game, as the Yankees fought the Red Sox for first place, "miffed" Yankees manager Casey Stengel, wrote Drebinger, "because the Mackmen withheld Brissie from their recent series in Boston and thus saved their ace southpaw for tonight's engagement with the Yanks. Lou could have faced the Sox last night."

• • •

While on the road Brissie would check in regularly with Dot at home, who followed Lou's and the team's progress in the newspapers and on the radio. She had developed a keen interest in the game from a personal, and supportive, standpoint. "One of the good things about her having a good head on her shoulders was that she never was critical of anything I did on the ballfield," said Brissie. "I appreciated that—I certainly did. There were some wives who'd ask their husbands, 'How come you can't get the ball over the plate?' Or complain that a fielder behind you booted a ball. Things like that. All Dot would do is ask, 'Are you all right? Kinda tough day today.' And it was good times when we won."

Finally, on Saturday, May 27, after more than a month into the season, something positive occurred on the ballfield for Brissie. He defeated the Yankees in Shibe Park, 6–1, on a three-hit complete game. He then started and lost another two games, the second another one-run loss, 6–5 to the Browns, giving up three earned runs and leaving the game in the sixth inning.

While the team was foundering on the field, the A's were in turmoil in the front office. Earle Mack, heir presumptive to his father as manager, was relieved as assistant manager and named chief player scout. This move was believed to have been engineered by Connie Mack Jr. Coach Jimmy Dykes succeeded Earle Mack as assistant manager, while coach Mickey Cochrane was shifted to the front office as general manager. All the while, it seemed obvious that 87-year-old Connie Mack was taking a backseat to the proceedings.

Cochrane, the former star player of the A's and Tigers and former World Series–winning manager of the Tigers, had lost a son in World War II. Gordon Stanley Cochrane Jr. was Mickey's only son. He had been in the infantry, like Brissie, and was killed in combat in the Netherlands. Mickey had served as a lieutenant in the navy in World War II, in the physical education branch under Lieutenant Commander (LCDR) Gene Tunney, the former world heavyweight boxing champion.

On the road, Brissie would frequently get a call in his room from Cochrane. "C'mon down to my room and let's talk," Cochrane would say. They talked baseball, but sooner or later Cochrane would always begin to talk about the war experience. "He wanted to know what it was like being in the infantry, and relating it to his son," said Brissie. "'If so-and-so happened, what would you do?' 'What was the food like?' Edible, usually, but I'd say it was fine. 'How did you keep warm in sub-zero temperatures?' I told him about cutting parts of blankets to make a neck scarf and a waist scarf, so to speak, to keep the back warm if the shirt or jacket flaps up. And you'd wear three or four layers of clothes.

'What about keeping your feet dry?' There was always the concern about frostbite. I said, 'You'd take your shoes and socks off and massage your feet, and we always carried three or four extra pairs of socks. And if they got wet we'd light a flame to our Sterno can and dry them by the fire.' Mickey's wife would listen and hardly say a word. I don't think he ever stopped grieving for his son, and I think that was one of the things that killed him." Cochrane, who suffered a series of nervous breakdowns and anxiety attacks, died in 1962, at age 59.

2.

Later in the year, Roy and Earle Mack purchased controlling interest of the club from Connie Jr., his mother, and heirs of the late Benjamin F. and Thomas S. Shibe. Roy and Earle said that their father would continue as manager indefinitely, which, it turned out, definitely would not be the case.

"I'm sure it didn't help that no one on the ballclub knew who was in charge at times, and what was going on," said Brissie. "The guys would say, 'What's new today?' expecting more disturbing news. You try to not let it affect you. Mr. Mack was still in the dugout. You still had to please him with your performance, but it did seem like the ship was springing a leak."

The bespectacled Bob Dillinger had failed to meet expectations even though he was batting around .300—the A's had hoped for more power from him and didn't get it—and the brain trust of the A's, whomever it was at the time, decided to try to recoup some of the money spent for him. They sold him on July 19 to Pittsburgh for an estimated $35,000. Kermit Wahl took over third base and batted .257 with two home runs. Not a sterling performance. He was traded the next season to the St. Louis Browns, which was his last season in the big leagues.

Hank Majeski, the capable third baseman for the A's in the latter seasons of the 1940s, was traded to the White Sox to make room for Dillinger. The A's got relief pitcher Ed Klieman in return for Majeski.

Majeski batted .309 for the White Sox in 1950. Klieman was not much of a return on investment. That season, he pitched a total of five innings in five games for the A's, and it proved the end of his big-league career. After these moves, some were reminded of the fairly recent trades that Mack and the A's had made in which George Kell and Nellie Fox were dealt away. Both became stars, and both made the Baseball Hall of Fame.

The A's, however, weren't the only team suffering in the standings. In a widely publicized experiment, the St. Louis Browns, a perennial second-place team, hired Dr. David F. Tracy, a New York psychologist and hypnotist. He claimed that he could help the team overcome its "defeatist complex." Dr. Tracy accompanied the Browns to spring training and worked with the players as the season got under way. But the lofty experiment was scrapped. On May 31 the Browns, bumbling as usual, announced the release of Dr. Tracy.

"I don't remember anyone suggesting that we should hire Dr. Tracy, or someone like him," said Brissie. "We laughed about the hypnosis. But well, if it can help—but we didn't think it could. And apparently it didn't. But we were getting desperate for something, or someone, to turn the season around for us."

It was not to be. The A's wound up dead last in the American League, losing 102 games while winning 52. As Brissie was losing game after game, so was the rest of the pitching staff, Alex Kellner in particular. Kellner, who won 20 games in his 1949 rookie season, featuring an unusual roundhouse off-speed curveball, reversed himself and led the American League in losses, with 20, against eight wins. Of course, these were not ordinary back-to-back seasons for Kellner, but Kellner was no ordinary man. He was named Alexander Raymond Kellner for the great pitcher Grover Cleveland Alexander, just as his brother Walter, who also pitched briefly and unsuccessfully for the A's in 1952 and '53 (0–0 won-lost record, 6.43 earned-run average in three games) was named for Walter Johnson, the Washington Senators' Hall of Fame pitcher. In the off-season, Alex Kellner augmented his baseball salary by trapping mountain lions for circuses and zoos. "Alex was funny," said Brissie. "He had this dry sense of humor. He'd come up with a remark that was so unexpected, and everyone would break up. Every year he sent a Christmas card from some hunting trip. Not too many guys went hunting for mountain lions—with a rope! And then he'd sell them to zoos."

Kellner had motion picture film of one of the expeditions that he made with his brother, Walter. During spring training he showed it to teammates, and he narrated it. When the scene was shown of a lion being trapped in a tree, with Walter only a few feet away trying to throw the noose around the animal's neck, a player asked Alex, "Where were you when all this was going on?"

"Oh, I supervised the whole job," replied Kellner. "But I was right there to lend Walt a helping hand if he got stuck."

"Sure," said Brissie. "From the next county?"

Joe Coleman, who had won 13 games in 1949, 14 the season before that, and was nicknamed "the Giant Killer" because his wins often came against contenders, injured his arm in 1950, pitched in only 15 games, and was virtually useless, posting an 0-5 record and an 8.50 ERA.

Brissie, too, suffered a season almost in direct contrast to 1949. He finished with a 7-19 record, yet he had the best earned-run average on the staff, 4.02 (Bobby Shantz, with an 8-14 record was second on the A's in ERA at 4.61). Brissie pitched 15 complete games, struck out 101, among the league leaders in both categories, and tied for third in the league in pitching appearances, with 46. He was also fifth in the league in saves, with eight—all for an eighth-place team.

In contrast, some pitchers on better teams than the A's (and that included every one of the other 15 teams in the major leagues) and who had higher ERAs than Brissie, had better won-lost records. For the Yankees, who won the pennant again, Tommy Byrne, a left-hander and one of the stars of the staff, won 15 games and lost nine in 1950, but had a 4.74 ERA. Hal Newhouser, a stalwart of the second-place Tigers' staff, was 15-13, with a 4.34 ERA. For the third-place Red Sox, Ellis Kinder was 14-12 with a 4.26 ERA, and Joe Dobson, at 15-10, had a 4.18 ERA. In the National League, the standout Carl Erskine of the second-place Dodgers was 16–12, with a 4.46 ERA. Again, how sweet it is to pitch for teams that score runs for you.

Brissie, to be sure, had control problems at times, giving up as many as seven walks in a game, and led the A's in bases on balls with 117, sixth in the league.

"After the season, I was given films of me pitching in games," said Brissie. "I hadn't realized this before seeing them, that as I pitched deeper into ballgames, my stride began to shorten. My left leg began to tire, I imagine, though I wasn't even aware of it. And when my stride shortened, my pitches began to get higher. The higher they got, the easier it was for hitters to hit, or the pitches just went sailing over the strike zone."

Yet he pitched those 15 complete games, including two shutouts. He was on the losing end of 10 games decided by one run, and another decided by two runs. As the summer wound down, through the heat and humidity and despite sweating profusely in the woolen uniform the teams then wore, Brissie was often and uncommonly effective.

On August 18 he lost to the Yankees, 3–2; on August 23, he lost to the White Sox 1–0, on six hits and seven strikeouts; on August 31, he lost to the Browns 4–3; on September 4, he lost to the Yankees again, 2–1, and on September 13 he lost to St. Louis 4–3. That's five straight one-run losses. One had to wonder: Where were the hitters? Brissie pitched one inning in relief on September 15 against Chicago, for no record.

But on September 17, four days after losing a nine-inning pitching performance against the St. Louis Browns and their ace right-hander, Ned Garver, Brissie suffered not only his most humiliating outing, but also the game that ended his season.

It was against the Indians in Cleveland Stadium, his fifth appearance in 13 days, and just four days after his grueling game against Garver. "My leg had flared up, and I could hardly walk," he recalled. "I just felt I couldn't say anything—couldn't miss a turn. I didn't want to be viewed as handicapped. It was ever-present in my mind."

The Associated Press described the game this way:

"The last-place Philadelphia Athletics dribbled away a nine-run lead today and had to go 11 innings to defeat the Cleveland Indians, 10 to 9. Kermit Wahl raced home all the way from first on Mike Guerra's single to score the winning run.

"The A's piled up their lead in the first three innings, but Lou Brissie couldn't hold that advantage."

With a 9–0 lead going into the bottom of the third, Brissie gave up a run, another in the fourth, yet another in the fifth, and then was credited with giving up four in the sixth. He pitched 5⅓ innings before he was relieved by Bob Hooper. Brissie had wilted. He had allowed 10 hits, walked five, and threw a wild pitch.

When Brissie came back to the dugout, Connie Mack was irate. "You weren't trying out there," Mack said, nearly raising his voice, which was highly unusual for him.

"Mr. Mack," said Brissie, politely but steadfastly, "I'm always trying. It just wasn't a good day for me."

Brissie felt that no other explanation would be sufficient. You're either healthy or you're not. And if he took the ball, he was saying he was healthy. It was always a dilemma for him. Brissie then made his way to the showers.

Mack would not call on him to pitch in any of the final 10 games of the season.

"There was nothing more I could do about it," recalled Brissie. "I just hoped that Mr. Mack would have a change of heart."

The A's, with the loftiest of preseason expectations, finished a dispiriting last, six games behind the generally moribund seventh-place St. Louis Browns, and 46 games behind the pennant-winning Yankees.

3.

Perhaps the profound disappointment, not to say embarrassment, of the 1950 season influenced Connie Mack, or maybe it was simply the effects of a being an octogenarian, but spring training 1951 was the most unusual for the A's in their 50-year history: Connie Mack retired as manager. And for the first time in half a century Connie Mack, tall and lean and sitting back on the dugout bench in street clothes, would not be waving his scorecard to move his fielders into position. For the first time in 50 years, in fact, a telephone line between the dugout and the bullpen was installed, and no longer would an assistant coach be waving the various hand signals to summon a relief pitcher. Somewhere, surely, Alexander Graham Bell was smiling.

It had all come as a shock. No one expected the Tall Tactician, among Mack's many sobriquets, to live forever. But so far he was showing few indications of leaving his job as manager, let alone leaving this life. He seemed thin, yes, maybe even gaunt, but he always had. And, though more frail than ever, he appeared healthy and eager to continue managing a ballclub, which he'd done since starting in 1894 with Pittsburgh. He had taken over the Pirates late in that season, and as related in *Baseball: The Biographical Encyclopedia*, "The team had few good hitters, so one of his first moves was to freeze the baseballs in the clubhouse ice box before each game, thereby deadening them. Mack posted a winning record as the Pirates skipper in 1895 and 1896, but was fired after a dispute with an interfering owner."

Mack never again allowed an interfering owner to fire him, since his next managerial job was with the A's in 1901 when he not only took over the team on the field but became owner of the ballclub, as well. So 56 years after he had taken charge of the Pirates, and 50 years at the helm of the A's, the elderly Mack decided that enough was enough and announced his retirement. Jimmy Dykes was named to succeed him.

"Dykes Stunned, But Not Speechless, After Appointment as Pilot," read a headline in *The New York Times* on October 19, 1950. The story continued:

"The cigar-smoking, wise-cracking Dykes is nearly as familiar to Shibe Park fandom as the man he succeeded, 87-year-old Connie Mack.

"Dykes, who will be 54 on Nov. 10, was only 20 when he made his first appearance with the Athletics. He played third for Mack from 1918 to 1932, when he was sold to the Chicago White Sox."

Dykes managed the White Sox from 1934 to 1946, was out of base-ball for a few years, and then returned as a coach of the A's.

The Times story went on: "'I started as a fresh kid when I broke into baseball,' Dykes observed today. 'But I've always had the highest respect for Mr. Mack, who is the game's greatest individual.... I am flabbergasted about my appointment. Stepping into the shoes of a man who has run the club for 50 years is a job that is too big for me, too big for any man.'"

Red Smith, who covered the A's for the *Philadelphia Record* in the late 1930s and early '40s, wrote when Mack died a few years later: "It is not for mortals anywhere to suggest that another has lived too long, yet for those who knew and, necessarily, loved him it is difficult to regard Connie Mack's last years as part and parcel of a life that was a beacon in our time. Toward the end he was old and sick and saddened, a figure of forlorn dignity bewildered by the bickering around him as the base-ball monument that he had built crumbled away.... There may never have been a more truly successful man, for nobody ever won warmer or wider esteem and nobody ever relished it more."

The entire A's organization appeared to undergo a shakeup, and Art Ehlers, a longtime minor league and major league executive, became general manager, replacing Cochrane. Even though the last communication that Brissie had with Mack was not a pleasant one—Mack had accused Brissie of "not trying" when unable to hold a 9-0 lead after three innings against the Indians near season's end—he still was stunned, and saddened.

"I will always be grateful to Mr. Mack," said Brissie, "because he didn't look at my disabilities. He looked at my abilities."

Memories of "Mr. Mack" flooded back to Brissie:

"There were several disagreements among players on the bench that I remember. Ferris Fain had an argument with somebody on the bench—I forgot who it was or what it was about. But there were some pretty harsh comments. And Mr. Mack said, 'I would like for all of you to remember that in the heat of battle and a contest, words are spoken that are not meant.' He said that in a very soothing manner. I never heard him raise his voice."

Brissie recalled a story that Al Simmons, the Hall of Fame out-fielder who played most of his career with the A's and became the third-base coach for Mack, told him: "It was when he came up to the A's from the Evangeline League, which was a B or C League, and he had hit .390. Simmons said, 'I had to fight to get into the batting cage in batting practice. The old batters would not let you in there. So Mr. Mack says, "Let the young man hit a few." And I started hitting and I had half a dozen guys telling me what was wrong, with coaches trying to correct me, because I was stepping in the bucket, moving my hands before the pitch came, kind of a hitch in my swing and they're all talk-ing, and Mr. Mack says, "Last year he hit such and such. I tell you let's approach this in a different way. Let's leave him alone and when he's not hitting, let's correct any errors he makes."' And Simmons laughed that big belly-laugh of his and said, 'By God, that's the last I heard from any of them. And I played I forget how many years.'" (It was 20, with a lifetime batting average of .334, which included leading the league in batting twice, with averages of .381 and .390.)

Brissie said Mr. Mack could be tough as well: "I met Ty Cobb at an Old Timers game in Philadelphia. Cobb played the last year of his career for Mr. Mack, in 1928—he and Tris Speaker both. Cobb said he was sitting on the bench one day and Mr. Mack says, 'Tyrus, can you hit this pitcher?' He jumped up and said, 'Mr. Mack, I'll knock him right off the mound. I'll take care of this guy.' He said, 'I jerked my jacket off. Mr. Mack looked at me and says, "Well, that's good. Put your jacket on and sit down. And Speaker, go on and hit for the pitcher."' I guess Ty had done something to displease Mr. Mack and he wanted to put Ty in his place.

"Maybe that was the second most embarrassing day of Cobb's career, because he told me, 'My most embarrassing moment on the ballfield was any cloudy day in Washington with Walter Johnson pitching.'"

But in the last year or so of Mack's tenure as manager, his memory began to fail. He had problems recalling some of the players' names and his concentration flagged over the full length of games, as Bob Considine had reported in *Life* magazine. Simmons, coaching at third, had to frequently disregard his signs. And Mack was aware of it, especially when Simmons' signs worked out for the A's.

Even earlier, Red Smith recalled an interview when he and a few Philadelphia reporters met with Mack in his hotel room in March of 1946. The Dodgers were coming to play the A's in an exhibition in West Palm Beach the following day, and a Philadelphia writer asked, "Suppose they bring Robinson?" A few months before, Robinson had been signed by Branch Rickey, breaking the color barrier in organized baseball (Robinson would play that season in Montreal but was with the Dodgers in spring training). Mack, recalled Smith, "just blew his stack. 'I have no respect for Rickey,' Connie said. 'I have no respect for him now.' He went into a tirade. Stan Baumgartner of the *Philadelphia Inquirer* said, 'You wouldn't want that in the paper, would you, Connie?' Mack said, 'I don't give a goddamn what you write. Yes, publish it.'

"Baumgartner wanted to run the story of Mack's racism, but Don Donaghey of the *Bulletin* recognized the furor that it would cause. He argued Mack into taking it off the record. At first he said no, then he agreed. Stan was furious at Don for killing a good story." As for Mack's reputation for saintliness, Smith, who had a high regard for Mack in most other areas, didn't write the story, either. He said, "I decided that I'd forgive old Connie his ignorance." (The A's didn't have a black player until 1953, six years after Robinson broke the major league color barrier, when Bob Trice pitched briefly for them.)

With the team in transition in 1950, trade rumors circulated that winter regarding the A's, and Lou Brissie's name was periodically mentioned.

Stories such as the following November 28 Associated Press dispatch appeared: "It is known that the Red Sox are in the market for such established pitchers as the Philadelphia Athletics' Lou Brissie or the St. Louis Browns' Ned Garver."

Jimmy Dykes and Art Ehlers, the new general manager, were on record as saying that they wouldn't trade Brissie. And the reputation of Dykes as a ballplayers' manager was a good one. Luke Appling, the star shortstop who had played for Dykes with the White Sox, told Brissie that one night a bunch of the players decided to sneak out of the hotel on the road and go out late. When they came back, they decided, since they'd broken curfew, to furtively return to the hotel through the kitchen entrance. And there was Dykes, at a table having coffee with the staff. He said to the players, "C'mon in, boys, been waiting for you." The players got a good laugh out of it, and a fine.

One of Brissie's new teammates was Morrie Martin, another left-handed pitcher and a man who had also experienced the horrors of World War II in the European Theater. Gabriel Schechter, in a profile, "A Closer Look," for the Baseball Hall of Fame website, wrote: "(Martin) suffered shrapnel wounds twice and was buried alive in Germany when the house he was in was bombed. Left for dead, he and two other soldiers clawed their way out and rejoined the war effort. At the Battle of the Bulge, he was machine-gunned, and nearly lost a leg after gangrene set in. It took more than 150 shots of a new wonder drug, penicillin, to spare him from amputation. He had no reason to think he'd play ball again."

But he did, to be sure, and was back in professional ball in 1946 (he pitched in the Pacific Coast League as an 18-year-old in 1941, before going off to war), and made it briefly to the Dodgers in 1949, and then to the A's in '51 (he played with several other major league teams until his retirement in 1959).

Even though Martin had some similarities in wartime with Brissie, such as having a leg saved from amputation, they never discussed it. "We never talked about the war and what we did in it," Martin said, many years later, from his home in the Ozark mountains in Missouri. "None of us who served in combat wanted to bring back bad memories. I didn't even want to talk about it with my family, my wife. I got around it somehow. 'Honey, I just don't like talking about it.'

"Despite everything, I came back from the war without physical handicaps, or at least I never felt bothered by them. As for Lou, I watched him and thought he was remarkable. I have no idea how he pitched with that bad leg, except that it was done on will and stamina."

It was, however, not a good spring in 1951 for Brissie. He was hit hard. "It was only spring training, a time to get yourself into shape, work on some mechanics and timing, but still I was feeling a little disoriented—I was losing concentration," Brissie recalled. "While Dykes brought some new enthusiasm to the team, there was still this sense of front-office turmoil. And we still had uncertainty on the pitching staff—would Alex come back around, would Bobby Shantz reach the potential he obviously had, and would our offense, one of the weakest in the league, respond this season? Our regular players were getting older, seven of the eight regular fielders were 30 or over, and apparently we weren't adequately replacing them. And this from a team that finished last the season before, while other clubs were making improvements.

"But I think most if not all of us had a great respect for Jimmy Dykes. I know that Mr. Mack had a great respect for him. And Mr. Mack surely hand-picked Jimmy to succeed him. And Jimmy was a peach of a guy to play for. He wasn't overbearing, and he was a good listener. He seemed to care about you as a person. Still in all for me, with the changes, my concentration just didn't seem to be there."

In Brissie's first start of spring training, on March 17, against the Senators in St. Petersburg, Florida, he worked five innings and left with the A's behind 4–2. And things didn't get much better as Opening Day arrived. Brissie started the second game of the regular season, against the Senators in Shibe Park on April 18—Washington had won the opener—with 88-year-old Connie Mack watching from a special box.

Brissie took a 4–3 lead into the ninth inning, when the Senators staged a rally.

"Starter Lou Brissie, a 19-game loser last year, began his own downfall by passing pinch-hitter Cass Michaels and Mike McCormick," wrote the Associated Press. "Then, with one out, (Irv) Noren hit Brissie's first pitch for the decisive blow." He tripled home both runners. Mickey Vernon's double accounted for the other run, as the A's lost, 6–4. The A's were now 0–2 in this unpromisingly fresh season.

Five days later Brissie was on the mound again, with similar results, though a bit closer. He left the game in the fifth inning with the Yankees ahead 4–2, on eight hits and three walks. The Yankees also had success bunting. "Phenom" Mickey Mantle, as Louis Effrat described the Yankees rookie, laid down a drag bunt in the seventh inning for a single, and Jerry

Coleman followed with another bunt for a hit. Both runners eventually scored. What was noteworthy about those bunts was that the pitcher they bunted against was not Lou Brissie, but the veteran right-hander Hank "Hooks" Wyse, who had starred for the Cubs in their 1945 pennant-winning season. But Brissie took the loss, and he was now 0–2.

"I thought I was throwing the ball fairly well," recalled Brissie, "and it was just a matter of time before I hit my stride. The season was still young."

And then came the second piece of stunning, incredible news for Brissie during the six-month period following Connie Mack's retirement the previous October. While there had been rumors, he imagined they were only rumors. He was wrong.

The headline in the May 1 *New York Times* sports section:

"Indians Acquire Brissie in Trade
Of 7 Players with A's, White Sox"

The United Press reported: "Lou Brissie was traded to the Indians today and Gus Zernial went to the Athletics in the year's biggest baseball deal."

Philadelphia received outfielders Zernial and Dave Philley from the White Sox, pitcher Sam Zoldak and catcher Ray Murray from Cleveland. The White Sox acquired infielder-outfielder Orestes "Minnie" Minoso from Cleveland and Paul Lehner from the Athletics. Cleveland obtained only Brissie. It boiled down for the A's that they traded one player to get four.

UP added: "No cash reportedly changed hands in the triangular deal.

"Brissie, a huge 'hard luck' left-hander who won sixteen games in 1949 but could only compile a lackluster seven-and-nineteen record last season, was the 'plum' in the proceedings.

"Manager Al Lopez of Cleveland plans to use Brissie both as a starter and relief pitcher, the same assignment Lou filled with the eighth-place A's."

The Indians, who finished in fourth place in the 1950 American League race, six games behind the Yankees, were now in first place.

Lou Boudreau was fired at the end of the previous season, and Lopez replaced him. The Indians were a strong team, with one of the best pitching staffs in baseball—and one of the best starting rotations in baseball history, with Bob Feller, Bob Lemon, Early Wynn—all future Hall of Famers—and Mike Garcia and Steve Gromek. Where would Brissie fit in? Well, all the Indians starters were right-handers. "We needed a left-handed pitcher badly," Lopez told the Associated Press, "and I think we got a good one. If he's as good as I hear, then our staff is all set." (Lopez had retired as an active player with the Indians in 1947, after a 19-year career as a major league catcher. He then was named manager of their Triple A Indianapolis farm team until hired by the Indians as a rookie manager before the 1951 season.)

The Indians also had a potent lineup, with power-hitting Luke Easter at first; Bobby Avila, who was an outstanding rookie substitute for the retired Joe "Flash" Gordon, ready to take over second base; Al Rosen, who led the American League in home runs in 1950 with 37, at third; a superb shortstop in Ray Boone, and an outfield with All-Star center fielder (and future Hall of Famer) Larry Doby, and Bob Kennedy and Dale Mitchell, .300 or near .300 hitters, in the other two outfield positions. Rugged Jim Hegan, behind the plate, had played in the 1950 All-Star Game.

What a marvelous opportunity for Brissie, to go from a last-place team with limited prospects to a team that would surely be contending for the pennant.

Brissie didn't see it that way. He had not been informed of the trade until Dykes called him at home and asked him to come to the ballpark. It was an off day. Brissie wondered what it was all about. He went to Dykes' office in the clubhouse, and Dykes gave him the news. It was a blow for Brissie, as though an unseen brick had fallen on his head. "Why did they have to trade me?" he lamented to a reporter when he was cleaning out his locker. "I never thought that would happen. I know I've been bush so far, but I never thought Jim (Dykes) would do that."

Brissie recalled, "It was the most devastating thing in the world to me. I had only wanted to play for the A's. My dad's dream was that I would help Mr. Mack win his last pennant. And that was my dream. I had a miserable spring. I was really depressed about the whole thing. I failed my dad. I failed Mr. Mack. I felt I was only there because of a series of miracles that had to happen. And I failed everybody that had had any confidence in me. I was in pain. I was having leg problems. I was thinking seriously about quitting. I liked Dykes and, after I got my thoughts together and some of the emotion subsided, I decided that I was going to go on pitching. And I thought the best thing I could do was to stay in the game."

The A's at the time of the trade had lost 10 straight games, and their hitting was especially meek, providing the pitching staff with little support.

Dykes had managed Zernial and Philley in Chicago, and he liked them both. "We just needed someone to hit the ball," Dykes told Brissie. "And when I spoke with Eddie Joost about that, he said, 'That's a pretty good argument.' And I guess it was."

"We didn't want to let Brissie go," Dykes told the Associated Press, "but we had to give up something to get something. We wanted out-fielders who could give us some power and we got 'em." (Zernial, a free swinger who led the league in strikeouts, generally held up his offensive end of the deal by also leading the American League in homers with 33 and RBIs with 129, just ahead of Ted Williams in both categories.)

Ehlers said, "Brissie wasn't helping us, but you never know. Maybe a change of scenery will do him some good. Lou has plenty of natural ability."

And Hank Greenberg, the Indians' general manager who made the trade for the left-hander, believed that indeed the change of scenery for Brissie would be beneficial to the Indians. "It's the kind of deal a club makes when it's going all-out for the pennant," he said.

The AP photograph that appeared in the nation's newspapers the day after the trade showed a glum Lou Brissie, dark haired, square-jawed, broad-shouldered, putting his baseball glove into an equipment bag in front of his A's locker, with the No. 19 uniform that he would never again wear.

Then Greenberg called Brissie to welcome him to the Indians. He was surprised to learn that Brissie had been reluctant to come.

Greenberg, as Brissie recalled, thought it was a matter of money. "C'mon over here, and we'll tear up your contract and write out a new one," Greenberg told Brissie over the phone. Brissie was then making $15,000 in this the last year of his contract.

"No, it's not a matter of money," Brissie insisted. "I don't want a new contract—I signed what I signed in good faith."

Greenberg said, "Well, what is it then?'" Brissie recalls that he had the feeling that Greenberg imagined that since he was from South Carolina, he might not want to play with black players, like Easter and Doby. The A's had no black players. "But of course that wasn't it either," recalled Brissie. "I had absolutely no problems playing with black players, or anyone else, as long as they were good teammates and wanted to win."

There was also the family consideration, a problem in trades with many players. The Brissies, after three years, had established a home and made friends in Philadelphia during the season. Being uprooted would be a trial for all of them. Dot understood the circumstances, the life of the sometimes itinerant athlete that was often out of his control, but still, would she and the kids would make their adjustments and be happy in Cleveland?

Brissie was troubled and told Greenberg, "Hank, I'm feeling really lousy being traded from Philadelphia. I had hoped to do better for them. I feel I've disappointed a lot of people."

Greenberg said, "Lou, we want you. We feel you can help us. We want to win the pennant."

Brissie was then 26 years old and felt he did have a lot of good baseball left in him. And he was going from last place to first place. There was another positive consideration in going to Cleveland. He'd be closer to Dr. Brubaker, who practiced in Elyria, a town some 10 miles west of Cleveland.

Brissie said to Greenberg, "Okay. Yes, I'm coming and I'll give you everything I have."

And Brissie told the *Cleveland Plain Dealer*, "I only hope I can help the Indians win the pennant."

While Brissie's career seemed to have taken a step up in a baseball direction, another career came to a close. It was reported that Phil Marchildon had been given his unconditional release by Toronto of the International League, ending his baseball career. Marchildon, the onetime A's star who spent nine months in a German prisoner of war camp, Stalag Luft III, who survived on only a few pieces of bread a day with wood in them and some watered-down soup, who saw some of his compatriots randomly shot and killed by German guards, and who was forced with other allied POWs to walk 130 miles in deep snow to avoid the oncoming Russian army near war's end, was never the same person when he returned from service. Though he won 19 games in 1947, he ended his big-league career at 0–3 with the A's in 1949 and was traded to the Boston Red Sox where he appeared in one game, in 1950, and, at 36, was gone from the major leagues.

"Phil was always so nervous after his experiences overseas," recalled Brissie. "You'd see him on the bench fidgeting. Mr. Mack said he had changed a lot—had become quiet and serious. I don't remember seeing him smile. He didn't talk about it, but it was obvious that the war had taken a toll on him."

11

The New Pennant Hope

1.

Lou Brissie left the A's clubhouse following news of the trade to Cleveland, shocked and saddened, and made the 20-minute drive to his apartment in Olney, a leafy section of North Philadelphia, the area where the Brissies usually stayed. Then he called Dot, who was still in their Greenville home with the three children. (Since it was early in the season and the team had been traveling, he hadn't yet been able to find a house for his family to move into—the previous home they rented in Philadelphia had become unavailable.)

He broke the news to her. "She wasn't thrilled with it, as one might imagine," recalled Brissie, "but she was accepting; she had learned to deal with situations. The change was abrupt. It caught her by surprise, but every baseball wife is prepared for something like this—up to a point."

They made hasty arrangements for a move—it wasn't going to be easy, what with a four-year-old daughter and year-old twin boys—and then Brissie, carrying a suit bag and an equipment bag, with his glove and brace, took a cab to the Philadelphia 30th Street train station.

He rode all night to Cleveland, confused at the turn of events, uncertain, but still determined. As long as he was going to work, he was, like the image of his father that was invariably with him, going to do the best job possible. Upon his arrival he took a taxi to the Auditorium Hotel, near Municipal Stadium. Sitting in the hotel lobby, unnoticed by Brissie, was a swarthy man in a sport jacket. The man looked up from his chair, rose, and approached Brissie, who was checking in at the desk.

"I'm Al Lopez," the man said, extending his hand.

Brissie recalled: "We had a nice little visit, and he said he was happy to have me aboard. It was one of the few times in my three years in Cleveland that I had any kind of a real conversation with Al. In fact, he always seemed rather distant, and I don't ever remember him calling me by name."

Well, he had pitched for a relatively quiet manager, Connie Mack, and, briefly, for a loquacious and humorous one in Jimmy Dykes, so Brissie felt that Lopez's style was simply that, his unique manner reflecting the manager's personality, and he didn't take it personally.

The Indians had perhaps the best starting rotation in baseball with Feller, Lemon, Early Wynn (all future Hall of Famers), and Mike Garcia—who won 20, 22, and 18 games in the three years that Brissie was his teammate. Brissie had pitched in relief a great deal for the A's and Greenberg saw that he could be the answer to a questionable Cleveland bullpen—the last piece in the puzzle, as it is termed.

Lopez stated that he hoped Brissie would help them finally unseat the Yankees, who had won two straight American League pennants and World Series. The players also seemed eager to have him on the team. They had hit against him, pitched against him, and were well aware of his abilities. Something else. "When Lou came over to us he was an object of awe," recalled Al Rosen, then the Indians' star third baseman. "We knew the story of his being shot up in the war, but he didn't talk about it, didn't parade around the clubhouse to show off his scars. He had that high-riding fastball and at times pitched very well for us in relief. We held him in high esteem."

In his first game for the Indians, on May 2, wearing No. 12 because No. 19, his A's number, was already taken by Feller, the Associated Press reported, "Bob Lemon and new pennant hope, Lou Brissie, produced a second straight victory for the Indians today over the Red Sox, 4-3." Lemon pitched five shutout innings, then suffered a pulled back muscle and gave way to Brissie, who allowed just two hits in the final four innings. One of those hits, however, was a three-run homer in the eighth by Boston shortstop Lou Boudreau, making his first visit to Cleveland since he was fired as Cleveland's manager after the 1950 season and traded to the Red Sox. Boudreau, long a fan favorite in Cleveland, was warmly greeted by the crowds in his first at-bat, though they were noticeably reticent when he cracked the homer.

This was Brissie's first game pitching for the Indians in his new home ballpark, the cavernous Municipal Stadium with the largest seating capacity in baseball at more than 78,000. Only a sparse 11,388 paid to watch that game, and it seemed to Brissie that he was pitching in the Grand Canyon, and that he could nearly hear people behind the first-base dugout speaking to each other. But a park so big could be a welcoming place for a pitcher.

Four days later Brissie started and lost the opening game of a doubleheader to the Senators—he was now 0-3 on the season, including his 0-2 start with the A's—but a brief few hours later he came out of the bullpen in the second game to save it for the Indians. With two on and no outs and the Indians ahead, 4-2, Brissie retired the next three batters to end the game. During the next week, he saved one game and started against the first-place Yankees in a night game at Yankee Stadium on May 14.

The Yankees games, like most games of sports teams, were in their infancy on television. There were many who believed that if you televised the games for free, the fans wouldn't pay to go to the ballpark to see the same game. Those were some of the same concerns people had when ballgames were first aired on radio. In his game story in which Brissie had started against the Yankees on May 14, Louis Effrat of *The New York Times* wrote: "That 68,027 fans, of which 66,265 paid, turned out for the after-dark contest also was a significant development. It is reasonable to assume that many of the customers could have viewed the game on television. Their presence, therefore, proves that sports fans, given a good attraction, will not stay away from the park. At any rate, it was the largest crowd (so far) in the 1951 major league campaign."

Before this huge crowd in the stands, and, surely, a large audience of fans watching on TV, Brissie gave up seven runs in six innings and took the defeat. His won-lost record stood at an unspectacular 0-4.

Appearing in eight games in relief after that, Brissie pitched well but didn't get his next start for three weeks. That start came on June 7, in Shibe Park. In the stands upon Brissie's return to Philadelphia was a 14-year-old boy named Howard Geltzer. Years later, Geltzer recalled that event:

"About five times a year my family and I traveled from Hazleton to Philadelphia—about a three-hour ride in those days—to see ballgames. My mom and dad and younger brother were avid Indians fans, while I rooted for the hapless Pirates and Athletics. But we all adored Brissie and knew his story. When we listened to the games on radio, the announcer, By Saam, used to always refer to it, and what Brissie had gone through to get to where he was. The memories of World War II were very fresh in the late '40s and early '50s, and although my dad was too old to serve, he had many friends from childhood who had been in uniform, including several who were killed. My mom worked as a telephone operator on the Hazleton civil defense squad—I guess it was part of the early warning system in case the Nazis or Japanese were going to attack Hazleton! Rooting for war heroes, regardless of their baseball uniform, was an exercise in patriotism. We came early for the game when Brissie returned to Shibe Park for the first time after being traded to the Indians. We always came early for batting practice, but this day was special. And when Brissie came out of the dugout in an Indians uniform, he received a standing ovation and cheers—even from the local fans, who were not known to laud the opposition. It gave you chills. I remember standing and cheering as loud as anyone. And the Indians fans I came to the game with, they were doing the same."

And they did the same when Brissie came on the field the next time. In a homecoming gesture, Lopez gave Brissie the ball to start the game. And Brissie rose to the occasion, pitching a complete game, giving up three runs, striking out five, and scattering 12 hits, as he won his first game of the 1951 season—and his first game for the Indians.

"The fans," Brissie recalled, "gave me a very nice reception when I walked out to the mound. And I appreciated it. There were times when I was pitching for the A's, and losing games, that they weren't so nice to me." He smiled. "But I guess I deserved it.

"It always feels good to win," he added, "but this one, returning to where I had begun, felt especially good." He didn't add, "And from whom I had disappointingly been traded."

Five days after his appearance against the A's in Philadelphia, the Indians at home beat the A's again, 8-6, with Brissie relieving Bob Feller in the ninth inning. Brissie cut off an A's rally and helped save a win for Feller, his ninth of the season against one loss. Brissie did it again on July 6, 1951, helping Feller notch his 12th win, entering the game, according to the Associated Press, "to halt the (Tigers') attack" and preserved a 7-4 victory.

Brissie and Feller, with his prominent dimpled chin that seemed to suggest his strong and assured personality, grew friendly. They also had a mutual admiration society. Both had seen combat action; both were dedicated pitchers.

"Lou and I used to sit in the bullpen and chitchat about pitching," Feller recalled. "He knew what he was talking about. Intelligent. He was a great teammate, had a good live fastball, and pretty good control for a left-hander. He couldn't bend his left leg very much, but he never complained."

Brissie admired Feller for, among other attributes, his professional thoroughness. "He was a student not only of pitching, but of his body, and how to work his body to make himself a better pitcher," said Brissie. "Bob knew every muscle grouping in every part of his body. He understood strength and flexibility before almost anyone else playing baseball. He went to doctors and professors to learn about it."

Brissie and Feller were talking about catchers one day, and both extolled the Indians' regular receiver, Jim Hegan. "One day, I crossed him up," Feller told Brissie. "I threw him a fastball instead of a curve"— and Feller didn't have to add how great his fastball was. "And Hegan caught the ball and walked out to the mound and said, 'You crossed me up, mate! Don't do that again!' He didn't drop it, he didn't fumble it. He just made a quick jerk. He had the best hands of any catcher I ever saw." Brissie agreed with Feller that Hegan had the best hands of any catcher. Another pure example of this, Brissie recalled, was when Hegan was blindsided by Hoot Evers of the Tigers who knocked him to the ground on a play at the plate: "Hegan's chest protector was turned around, he had one shin guard knocked off, he'd lost his mitt, but he had held onto the ball when he made the tag, and Evers was out."

Feller, who won eight battle stars in five campaigns during World War II, was one of the first major league players to enlist in the military after Pearl Harbor. "Like a lot of people, I really thought we were in serious trouble," Feller said. On December 9, Feller, then 22 and already one of the stars of the American League—he had led the league in strikeouts in the previous four seasons and in wins in the previous three—went through the door of a Navy recruiting office in Chicago and signed up. He would be making $80 a month, or $960 a year, as opposed to his baseball salary of more than $40,000 a year. At first, Feller was assigned as a physical fitness instructor. But he wanted to do more. He entered gunnery school and eventually became a captain (Chief Specialist) on the battleship USS *Alabama*, commanding a gun crew that saw considerable action in the South Pacific.

In his book, *From Playing Field to Battlefield: Great Athletes Who Served in World War II*, Rob Newell wrote: "In June 1944 the Japanese launched an all-out attack.... It was a last-gasp effort to try to stem the Allies' steady advance toward the mainland.... Of the estimated 430 Japanese aircraft that were launched, only 35 survived... Asked how many planes his gun mount crew shot down, Feller volunteers only that they 'bagged a couple of them. You never really knew who shot down what, because there were other ships around shooting at the same aircraft,' he says, 'but it was certainly the most exciting 13 hours of my life. After that, the dangers of Yankee Stadium seemed trivial.'"

Brissie made another of his rare starts on July 18, in Boston. The game started poorly for Brissie and quickly ended the same way. He gave up three runs in the first inning and three in the third, and was relieved by Mickey Harris as Boston won 9-2.

Of the Indians' four prominent starting pitchers—teams generally went with four starters in those days, as opposed to five in recent times—three won 20 games that season: Feller led the American League with 22 victories, Garcia and Wynn each earned 20, and Bob Lemon had 17.

On September 18, however, in a game against the Red Sox as reported by Louis Effrat in *The New York Times*, Al Lopez demonstrated a routine that was to become, for Brissie, all too familiar as time went on—the manager's often unwavering reliance on his four primary starting pitchers, which sometimes paid off and sometimes didn't. In this case, the Indians were leading 6–2 in the bottom of the ninth, with Garcia going for his 20th win and the Indians seeking to come within three percentage points of the first-place Yankees. The Red Sox rallied. Garcia, obviously tiring, loaded the bases "after the first three batters slashed singles to left. Manager Al Lopez had Lou Brissie and Steve Gromek active in the bullpen. Twice Lopez strode to the mound for conferences with Garcia, but the manager elected to stay with Mike. Even after Fred Hatfield and pinch-hitter Vern Stephens each had driven over a run on an infield grounder, Lopez refused to change pitchers. When (Red Sox manager) Steve O'Neill sent Lou Boudreau to bat for Nixon, Garcia proved his worth.

"The right-hander gathered in Boudreau's hopper to the mound and, taking no chances, raced to first for the game-ending putout," and a 6–4 Indians win.

Bob Lemon, a 20-game winner the previous three seasons, had an unusual history. He came up to the Indians in 1941 as a left-handed-hitting third baseman, but his throws across the diamond had such a dip to them that he was tried out as a pitcher—and never went back to third base. Hegan had said that Lemon's was "the most live fastball I ever caught. It would jump this way and that."

"He had wrists like a bulldog," said George Strickland, who became the Indians' regular shortstop in 1953. "And Lemon's slider was so good, it could drop two feet. I remember once Cliff Mapes with Detroit thought the pitch was going to hit him and he fell down, but the ball broke and the ump called him out."

Strickland also recalled that Lemon "taught me how to drink.... We'd go to dinner and I might have a couple of highballs, and before you knew it Lem had eight or ten. But you'd hardly know it. He wasn't a slobbering guy. He was a great guy and a very smart baseball man. But when we'd go to dinner with Lem and his wife and other couples, my wife, Lorraine, would ask, 'Well, are we going to eat tonight?'" In later years, Lemon developed a rather reddish nose, the result, assumedly, of those many highballs.

Lemon also remained one of the best hitting pitchers in the game, and he was sometimes used as a pinch hitter. He batted .232 lifetime, and his 37 homers as a pitcher put him second on the all-time career list, behind Wes Ferrell—another reason why Lemon, at times, stayed in the game longer than one might expect during a relatively rocky outing.

Brissie had a particular fondness for Lemon. "One time when I was having some tough luck on the mound," recalled Brissie, "Lem came over to me and said, 'You're doing a fine job. We appreciate it.' He didn't have to do that."

Garcia was nicknamed the Big Bear for his swarthy complexion (he was Mexican Indian, though born in California) and hulking 6'1", 210-pound presence. His size presented a problem in his youth because he originally dreamed of becoming a jockey, and so had to settle for being an All-Star major league pitcher. "Mike and I roomed together for a while," said Brissie. "He was so even tempered. If anything upset him, you'd never know it. And he was comfortable in all settings. When we'd play in Washington, and Dr. Suraci invited us for dinner, Mike almost became a part of the family immediately."

Wynn had a different disposition. "He could be moody and grumpy," said Brissie, "but a lot of that contributed to his being such a fierce competitor. Wynn was so ferocious, in fact, that he was known as a 'headhunter,' someone who had no compunction about throwing at batters' heads. A story went that when asked if he'd throw at his own grandmother, Wynn replied, 'I'd have to. Grandma could really hit the curveball.' Maybe he was only half-joking about being a tough guy." Lopez recalled a time when he came out to the mound to remove Wynn, and Wynn was as reluctant to leave the game as Lopez usually was in having him leave. Lopez said that he always extended his hand when taking a pitcher out and expected the pitcher to put the ball in it. "Except the one time I went out to take Early Wynn out," said Lopez. "I stuck out my hand and he hit me right in the stomach with the ball." Shortstop George Strickland said that Wynn, who had earned the nickname "the Beast," sometimes knocked his teammates down when throwing batting practice. "Just for practice," said Strickland.

Brissie recalled that when Hank Majeski joined the Indians, Wynn shook hands with him and said, "Nice to have you with us."

"Now, when Majeski was with the A's, Wynn had hit him in the head with a fastball," said Brissie. "Wynn never asked Majeski, 'Are you okay? How ya doin'?' Nothing. It hurt Hank. But it was really a dog-eat-dog business for Early."

The Indians overtook the Yankees for first place in mid-September, but they fell back again and finished second, five games behind New York.

In the bullpen, meanwhile, Brissie proved instrumental in the Indians' run for the flag, pitching in 56 games, second highest total in the league, and compiling nine saves, third in the league. Brissie wound up starting in just four of the 54 games in which he appeared for the Indians in 1951, winning four and losing three. He had a very respectable 3.20 earned-run average for the Indians, better even than Feller's 3.50 and Lemon's 3.52.

Midway through the 1951 season, Bill Veeck, who had been forced to sell the Indians because he needed money in a costly divorce battle after the 1949 season, bought the Browns. He had demonstrated unique promotional skills in Cleveland and continued in that vein in St. Louis, most notably with the insertion of the midget into a major league lineup. He invented yet another promotion (read that "stunt" to his critics) that provoked negative comments in baseball: Grandstand Managers Day. His team was stuck in last place—on the way to 102 losses in the 154-game season—and drawing flies, along with a handful of fans.

For Veeck, the question was: what to do? How about the fans in the stands choosing the starting lineup and deciding strategy? Which is what he did. Veeck encouraged fans to write letters to him about why they should manage the team. At the game, each fan was given a placard with green for YES and red for NO printed on opposite sides. Questions regarding most conceivable situations had also been printed. A circuit court judge was given the assignment of counting the ballots for each situation. The Browns' manager, Zack Taylor, was given a seat in the stands—in a rocking chair, actually. He sat there in slippers, smoking a pipe. He seemed quite content. The Browns were playing the A's, but Art Ehlers, the A's general manager, wasn't so content. He threatened to protest because the Browns "were making a travesty of the game." The umpires thumbed through the rule book but couldn't find any reason not to play the game, and so it went on. The Browns won 5–3, ending a two-game losing streak!

Paid attendance for the game was 3,925. Well, Veeck had tried.

Brissie's views were sanguine toward Veeck and his promotions: "I thought they were fine. You gotta get 'em into the ballpark. And Veeck had a tough row to hoe over there because the teams, with a few exceptions, had been so bad for so long. Baseball's a business; it's show business. You do whatever you have to do to draw people."

Years later, Brissie ran into Veeck in a hotel in New York, and the two had breakfast together. "I admired Bill for all the things he tried to do to enliven baseball and bring people into the ballpark, from the midget to exploding scoreboards," said Brissie. "I also liked the way he treated his players. When Joe Tipton, a reserve catcher, came over to Philadelphia from Cleveland, he told me how he had been summoned into action on a road trip when the first-string catcher got hurt, and he delivered some clutch hits and handled the pitchers well and the team had gone on a winning streak. When they returned to Cleveland, Veeck called Tipton into his office. "'I thought he was going to trade me,'" Tipton told Brissie. "Veeck came around his desk and motioned Tipton to the window. He said, 'See that blue Chevy parked out there?' Tipton said yes. He said, 'Here are the keys to it. It's yours, in appreciation for doing a great job.'"

At breakfast, Veeck asked Brissie about his leg. Veeck had had his right leg amputated from a mishap when he was a Marine stationed on the island of Guadalcanal during World War II. An antiaircraft gun recoiled into his leg, the leg became infected, and two years later it had to be amputated. On the night after the amputation, Veeck threw a "post-leg-amputation party" for himself and danced the night away on his new wooden limb. He seemed to have no inhibitions about it. Sometimes, in fact, he would take a companion aback when he'd remove the artificial leg and use the top of it for an ashtray.

"Bill and I talked about our bad legs," recalled Brissie. "He asked me specific questions, and he told me that he had osteomyelitis, too. He said, 'I want to tell you one thing, young man. When they want to take off your leg, let 'em. I wish I had done it sooner. You won't suffer nearly as much.'"

2.

In Cleveland, the Brissies rented a house with a backyard where the kids could romp. "The boys never ran in the same direction together," recalled Brissie. "One would go east while the other would head west. We were always chasing them this way or that."

And, Brissie recalled, there were the moments of frustration, as there were early in the 1952 season, when he called Dot from the road and he could hear it in her voice. "Sometimes things piled up," he said. "The kids are sick, and the plumbing went out, and one problem added upon another. I tried to be as understanding as I could. Sometimes all I could say was, 'Honey, I'll be home soon.'" In a few days, as the kids stopped crying and got over their colds, and the plumber fixed the toilet, Brissie and the Indians indeed arrived home. "It was really one of the hardships of being a ballplayer," said Brissie. "When you're away, you just can't leave the team to get a handyman. Dot knew this, of course, and while it was difficult, it was something that we just had to deal with."

In the Indians' fifth game of the 1952 season, Brissie made his first appearance on the mound for them. He entered the contest in the seventh inning in relief and squelched a Tigers three-run rally off starter Early Wynn. The Indians won 7–5, for their fifth straight win of the season, and Larry Doby figured prominently, hitting a homer and a double and driving in three runs, the margin of victory. Doby went on to lead the American League in homers that season, with 32.

Doby, the first black player in the American League, debuted in his first game, July 5, 1947, just 11 weeks after Jackie Robinson's historic Opening Day appearance with the Dodgers. Doby had emerged as a standout center fielder, and played in his fourth straight All-Star Game in 1952.

The Indians were only one of three American League teams to employ black players. The Browns and White Sox were the others. Besides Doby, the Indians roster in 1952 included first baseman Luke Easter, pitcher Sad Sam (also called Toothpick Sam) Jones, outfielders Dave Pope and Harry "Suitcase" Simpson, and the former Negro Leagues star catcher Quincy Trouppe who, at age 39, was the league's oldest rookie. He appeared in just six games for the Indians, the length of his big-league career; like many standout Negro Leagues players from years past, Trouppe's time had, unfortunately, passed.

It's not hard to imagine the obstacles, and the suspicions, that Doby had to deal with. On his first day with the Indians, Doby, coming out of the Negro Leagues as a young second baseman, was introduced by the manager, Lou Boudreau, to his new teammates. Some refused to shake his hand. When Doby slid into second base, a second baseman spit in his face. Joe Gordon, the Indians' second baseman, was one of the few to befriend Doby openly. When the then 6'1", 185-pound Doby stepped onto the field before that first game with the White Sox, he stood silently in Cleveland uniform No. 14, glove in hand, for what he recalled as 5 or 10 minutes. "No one offered to play catch," he said. Finally, he heard Gordon, the All-Star second baseman, call to him, "Hey, kid, let's go." And they warmed up. It was reminiscent of the moment in the infield early in Jackie Robinson's career with the Dodgers when their highly respected shortstop, Pee Wee Reese, casually put his arm around the beleaguered Robinson, the team's second baseman then, saying in effect to all those on the field and in the stands who remained prejudiced against a black man in the major leagues, "What's the problem, guys?" Reese, like Gordon, had the reputation for being intelligent and gentlemanly.

Bill Veeck, the man responsible for buying Doby's contract from Newark, received 20,000 letters regarding it. "Most of them," Veeck said later, "in violent and sometimes obscene protest." Doby, a left-handed batter, pinch-hit that first day and struck out. He played little that season, often sitting alone at the end of the bench, and stayed by himself on the road when some hotels remained segregated. He batted .156 in 29 games and, trying so hard, frequently struck out, sometimes wildly. "During that whole first year," Veeck wrote in his autobiography, *Veeck—as in Wreck*, Doby "was a complete bust.

"The next year, however, when Tris Speaker and Bill McKechnie converted him into a center fielder, Larry began to hit and one of our weak positions became one of our strongest.

"With all that, his inner turmoil was such a constant drain on him that he was never able to realize his full potential. Not to my mind, at any rate. If Larry had come up just a little later, when things were a little better, he might have become one of the greatest players of all time."

Doby became the first black player to hit a home run in a World Series, made six straight American League All-Star teams, and, at one time or another over a 13-year career, led the American League in homers, runs batted in, runs scored, and slugging average, as well as strikeouts. When he retired in 1959, he did so with a .283 career average and 253 home runs, and he was ultimately elected to the Baseball Hall of Fame.

In an interview years after his playing days, Doby said he could not forget the sense of loneliness, particularly after games. "It's then you'd really like to be with your teammates, win or lose, and go over the game," he said. "But I'd go off to my hotel in the black part of town, and they'd go off to their hotel.

"And then I always tried to act in a dignified manner. When I was in the major leagues, some people thought I was a loner. But, well, when Joe DiMaggio was off by himself, they said he just wanted his privacy. And midway through the 1948 season the Indians signed Satchel Paige, and they made him my roommate. Well, he was almost never in the room. I'm not sure where he went. But he was a character and he enjoyed being perceived that way. He'd come into the clubhouse and clown around, and did some Amos 'n' Andy stuff. I didn't think it was right—at least, it wasn't right for me."

Brissie remembered being on the bench when the A's played the Indians for the first time in 1948, Doby's second season in the big leagues and Brissie's rookie year. "The bench jockeying was pretty brutal," Brissie said, "I heard some of my teammates shouting things at Larry, like, 'Porter, carry my bags.' Or 'Shoeshine boy, shine my shoes,' and, well, the N word, too. It was terrible." Brissie empathized with Doby. "He was a kind of an underdog, like me," he said.

When he joined the Indians in 1951, Brissie came to know Doby, to an extent. "Larry had a high degree of sensitivity," recalled Brissie. "He could be a little distant. He had a heavy load to carry. It seemed to me that he shared with Jackie Robinson a deep sense of obligation to their race."

Among the wives of the Indians players that Dot Brissie grew friendly with was Helen Doby. "I think one of the major reasons that Larry was able to deal with his problems was because of Helen," Brissie recalled. "She was a very impressive woman and held things in an even keel. I remember that she told Dot once that she told Larry, 'Don't worry about it. It'll be better tomorrow.'"

• • •

The Indians were keeping pace with the first-place Yankees and seeking to win the pennant, something the Yankees, now having won three straight American League pennants and World Series, had understandably come to think as their birthright. And Brissie was holding his own.

June 7, 1952, in Philadelphia was a fairly typical outing: the United Press reported: "Luke Easter walloped a grand-slam homer in the first inning, and Mike Garcia and Lou Brissie collaborated in shutting out the Athletics as the Indians rolled to a 14–0 victory." Brissie allowed no hits in pitching the last two innings, while walking one.

Brissie was used solely in relief and pitched no more than three innings (three times) in each of his 19 appearances. But on July 1, in Cleveland, that changed dramatically. Brissie and Satchel Paige hooked up in the late innings of a memorable game. And it was in this game that Brissie got a closeup look at Paige's "bow-tie pitch." "The bow-tie

pitch," as Paige once explained, "is when you throw it right here." Paige
drew a line with his hand across his Adam's apple. "Where they wear
their bow tie. It keeps the batters off the plate and makes them very
uneasy about digging in."

Paige entered the game for the St. Louis Browns in the eighth, after
Feller and Ned Garver had been locked in their own pitchers' battle,
each leaving the game at 2-2. Paige went on to pitch scoreless ball for
10 innings. Brissie, coming into the game in the ninth, matched Paige
and pitched nine innings without allowing a run. Then, in the top of
the nineteenth inning, Brissie gave up a run on a walk, a sacrifice bunt,
and a single. The Indians were now down 3-2, but in the bottom of
the inning they rallied: Bobby Avila singled; Al Rosen doubled, scoring
Avila and tying the game; and, with two outs, Hank Majeski slashed a
pinch-hit single to win the game, which, at 4 hours and 49 minutes,
equaled the then record for the longest night game in major league history. And it was Brissie's first win of the year, against no losses.

"I was exhausted after the game," recalled Brissie with a certain
fondness for that extraordinary evening. "I wondered if I could ever
move again, let alone walk again. I took a very hot, very long bath that
night. A few things stand out for me in that game: old Satchel Paige
pitching so well and, it seemed, so effortlessly, and Al Rosen coming
through the way he did—he was such a fine player—and Hank Majeski
doing the same. Hank was tough with men on base when we were in
Philadelphia, and he was the same in Cleveland. He was this nice,
quiet guy—sometimes he'd come over from third just say to something
like, 'Good pitch,' that's all—but he could be a terror with a bat in his
hands."

And it was Majeski, who had a locker across from Brissie's in the
Indians' clubhouse, who one day said, "How do you do it?"

"Do what?" Brissie asked.

"Well, I watched you get ready in Philadelphia and I've watched
you here, going through all the stuff that you do."

Trainers of ballclubs didn't help much. "I pretty much took care of
my leg myself," said Brissie. "But if I had drainage, they'd dress it before
and after a game. When I cramped up they'd massage it and put on

something hot to keep it loose. I don't think I was cramping up more than usual, but I still cramped up fairly often.

"I had this heavy scar tissue on the front of my leg and on the back of it. So every day before a game I'd first apply cocoa butter to keep the scar tissue soft and pliable, to avoid cracking. It would open up and fester when it cracked.

"I'd put on cotton stockings under my uniform and stirrup socks and add a heavy wrapping around to help support and pad the leg. Then I'd put on the brace, which hooked on the heel of my shoe. I used cocoa butter on my right foot, too, because of scar tissue on my instep there. And I put rubber padding in my left shoe to build it up about half an inch because my left leg was shorter than the right from the operations."

Brissie hadn't realized that he had been watched. "It's just preparation for the game," Brissie replied to Majeski. "Same way you prepare. Only different." While Brissie was, in the accounts of his teammates, an easy and supportive presence on the bench and in the clubhouse, he was ever reluctant to call attention to his disability. He wanted no one to think he was handicapped. First, he wanted no one to feel sorry for him, and, to be sure, if it was known he was hurting he might not be called on to pitch, and out of pride that was something he dreaded.

• • •

On August 27, in an ever-tightening pennant race, a headline and subhead in *The New York Times* read: "Indians Vanquish Athletics by 6–3; Starters Shantz and Feller Fail to Finish as Brissie Stars in Relief." Again in Philadelphia, before a crowd of 35,092, Brissie shut down the A's, this time in the last $2\frac{2}{3}$ innings. "Brissie came on in the ninth with the score tied (3–3), the bases filled, and only one out in relief of starter Bob Feller," the story read, "and the lean lefty promptly fanned pinch-hitter Kite Thomas and Eddie Joost." He remained in the game.

The Indians scored three runs in the top of the 11th for the victory. Brissie registered his third win of the season, against, now, two losses.

As the season entered its final month, the Indians nearly caught the Yankees, but then fell back. It was Sisyphus pushing the boulder up the hill. The Indians were 1½ games out on September 14, when they lost at home to the Yankees, 7–1, with Brissie pitching the fourth and fifth innings and allowing one run. The Indians closed to a game and a half out on September 21, then crept to within a game back. But on the following day, they lost to the White Sox 10–1. The Yankees clinched the pennant three days later. The loss to the White Sox was one of the few times that Lopez used a relief pitcher down the stretch. And this in a mop-up situation, after Garcia had given up five runs in the first inning. Brissie pitched a shutout final inning. It was his final appearance of the season.

Casey Stengel said: "You can't win a pennant with just four pitchers." Brissie agreed wholeheartedly with that statement. Stengel relied on his bullpen, and in one of his best-known change of pitchers, he removed the rookie left-hander, Whitey Ford, in the fourth game of the 1950 World Series. Ford had pitched beautifully for 8⅔ innings, but found himself in trouble. He was leading 5–2 (after an error by the left-fielder, Gene Woodling, allowed two runs to score), and then Mike Goliat banged a single. The crowd was cheering for the youngster to pitch a complete game. But Stengel was taking no chances. He went out to the mound and, as Red Smith described it, "was apologizing to the kid for what he had to do...and signaling the bullpen to send in the right-hander.

"Allie Reynolds came striding in, lugging his glove and windbreaker, and Ford walked to the dugout, pulled on a jacket, got a long drink at the water-cooler, and stayed to watch the final...

"Know what Casey said to Ford when the manager took him out? Casey said: 'There's a stinkin' little ground ball between third and shortstop and it's my fault. I should have had Rizzuto over there, but he didn't see me waving at him.'

"That was a lie, of course, from a very considerate liar.

"Well, Reynolds threw four pitches past Stan Lopata and struck him out. Yogi Berra caught the last strike, leaped approximately 12 feet straight up, brandished a fist with the ball clutched in it, and ran around in small circles looking for somebody to embrace."

The Yankees had won their second straight World Series championship.

Smith added, "Mr. Stengel then summed it up for the visiting press: 'I hated to take that kid outta there, but sometimes you hafta do it because you fellers hafta get home.'"

Brissie recalled that Connie Mack and Joe McCarthy, two other great managers, had four outstanding starting pitchers "but they also relied on depth," said Brissie. But it seemed to Brissie that Lopez was attempting to do it with essentially four starters, and failed. Of the top five American League pitchers in innings pitched, Lemon (with 310), Garcia (292), and Wynn (286) were one, two, and three. Far down, the Yankees leader in that category was Allie Reynolds, at 244.

Of the top five leaders in complete games in the American League, Lemon was first, with 28, Wynn and Garcia (19 each) tied for fourth; Feller had 11. Reynolds, again, was the lone Yankee in that group, with 24.

Wynn, with 23 wins, was second in the American League to the A's Bobby Shantz's 24 wins, while Garcia and Lemon compiled 22 each. Feller, in an off year and feeling the effects of a career that had begun 16 years earlier, was 9–13.

Looking at the record, Brissie had had a good season, despite the now routine problems with his leg. He pitched in 42 games and was tied for fifth in the league in appearances with Lemon, second on the Indians to Garcia's 46. His won-lost record was, for a relief pitcher who relies on saves, a creditable 3–2 record with a 3.48 earned-run average. He totaled two saves (a save is registered when a pitcher comes in with a lead and protects it). But he started just one game all year, and the fact that he didn't start more still rankled.

At the end of August an incident occurred that, Brissie believes, might have had some impact on how much he was being used. It's hard to imagine that personalities could have a bearing on a team's chase for the pennant, but stranger things have happened. It took place between Luke Easter and Brissie.

Easter, at 6'4", 240 pounds, was a colossus of a first baseman. Born in segregated Mississippi, raised in segregated St. Louis, after playing in the Negro Leagues and, in 1949, in the Pacific Coast League, he was brought up to the Indians late that '49 season. He was then a 34-year-old rookie, though he told people he was 28, or 30, or 32. Regardless of his age, or alleged age, when he was in the batting cage players from both teams stopped what they were doing to watch him belt balls into the stands. In 1950, in what was essentially his rookie season, he hit the longest home run in the history of Cleveland's Municipal Stadium, a 477-foot shot over the auxiliary scoreboard in right field—only Mickey Mantle ever approximated that feat.

When once told by a fan that he had seen Easter's longest home run in person, Easter is reported to have replied, "If it came down, it wasn't my longest." In 1952, he hit 31 homers, his career high, and led the American League in home runs per 100 at bats with a home run every 7.1 times at bat.

Bill James, in *The New Bill James Historical Baseball Abstract*, described Easter as "an amiable, fun-loving man who gambled, wasn't 100% honest, and had a bad temper" with "shoulders that crossed three lanes of traffic." Brissie had gotten along well with Easter, until this incident:

In 1952 Luke Easter, Brissie recalled, "played all year with a broken foot. He played with it despite pain. He showed a lot of guts. I think if you've had problems yourself, you can surely sympathize with him. In one game there was a ground ball hit to him. He had been holding a man on first, then moved off a bit when the ball was hit. Well, Luke tagged first base and then threw to second when he should have thrown to second to begin with, to start a double play. The shortstop didn't see Luke tag first base and so he tagged second for what he assumed was a force out and threw to first for a double play. But the runner on second was safe, since he hadn't been tagged.

"When Luke got back to the bench after the inning, Lopez tore into him. Luke was seething about that. After all, he could hardly pivot, with that bad leg. I was in the trainer's room after the game having my leg treated and Luke comes in and he's grumpy and complaining about Lopez.

"I said, 'Don't worry about it, Luke, sometimes the manager tells you something that he thinks is right but is wrong.' Well, Luke obviously took it the wrong way because he cursed me out. Now, we'd always gotten along just fine before this. I tried to talk to him, but he wouldn't respond."

The next day Brissie left the clubhouse to go onto the field during batting practice when Hank Greenberg, the general manager, called him aside in the runway. As Brissie recalled it, the conversation went like this:

"I understand you had trouble with one of the blacks," Greenberg said.

"Luke and I had some words. It was a misunderstanding," Brissie said.

"It's gonna cost you some money," said Greenberg.

"You can fine us, that's your prerogative," said Brissie.

"No, I'm fining just you," said Greenberg.

"Don't you want to hear my side of the story?" Brissie asked.

Greenberg said, "I know your side."

"If you fine me, and it comes out in the papers, Hank, you don't know what you're getting into. Some guy will have a press conference and accuse you of discriminating against a white," said Brissie.

Brissie recalled: "Hank turned around and walked away. He didn't fine either Luke or me. But I thought that Hank didn't forget this, and in some way held it against me. Like I was a redneck. It wasn't so. The sad fact is that Hank judged me without the whole story. We all have to guard against that.

"I thought about this and wondered again if Hank thought I didn't want to play in Cleveland with blacks, since I was a white guy from South Carolina. But I'd been there for a few years now and never had a problem with my black teammates. Suitcase Simpson, I got along with him real well. The pitcher Dave Hoskins and the catcher Quincy Troupe and I got along real well. No problem with Sad Sam Jones. I went to Harlem with Sam Jones. He danced. I didn't. We went someplace where musicians hang out. I wasn't exactly at ease. I don't say that critically. There were a few whites there, but not many.

"My feelings about blacks go back to my father's attitude, and my grandmother, Elizabeth Hodges Brissie, who died in 1934, when I was about 10 years old. She had me come in and sit by the side of her bed and she told me that she wanted me to live by the Golden Rule. 'That applies particularly to the black folk because they need that more than anybody.'

"In baseball, black guys were out on the field doing the same thing I was doing. You don't have to have any brains to hate. There's no logic to hating."

One way to view Hank Greenberg's reaction to the Brissie-Easter situation, perhaps, is to comprehend that Greenberg had a particular affinity for black ballplayers, as did, ironically in this case, Brissie. Greenberg empathized with the blacks, especially in the early years of blacks in baseball. Greenberg was the first Jewish ballplayer to become a star. He had stunned the baseball world in 1938 by chasing Babe Ruth's single-season home-run record of 60, falling short by just two homers. He was the first Jew to be elected as a player to the Baseball Hall of Fame. In his autobiography, *The Story of My Life*, Greenberg told about the time he, a first baseman with the Pittsburgh Pirates in 1947 and in the last season of his sensational career, collided with Jackie Robinson, who was trying to beat out a hit. Robinson was in his first season with the Dodgers, and Greenberg heard the taunts to Robinson from the stands and his own Pirates' dugout, such as "Coal Mine" and "Porter," and it reminded him of the taunts he endured as a Jew. "Whenever I struck out," said Greenberg, "it wasn't just that some fans called me a bum, I was always a *Jewish* bum."

After they collided Greenberg helped Robinson up, and had a brief chat. Following the game reporters asked Robinson about the conversation at first base. Robinson said, as reported in *The New York Times*, that Greenberg told him, "Stick in there. You're doing fine. Keep your chin up." The encouragement from an established star heartened Robinson. "Class tells. It sticks out all over Mr. Greenberg," Robinson declared. Greenberg, who was best friends with Bill Veeck, who brought Larry Doby and Satchel Paige, as well as Luke Easter, to the Indians, obviously shared Veeck's social views. And, though apparently misguided in this case, he was defending Easter.

Greenberg surely had a stubborn side. Al Rosen, the Indians' star third baseman during Greenberg's tenure as general manager, had, like Brissie, idolized the 6'4" Greenberg during his playing days. "He was a cultured, intelligent, bright, good-looking, massive sort of man," said Rosen. After the 1953 season, Rosen went into Greenberg's office and asked for a raise—he had been named Major League Player of the Year, after all. Greenberg brought out the record book and compared Rosen's season to one of Greenberg's. It fairly paled in comparison. Rosen didn't get the raise. In fact, Greenberg tried to cut Rosen's salary by $5,000. "Hank could be very tough," said Rosen.

Greenberg had a certainty about him that transcended baseball. He served with distinction in the army before and during World War II, though, unlike Brissie, he did not see combat while stationed in India and China. He had been drafted early in 1941 and served from May until his release on December 5. When Pearl Harbor was attacked on December 7, 1941, he turned around and immediately enlisted. "I'm going back in," the Associated Press quoted Greenberg. "We are in trouble and there is only one thing to do—return to service. I have not been called back. I'm going back on my own." He also requested overseas duty and, unlike a number of baseball stars, played no ball during his service. Sergeant Greenberg was later commissioned a second lieutenant and eventually made captain. He served four and half years, nearly until the war's end.

3.

In Cleveland, as he had in Savannah and Philadelphia, Brissie the professional baseball player continued to visit hospitals and rehabilitation centers for both disabled veterans and disabled citizens. He continued answering letters thanking him and expressing appreciation for his efforts, and holding him up as a model for them.

From a letter dated October 1, 1951:

Chelsea, Mass.

Dear Lou:

Words are neither adequate nor sufficient to properly express the gratitude and appreciation of the officers and members of this Lodge and the few hundred hospitalized servicemen at the US Naval Hospital here in Chelsea for your kindness and generosity in appearing before them at our sports night. (It did) so much to boost the morale of these men who have sacrificed so much for this great country of ours...

Max Ross
President
B'nai B'rith
David A. Lourie Lodge No. 1258

Nov. 27, 1952:

Queens, New York

Dear Lou:

You don't know me but I've watched you pitch many times. I've been a long admirer of your courage and will, which has helped me to overcome my handicap. I too have a handicap in my left foot which remained after I was stricken with polio several years ago. Although I've had a couple of operations, I still have a slight limp. I love to play basketball and baseball, but baseball is my favorite sport. I am also a pitcher like you, and hope to make my college freshman team this season.

I am 17 years old now but maybe if I am good enough, I'd like to play pro ball and show everyone how I have overcome my handicap. You are an inspiration for boys like me who have had to fight their misfortunes.

Yours sincerely, Arthur Cavallara

And in 1953, Charles W. Mayser of Lancaster, Pennsylvania, wrote to Brissie telling him that "In a cynical world it is men like you who inspire us to continue to make this a better world to live in."

"And then," Brissie said, "there were letters from guys who said, 'I'm a World War II veteran and am pulling for you to win 20.' A lot of times, they didn't say they were busted up. But you could see from the return address that it was from a VA hospital. And I imagined they were following me and thinking of themselves getting out to work and resuming their lives."

Such responses from people with disabilities continued to be meaningful to Brissie. "People saying, 'Because of you I decided to try.' That changes you," he said. "That affects you. You feel a responsibility."

To be sure, Brissie also found time to spend with his family. "Dot and I would take the kids to the circus, to the zoo, to anything of historical significance. It wasn't easy. First, I had problems getting around on my leg. And second, three little kids are a handful. But—and I know Dot agreed—they were a wonderful handful."

• • •

A new season dawned and 1953 had all the potential of a sweet year for Brissie, ostensibly still in his prime at age 28 (he wouldn't turn 29 until June 5). He looked sharp in spring training, and a game against the Giants in Wichita, Kansas, a few days before the regular season began was an example. *The New York Times'* John Drebinger wrote that the Giants, in losing to the Indians 3–0, "were baffled for seven innings by a superb exhibition of mound work on the part of Bob Lemon, and then for two more by left-handed Lou Brissie."

The Indians broke camp in late March from Tucson and hooked up with the New York Giants, who had trained in Phoenix. The two took the train together for some 18 days and played exhibition games in 17 cities, including Los Angeles, San Diego, and San Francisco, California; Wichita and Topeka, Kansas; Tulsa, Oaklahoma; Denver, Colorado; Lubbock and Dallas, Texas; Baton Rouge, Louisiana; Birmingham, Alabama; and Lynchburg, Virginia, ending in mid-April with the start of the regular season.

"It was on the train trips from city to city, from spring training through the season, that you often came together as a team," said Brissie. "You got to know each other; you talked with each other; some played cards." He recalled that several players played Hearts, as the train clacked along the rails, and other guys would stand around and kibbitz. One of the card players was a rather lighthearted Early Wynn. "Early was very sociable, very likeable at times," said Brissie, "like a different person from when he was at the ballpark.

"Some guys read. I read history and the newspapers, to keep up on current events. Bob Feller always had a lot of books with him. He was an avid reader. One time the train was coming to our stop and a red cap ran over to pick up Bob's suitcase and it nearly pulled him off his feet. The suitcase was filled with books.

"But there was still a kind of separation of players. The black players, Doby, Suitcase, Sam Jones, Luke, they all stayed pretty much to themselves. It was evident that they didn't feel comfortable totally mixing with the white players. We'd talk together, we'd joke, but there was still a kind of unspoken separation. That was unfortunate."

Early in the season, on April 17, Brissie failed to bail out Feller, who had been knocked out of the box in the ninth inning by the Detroit Tigers. This time Brissie entered the game with a man on third and one out. He walked the next two batters to fill the bases and set up a force play at any base. But he gave up a long fly to center field to the next batter that scored the winning run.

He pitched one inning, the ninth, on May 30, giving up one run. He had tried to run in the outfield in batting practice, but it was a trial. His leg pained him, and, as Joe Astroth had recalled when Brissie did the same in Savannah, running could bring tears to his eyes.

"I went to Al and told him that I had to pitch more to stay in shape," recalled Brissie. "I said, 'I can't run much, and I can't stay in shape just by throwing in the bullpen. But I feel I can help this ballclub. You need to play in games. You can't get that body extension in the bullpen that you can on the mound in a regular game. It's like a track star can run 10.5 in practice, but will do 10.2 in competition. You need the competition to stay sharp. You stay in the bullpen, you fall into bullpen bad habits.' Al listened and that was about the extent of it. He was still using his four starters to a huge degree, and I didn't spend much time in games."

Brissie pitched to one batter on June 5 against Philadelphia, and allowed a hit that scored a run to tie the game, 2–2, and Steve Gromek replaced Brissie to end the threat. The Indians won in the tenth on Hank Majeski's pinch-hit fly with the bases filled and none out.

On June 12 in Cleveland, Brissie entered in the seventh inning against the Yankees, in relief of Wynn, who had allowed New York to tie the game and left with men on first and third and two outs. Brissie "stopped a rally," wrote Louis Effrat, in *The New York Times*, by getting Irv Noren to pop out. Brissie faced just that one batter as Barney McCosky pinch-hit for him in the bottom of the seventh. The Yankees, however, went on to win, and increased their lead over the second-place Indians to 7½ games.

Brissie pitched two innings against the Yankees the following day, allowing no hits but giving up three walks, and again left the game for a pinch-hitter, in another Indians loss. It was the soaring Yankees' 16th straight win.

"Managing can be more discouraging than playing, especially when you're losing," said Lopez at one point, "because when you're a player, there are at least individual goals you can shoot for. When you're a manager all the worries of the team become your worries.... The manager is by himself. He can't mingle with his players. I enjoyed my players, but I could not socialize with them, so I spent a lot of time alone in my hotel room. Those four walls kind of close in on you." Indeed, in the many train trips the team took, for example, Lopez was little seen, recalled Brissie. "Lopez," he said, "stayed pretty much to himself."

Richard Goldstein wrote in *The New York Times*, "Lopez was a low-key type, his Spanish heritage and his persona leading him to be known in the press as a caballero, or a gentleman."

Lopez was born in Tampa, Florida, the son of immigrants from Spain who settled in Tampa's Spanish-speaking Ybor City section. One of Lopez's earliest memories was of the odor of cigar smoke in the factory where his father, Modesto, worked as a tobacco selector. "I hated it," said Lopez. "I vowed never to work in one."

At 16, Lopez quit school to play for the Tampa Smokers of the Florida State League, and in 1928 he made his major league debut with the Brooklyn Dodgers. And now he was manager of a pennant-contending major league team, a long way from that cigar factory that he loathed in Tampa.

As a player, Lopez was not much of an offensive threat. He hit higher than .275 only three times in his 19-year career. For many years he held the record for most games caught in the major leagues (1,918) and the National League (1,861). He made two All-Star teams.

His major asset was reported to be his handling of pitchers—"gentle, soothing personality," and "persuasive but also comforting," as described in *Baseball: The Biographical Encyclopedia*. Brissie, unfortunately, wasn't having that kind of experience with him.

• • •

On July 5, against the White Sox, Brissie gave up two hits and one run in two innings, in a 4–0 loss to the White Sox, but he also walked three batters, forcing in a run with the bases loaded.

"The Cleveland announcer, Bob Neal, said on the air 'Any guy who can't get the ball over the plate doesn't belong in the big leagues,'" recalled Brissie. "The president of the beer company sponsoring the game wanted to fire him. It was free speech, though it didn't make me happy. I stayed out of it. Neal kept his job."

Brissie knew he could do better with more work, but when sitting in the bullpen and the phone would ring seeking a relief pitcher, it was invariably for someone other than Brissie to warm up. "It was discouraging, disappointing, disgusting," said Brissie. "And I always thought, I'm lucky to be here at all. Lucky to be alive. I just have to believe that my turn will come."

On September 1, in Cleveland, the Indians pummeled the Red Sox, 13–3. Brissie finished up the game in the ninth, allowing one hit, one walk, and no runs.

He did not pitch again for the rest of the 24 games remaining in the season. The Indians finished a disappointing second, seven games behind the Yankees.

Some teammates and friends on other teams asked him, "Briss, anything wrong with you?"

He'd replied, "I'm feeling fine, I'm just not getting much work right now."

Brissie recalled, "You can't explain what you don't understand."

The right-hander Bob Hooper, who was primarily a starting pitcher with the A's when Brissie was his teammate in 1950 and the first month in 1951, came over to Cleveland in a trade before the 1953 season and supplanted Brissie as the number one relief pitcher, pitching a total of 69.1 innings in 43 games, with a 5-4 record and seven saves.

"Al didn't have confidence in me and, I think, in the bullpen, period," said Brissie. "There were guys in the pen who could throw well—Dave Hoskins, George Zuverink, Bob Chakales—who were rarely called upon. And he hardly let Sam Jones pitch, either.

"The way Al used the bullpen was either too late in the game or not at all, as I saw it. In my case, I don't know if Greenberg still was angry at me for the Easter incident and influenced Al. But I've considered it."

(Easter's life, sadly, ended in tragedy. On March 29, 1979, as chief union steward for the Aircraft Workers Alliance in Cleveland, the 63-year-old Easter was transporting $40,000 of the union's funds to a bank when he was met by two hold-up men with shotguns. They demanded the money, Easter refused to give it to them, and he was killed.)

• • •

Despite his problems on the field, Brissie tried not to bring them home with him. "I saw no purpose in deflating the family," he said.

His daughter, Vicki, recalls that her father never was moody. "What I do remember about his playing days in Cleveland was one night my mother had the radio on when my dad was playing, and she listened and did the ironing. I was upstairs in my bedroom when he came home and she made him dinner—I think it was liver and onions—and what I remember is that it smelled terrible."

Brissie didn't remember the liver and onions. "Growing up poor, you were happy to eat anything," he said, laughing at Vicki's recollection. "And Dot was a good cook. I'm sure the meal was fine, though maybe not entirely to my little girl's appreciation."

For the 1953 season, Brissie pitched in just 16 games, for 13 recorded innings—in a 154-game schedule—a remarkably small number of appearances. And each of his appearances was in relief, with two saves and no decisions. He declined to a gaudy 7.62 ERA and struck out just five to go along with 13 bases on balls. It was a profoundly disappointing season for him, to say the least.

"It was a miserable season and I was determined not to have another," Brissie recalled. "And that winter I worked out hard. I kept my weight down—ate a lot of vegetables—and was looking forward to spring training. And then I got that phone call."

12

A New Life

1.

On February 1, 1954, just a couple of weeks before he was to report to the Indians' spring-training camp in Tucson, Arizona, Brissie was in the lot beside the garage of his house in Greenville, working to restore a World War II jeep, when the phone rang. He wiped his greasy hands with a rag and went inside to take the call. It was from a reporter with the Associated Press based in Atlanta.

"It just came over the wires that your contract has been sold by the Indians to Indianapolis, Triple A of the American Association," he was told. "How do you feel about it?"

"Indianapolis?" said Brissie, stunned. "This is the first I've heard of it." No word from general manager Greenberg.

Despite Brissie's terrible season on the mound for the Indians in 1953, he imagined he would return to the team. He had been given no indication otherwise, and certainly nothing was said about his being demoted to the minor leagues. While the way it was handled seemed callous, it was frequently the way such business was done in baseball—and, it might be argued, in business generally. In fact, when Greenberg himself was sent on waivers in 1947 from the Detroit Tigers—the team he played with his entire career dating back to 1930—to the Pirates, he learned about it nearly the way Brissie had his sale to Indianapolis. "I heard on the radio one Saturday afternoon as we (he and his wife, Caral) were driving...," Greenberg wrote in his autobiography. He then received a very brief telegram from Tigers general manager Billy Evans that in its "cold terms," and after his long relationship with, and production for the team, "just left me speechless." He said, "At that moment I decided I was through with baseball" (though he did play one more season with Pittsburgh).

Greenberg wrote that in baseball there was "no sentiment. It was all dollars and cents." Even such great players as Ty Cobb and Babe Ruth, Greenberg added, were treated "shabbily" by their ballclubs. As a general manager himself with Cleveland, Greenberg wrote regarding reducing his roster to the required 25 players at some point before the regular season, "Someone had to tell these players that they were being sent back to AAA or AA and we would see them next year. Well, this wasn't an easy chore...and Lopez didn't like to face it, so I was the one who had the responsibility of telling the player." And, in many cases, he did. Brissie, who did not get a mention in the book, was, however, one player, for whatever reason, Greenberg neglected to inform about his demotion.

After hanging up from the reporter, Brissie went around the house to find Dot, and told her.

"What are you going to do?" she asked. "Can you talk to Hank?"

"I'm going to try," he replied.

As Brissie recalls, he phoned Greenberg in Cleveland. He was told that Greenberg was at the club's minor league complex in Daytona Beach, Florida. He tried there and couldn't reach him by phone. He decided to see Greenberg face to face.

The next morning, around 3:00 AM, Brissie climbed into his black 1949 Pontiac and began the nine-hour drive to Daytona Beach in the dark. He started early because he wanted to catch Greenberg by the early afternoon, when the players were still on the field. During the long drive, the entire relationship with Greenberg played in his mind, and what was particularly disturbing was that he felt the Easter situation was at the core of this "punishment," as he termed it, and now he'd fully explain that it wasn't anything as awful as Hank thought. With Brissie behind the wheel, the dawn broke somewhere in Georgia and the sun was high in the sky when he rode into the Daytona Beach ballfield.

When Brissie arrived, Greenberg was on the field behind a batting cage. He approached Greenberg, and they greeted each other.

"Hank, I understand I've been sold to Indianapolis," said Brissie.

"That's right," said Greenberg. "It's a move I had to make."

"Hank," replied Brissie, "I can't go to the minor leagues."

"But we have roster considerations," said Greenberg, "and you pitch well there, and we'll bring you back up to the big club."

"Hank, you don't understand, I can't go to the minor leagues."

"Why not?" Greenberg asked.

"If I do," said Brissie. "I'd be failing all those guys still in hospitals, guys who follow my games. If I fail in their eyes, it's as if they might fail."

Greenberg had his decisions to make and his baseball priorities.

"I'm sorry, Lou," said Greenberg. "That's the way it is."

Brissie told Greenberg, "If I can't be on the roster of the Indians, then I want to be traded to a major league team. I'm not going to play in Indianapolis. I've paid my dues, and I deserve the opportunity to stay in the big leagues." Brissie was aware that three major league clubs had made offers for him.

As Brissie recalls, Hank stood firm. "I've made my decision, and I'm sticking to it. You play where I tell you to play."

"I said, 'We'll see about that.'"

The Indians owned exclusive rights to Brissie under the longstanding baseball reserve clause. "It was only an eight-team league then," recalled Al Rosen years later—Rosen himself had been a high-level baseball executive with the Yankees and Giants, "and while Lou might have been a starting pitcher on other clubs, Hank probably figured that letting Lou go would help another club the Indians were competing against. It was a tough business. You had no place to turn. You had to do what the ballclub told you to do, or you quit. Lou quit." Just as Rosen had quit a few years earlier when confronted with a similar situation.

Brissie was introspective. Not only was he pitching for himself, but he felt he was pitching for a lot of other people as well, from wounded soldiers to handicapped kids. While his leg still gave him problems on nearly a daily basis, he believed it wasn't any more detrimental to his pitching than at any other time in his career. During that long, despairing 1953 season, Brissie, sitting in the bullpen, sitting in the whirlpool, lying in bed, had a lot of time to think of the future and what he would do if he wasn't in the major leagues. He came to no firm conclusion. He simply hadn't been ready to give it up. He remained confident that he still had a few good years left in his arm. But now he indeed discussed with Dot the possibility of his quitting baseball. She had mixed feelings. She didn't like all the traveling that a life in baseball entails, but, he said, "she was unhappy for me."

"Lou," she said, "follow your heart."

Just that simple notion from someone who he knew was completely supportive of him, made the decision so much easier, so much lighter on his conscience.

After pitching for seven years in the major leagues, Lou Brissie announced his retirement from baseball. He was 29 years old.

"I've never regretted that decision," said Brissie. "I felt I had done the right thing."

There were a few weeks there when he didn't know what he was going to do with his life. "All of this had come as such a shock that I hadn't thought it through," he said.

Then another call came that would change Brissie's life. It was from Arthur J. Connell, the National Commander of the American Legion. Connell offered Brissie a job. Brissie listened and accepted. And in March 1954, Brissie was named commissioner of the American Legion junior baseball program, and, wrote Art Morrow in *The Sporting News*, it "struck a popular note with war veterans, baseball men and kids alike." (The Legion headquarters, ironically, was in Indianapolis, where Brissie had refused to play after having been sold to the minor-league team there by Greenberg.)

"Brissie's appointment will mean a greatly expanded American Legion junior program," said Connell. "Lou's fight against great odds, his fortitude and his fine character will be a tremendous inspiration to all American youth. Baseball owners, too, will welcome his association with the American Legion."

Connell said Brissie, who would direct a program involving more than a million boys, was eminently qualified on three counts: "1. As a war veteran—his heroic recovery from leg wounds suffered in Italy stands as an inspiration to the handicapped in every field.

"2. As a baseball man—he was a mainstay on the Philadelphia Athletics' pitching staff in 1948-49-50 before being traded to the Indians, with whom he also served three seasons.

"3. As a leader in boys' activities—he was long associated in the Christian Athletes' Foundation and is deeply interested in the problems of youth."

Before accepting the American Legion position, however, Brissie had tried once more to remain in major league baseball as a pitcher. He felt that he still had some good innings left in his arm, if not his leg as well.

He was unhappy that the Indians had waited until just before the start of spring training to make the announcement that he'd been sold to Indianapolis. Clubs had already finalized their rosters and made their decisions on who they expected to be on their teams, or contend for positions.

In fact, Brissie learned, the Baltimore Orioles, with Art Ehlers as general manager and Jimmy Dykes as their new manager—they had both just come over from the A's—wanted to trade for him. He called them, and they said they would be interested in signing him. Brissie, with the approval of Dykes and Ehlers, went to Johns Hopkins hospital in Baltimore to take a physical, and he was given a good report. His leg was no better or worse than it had ever been.

Brissie then went to see Dykes and Ehlers at their office in Baltimore. "Ehlers," he recalled, "picked up the phone and called Greenberg and said they were 'interested in Brissie.' Greenberg said, 'Well, I don't know if I can let him go or not. I gotta talk to Al.' And Art said, 'Aren't you still the general manager?' Greenberg called back in 30 minutes and spoke to Dykes. He said, 'We can't do that.' And Dykes said, 'What would it take to get him?' And he says, 'A hundred thousand dollars.' And Dykes said, 'We can't pay that kind of money for someone who didn't pitch last year.' (By that he meant, having pitched in only 16 games.)

"Ehlers said to me, 'We can't make that kind of investment in you after last season.' I said, 'I understand that.' They had their own pressures." The team had just moved to Baltimore from St. Louis, and they had new owners—Veeck having sold the team. And surely paying so much money could hardly be justified by them to the new owners—$100,000, after all, was a lot of money to pay in those days, especially for someone who hadn't done the job the year before and was pitching with a handicap.

Just how tough, or grim, the baseball business was even for its stars was exemplified in contract negotiations between the Indians and Bob Lemon, who had won 21 games for the Indians in 1953, best on the club and second most in the American League, while losing 15. It had been another outstanding season for Lemon. Now he was a holdout. In a March 2 United Press story, referring to Lemon's won-lost record, it read that "this was the argument that Hank Greenberg used for asking (Lemon) to take a salary cut from last year's reported $42,000. He argued that the difference between Lemon's victories and losses was only six, and that this was not good enough." The season before, Lemon was 22–11. Greenberg, however, did agree to "a bonus based on attendance."

What happened to Brissie in that last season with the Indians? It was obvious that Lopez, and probably Greenberg, too, had lost confidence in Brissie. Why they had kept him for an entire season and used him in just 16 games remains a mystery.

"Lou wasn't throwing as hard as he once did," reflected short-stop Eddie Joost, Brissie's teammate with the A's and his opponent in 1953.

"I wondered if maybe his leg was just giving out," said George Kell, who was with the A's when Brissie first came to Philadelphia on crutches after the war, and then became a Hall of Fame third baseman for Detroit. "But I was there early, and at the end of his career. I saw what he went through. Lou Brissie was my hero, and still is."

"What I remember," Bob Feller said, "was that Lou had that big, heavy brace and he pitched with a lot of anguish. One thing about Lou, though, no matter what he was going through, he never complained. And I know that he was going through a lot."

Wally Westlake, an outfielder with the Indians in 1952–53, remembers that "Lou's leg was giving out on him." "He was a left-hander and the left leg is the one you shift your weight on when you crank up," he said. "You could see that it was really starting to get to him. But he was a great guy, a real kick in the butt."

Al Rosen, the third baseman on the Indians in 1953, said, "It was my perception that Lou lost interest, that he wasn't being appreciated. It's very difficult to keep motivation when your pride is injured. And you go from being an All-Star to a one-hitter pitcher. And if you give up a hit, or a run, your ERA is going to swell."

Brissie does not disagree with Rosen's view of his losing interest. "It was hard to stay motivated when you weren't being used," he said.

Besides needing work in games because of the problems with his leg, Brissie said that "when you don't pitch a lot in games, you lose your edge up there against those guys. Major league hitters didn't just get there. They've learned how to hit. They can really jump on you quick if you're not at your best."

Brissie said, "You can always look for excuses, and I had nobody to blame but myself, but a fact is that since I wasn't pitching much, I tried running more. That put more pressure on my leg, and that just didn't help matters."

In the end, said Brissie, "I believe my leg affected my longevity. I was never able to bend it more than 60 percent of normal. I felt I could have kept on pitching, but by any measure of objectivity the leg was a small factor in my retiring early, though, because I still felt strong; I didn't feel I had to retire that early."

While Brissie truly believed that with more pitching he would be as good as he'd ever been, the condition of his leg as time went on raised questions about that. "I can't imagine that the constant pressure on the leg necessary to throw 90-plus-mile-an-hour fastballs didn't compromise to some considerable extent his ability to throw like that," said Dr. Marc Siegel of the New York University medical staff. "In regard to medical science, the arthritic wear-and-tear that such pounding automatically produces on a leg that was essentially missing a bone, and a leg frequently cracking and oozing infections, would ultimately lead to a deterioration."

Bob Feller delivered what for many is the ultimate assessment: "Lou Brissie would have been a Hall of Fame pitcher, if it hadn't been for World War II."

Brissie's major league career totals were 44 wins, 48 losses, 29 saves, a 4.07 earned-run average in 234 games, and 897⅔ innings pitched. He struck out 436 batters and walked 451. He also batted .227, with 67 hits in 295 official at-bats and struck out only 23 times. He hit no home runs but had five doubles and, not surprisingly, stole no bases. He did have, of course, that one triple.

In 1954, after three seasons of finishing second to the Yankees, the Indians broke through to win the pennant, with an American League record 111 victories. "General Manager Hank Greenberg and manager Al Lopez built a powerful team on the ashes of the 1948 championship squad, retaining only Larry Doby, Dale Mitchell, Jim Hegan, Bob Feller and Bob Lemon from that unit," wrote David S. Neft and Richard M. Cohen, in their book, *The World Series.* They added that the pitching staff had "three right-handed aces" in Lemon, Early Wynn, and Mike Garcia, and strong "second-line hurling" from rookie relievers Don Mossi and Ray Narleski. Left-hander Mossi and righty Narleski were surprises in the league, and Lopez and Greenberg either learned a lesson from previous seasons and began to rely more on their bullpen—the starters still pitched a lot of innings, however—or Mossi and Narleski were the kind of relief pitchers the Indians needed.

Either way, Lou Brissie got on with his life. "It would have been nice to get to the World Series," he said, "and I was happy for the guys I played with there who did go." (The Indians couldn't sustain their good fortune and were swept in the Series by the New York Giants.) But, he told Rich Westcott, a Philadelphia sportswriter, "I had my day in the sun, and that was important. (Baseball) was a big part of my life. Over the years I had a few good days. Opening Day in 1948, the All-Star Game in 1949 were big thrills. I went 14 innings once at Yankee Stadium and had to face Vic Raschi and Joe Page. We ended up losing,

2-1, but that was a game to remember. And that game that I pitched with Cleveland against Satchel Paige and the Browns that went 19 innings, and we won. Nice to remember.

"I played with and against DiMaggio, Keller, Williams, Doerr, Feller—guys I read about growing up. Reading about them in the papers was a big part of my life as a boy. Then one day I'm on the ballfield with them. I always wanted to do well, to win, of course, but all of it in the end was the grandest experience—to associate with people you admired when you were young. I'd think, 'How did this ever happen?' It was really tremendous. As my dad used to say, 'Every day's a good day, but some are better than others.'"

In fact, even throughout the trying 1953 season, Brissie received letters from soldiers in hospitals and disabled people and invitations to visit and speak to such groups. "I went because they said they wanted me there," said Brissie. "It was one of the positives of that season."

His new position with the American Legion gave him a new baseball perspective and returned to him some of the joys of the game that had diminished in his last year or so in the big leagues. In his eight years as director of the organization, Brissie took an active and serious interest in the organization and the boys 15-18 who played in it.

He gained particular pleasure in seeing such young, outstanding players in Legion ball as future big leaguers like outfielder Rusty Staub and pitcher Dave McNally. On occasion, he'd go out to the mound in street clothes during a practice session for one of the Legion teams and try to show a young pitcher how to improve his delivery or his pitches. Sometimes, when his leg was giving him problems, he'd use a cane. "Some of those kids would look at me like, 'What's this about?' They were a little skeptical." He laughed at the memory.

In the *Old Farmer's Almanac, Southern Edition*, 1996, Mel R. Allen (a writer, not the announcer) wrote: "(Brissie) watched youngsters throwing their arms out during playoff games and drafted the rule that limited the number of innings young pitchers could work in a week, a rule that filtered down to youth leagues everywhere." And, perhaps, it one day influenced the pitch count in the major leagues, in which managers are reluctant to let a pitcher throw more than 100 pitches in an outing.

In 1958, Greenwood, South Carolina, near where Brissie grew up, placed a team in the finals, against Cincinnati, with a hustling 17-year-old infielder named Pete Rose. It was in Colorado Springs, Colorado, and the teams stayed at the exclusive Broadmoor Hotel and Resort. Before going to dinner in the establishment's chandeliered restaurant, the Greenwood boys had prepared to dine in blue jeans. Olin Parnell, one of the Greenwood players, recalled that Brissie told them, "You can't go to dinner in blue jeans here."

"But," said one of the players, "we only have blue jeans. We're country boys."

Brissie, of course, understood.

"And," said Parnell, "he went into his pocket and pulled out some bills. 'Here,' he said, 'you guys go buy yourselves some pants.'"

• • •

On February 8, 1956, Connie Mack died in Philadelphia. He was 93 years old. "I was in Arizona for American Legion regional meetings when I heard of his death, and even though he was an old man, his passing came as a blow to me. I had arranged for people to come to the regional meetings from all over the country, and I just couldn't leave to go to Mr. Mack's funeral, as much as I had wanted to," said Brissie. "Mr. Mack had meant so much to me, had changed my life. He'd given me hope when his letters were about the only hope I had. And he looked past any infirmity I had and saw the abilities I had. He was a second father to me, and I wish I could have helped win him a pennant. It is one of the regrets I have in life. Mr. Mack could have a temper, he could be very careful how he spent a dollar, but he was a kind, generous, thoughtful, smart, fine human being. Mr. Mack and my father were two of the best men I've ever known."

• • •

On June 15, 1957, Brissie was appointed by President Eisenhower to the Citzens Advisory Committee on the Fitness of American Youth.

Vice President Richard Nixon was the chairman of the committee. "I was in awe," said Brissie. "I was still a country boy at heart myself."

The committee, composed of what the government termed "national leaders in youth work," was designed to "consider and evaluate existing and prospective governmental and private measures conducive to the achievement of a happier, healthier, and more completely fit American youth."

"There was a concern in the country that our young people weren't physically fit enough generally in case we needed them in a military emergency," recalled Brissie. "So we made suggestions and sent out booklets to schools and recreation centers on how to get more physically fit."

Brissie, at the suggestion of the U.S. State Department in an effort to help create goodwill for the country, ran baseball clinics throughout Australia for two months for two years. Again, for the State Department, he took American Legion All-Star teams to several countries in Central America, Cuba, and Venezuela in the 1950s. "They were great trips," said Brissie, "and we had a tremendous reception from the people." The State Department sent him a congratulatory letter of appreciation.

But the trip to Australia, for one, didn't make everyone happy. "Baseball Tour Irks Ohio Congressman," read an Associated Press headline in *The New York Times* datelined July 9, 1957.

> WASHINGTON—Clarence J. Brown, Republican of Ohio, complained today about the State Department using tax money to send a former major league pitcher, Lou Brissie, to Australia to teach baseball.
>
> As for comment, the Department said Brissie was sent to Australia as a result of requests from that country for help in learning to play baseball.
>
> During the Olympic Games last winter in Australia, the department reported, the Air Force sent a baseball squad to Australia to play demonstration games and these created a "surprisingly high degree of interest." The request for a teacher resulted.

Brissie was chosen because of his big-league experience and his position as head of the American Legion baseball program....

Brisse was discharged this morning from a Washington hospital but couldn't be reached for comment. He underwent surgery for removal of scar tissue from a leg wound suffered while fighting in Italy in World War II.

2.

Brissie's traveling became very limited when Dot was diagnosed with terminal breast cancer in 1959. He spent as much time as he could at home in Indianapolis, to help look after her and to help care for his three children. He drove her to several hospitals around the country where there were cancer specialists, from those at Duke University to those at Emory University. More and more, when Dot couldn't handle problems relating to family and household, Lou took over.

"My father had a low-key way of getting his point across," Vicki Brissie Bishop recalled years later. "I remember just before I was going off to Erskine College, I was dating a boy who I was crazy about. He wasn't going to college. My dad said, 'You know, I have nothing personal about that young man, but he doesn't have much ambition. Do you think it's a good idea to tie yourself up? You might meet someone else in college who you like even more.' My mother was sterner: 'You can't go out with him!' But my father had planted a seed. And it worked."

When Dot's health worsened, Brissie left the American Legion job to cut down on travel to be with her. After that, the family moved back to Greenville, and Brissie scouted part-time for the Dodgers for four years and the Braves for three in the 1960s, around South Carolina and the adjoining area, never far from home. After a painful few years—"It was a long siege," he said—Dot died on May 6, 1967. She was 42 years old.

"We were married for 23 years and 20 days," said Brissie. "Every one of those days was memorable for me, to live with the woman I loved. In the last few years of her life, I know she was in a great deal of pain, but she never complained. And if you looked at her you could never tell she was sick. Her face was still pretty, and she was still slender. She was a courageous lady."

Before she died, she had asked Lou to give many of her effects to her sister Betty and her daughter Vicki, and the rest for the most part, to the charities.

"After she died," said Brissie, "I went into her top drawer to begin to divide her things when I saw an envelope with my name on it. I opened it." It read: "Dear Lou, It's been a good life for a very long time. I love you all. I'm sorry that I can't fight this any longer, Dot."

Rob Brissie, one of the Brissie's twin boys, recalled that he had never quite realized what a team his father and mother had made, what a bond they shared, until her death, and saw "how hard my dad took it." He and his brother, Ron, were 17 at the time.

"I had always heard family stories of how loving they were together when Dad was in the hospital in Georgia when he came back from the war, and how they endured that little apartment in Savannah—and though she had complained early on, she stuck with him, and how when he was having a bad game pitching and she was in the stands, a fellow behind her start yelling uncomplimentary things to Dad and how she turned around and how she confronted the guy real quick. We talked about those things and laughed through our tears.

"To this day, I believe that Dad would never have accomplished what he did without her. We all need someone to present a sunny side, to push us in difficult times. Mom was that someone for Dad."

After Dot's death, Brissie worked for 10 years with United Merchants and Manufacturers of New York. "They were putting in new dye machines in the plant and old timers felt it was a threat in that they weren't going to have a job," said Brissie. "So my job was to go in and convincing them: 'Look, what they're going to do is going to make your job easier. It's a matter of you learning new skills. These machines have to be programmed.' It was true, but the first thing I had to have was the confidence of the people because if you ever lie once, then you're a full-time liar as far as they're concerned. I really enjoyed it because there was a lot of new technology coming in and a lot to do. You become a change agent and you have to prepare people for it."

• • •

The issue of race has been a part of Brissie's life from as far back as he can remember, and it is an issue that still deeply concerns him. Like his father, he has always been sensitive to it, which is why the Luke Easter–Hank Greenberg conflict bothered him so much, and why he took an action for equality when he was director of American Legion baseball.

Before Brissie's arrival as director of the junior baseball program, when the championships were played in various cities, the teams that had some black players had to separate blacks and whites in housing, the whites staying at a hotel, the blacks generally at the homes of local professional blacks. "I thought that a team ought to stay together," said Brissie, "and before assigning the championship series to a town or city, I let it be known that blacks and whites had to stay together. If there was a problem, we just wouldn't go there. We never had a problem with that from then.

"The whole thing about race has been at the heart of my existence, and the existence not only of Southerners, but all Americans," he continued. "Here we are a half-century after *Brown v. Board of Education*, which was supposed to end segregation in this country starting with the schools, and we're still debating the issue of race. The issue isn't politics. The issue is education. If you go to a school and you see the kids coming into the first or second grade, what do you see? Bright, beaming faces, expectant, anticipating, happy kids. Look at them in the seventh grade—surly, sour, sarcastic, and disgusted. We are doing something wrong somewhere. I understand that parenting has changed, economics have changed, and you have a lot of husbands and wives working. But that was true in my time as well. We have to do a better job, all of us—elected officials, teachers, parents. All of us."

• • •

One of Brissie's twin boys, Ron, returned from Vietnam War service in 1973, at age 24. He seemed to suffer some of the same psychological problems—the traumas of war—that plagued Brissie, except he also had problems with alcohol. "I said to him, 'Whenever you want to talk about anything, I'm here,'" Brissie recalled. "That's how I wanted to be treated. Ron was very quiet, very much to himself. And we never did talk about the things that troubled him. I wish we had." When Ron, an auto mechanic, was diagnosed with colon cancer, it was at a time when he and his wife were separated. Ron was in a bind. He moved in and stayed with me for three years until he died." He died in 2001. He was 52 years old.

While both of Brissie's boys enjoyed playing baseball as youngsters, neither sought to make a career of the game. "I'd go to some of their boyhood games, but I would watch from a place where I couldn't be seen," said Brissie. "I didn't want to put any pressure on the boys in this regard, and I didn't want anyone saying to them. 'You're good, but not as good as your father.'"

"Ron and I were a lot smaller than Dad—we were both about 5'10" and pretty thin when we were younger," recalled Rob Brissie. "I wish we had been better baseball players, but we were just okay. And I felt sorry for Dad. I know he'd stand away from the ballfield but close enough to see the game when we played. He wanted to avoid the perception that we weren't as good as he was. He was extremely sensitive about that. And he never gave us any advice on how to play—he thought that would put pressure on us. Oh, he'd have a friend who may come through town suggest something about our hitting or throwing, but that was all.

"Years later, when I was coaching Little League, Dad was a tremendous help. He'd explain to me the proper way to throw a baseball, to take the strain off the shoulder and elbow of a young pitcher, and emphasized the importance of balance, of a proper stride, and its length."

And Lou Brissie spoke little about his playing days. "One of the few times he'd talk about his baseball days was when he'd speak to a group, a church, or an American Legion group or whatever," said Rob Brissie. "And he'd laugh at himself, especially the season when he lost

19 games. I remember him saying that Connie Mack had a high regard for him, and it was probably for that reason he didn't let him pitch the last month of that season—he didn't want Dad to lose 20 games."

But, added Rob, "I don't ever remember a time when my dad wasn't my hero. I knew of his disability, of course, because I lived with it and saw it on a daily basis, and what he suffered through with his pain. When I was 10 years old, I broke nerves in my arm, and my left hand and arm were paralyzed. I was put in a cast and I couldn't move. My doctors told my father, who told me years later, that I had only a 20 percent chance to ever move the fingers of my left hand again. I was paralyzed like that for about a year. But I never doubted that I would move my hand and fingers. My father was my inspiration. I really was certain that because I saw what he was able to do, that I was going to overcome my physical disability as well." Rob would eventually own textile companies and work in sales in the textile field, traveling around the world. "And every time for the rest of my life that I ran into an obstacle," he said, "I found it much easier to face because of the example Dad set. It was second nature to me."

Brissie would often take his boys along with him when he was scouting for major league teams. Sometimes he'd go back to see a particular pitcher three and four times. After seeing one particular prospect several times, Rob asked his father why, when every time they saw this prospect he pitched well. "Anybody can get through a good night," his father explained. "I want to see what the kid's made of when he doesn't have his best stuff."

When Vicki was in college, she recalls the house mother in her dormitory said to her, "Did you see the latest *Reader's Digest?* There's an article about your father." Vicki said, no, she hadn't seen it. "It was called, 'The Pitch I'll Never Forget,'" she remembered. "It was an interview with Ed Sullivan, about Ted Williams hitting the ball off the brace my dad was wearing. I never knew that. He never talked about it. He never talked baseball or the war, either. But I remember him talking about his dad, the impression he made on him, how his dad was willing to stand up for what he believed was right no matter what. He'd get choked up talking about it."

3.

Brissie accepted a role as a volunteer with the South Carolina group working to gain entry for Shoeless Joe Jackson, the star White Sox outfielder, into the Baseball Hall of Fame. Jackson, who had been banned from baseball for allegedly throwing World Series games against the Cincinnati Reds in 1919, was from Greenville, South Carolina, and owned a liquor store there when Brissie was growing up. Brissie met him when he was a boy and found him "very big, and very nice." "I was a little guy, and at my size the one thing I remember is that he looked huge—he was about 6'3" and he had these huge hands," said Brissie.

Brissie believes that Jackson was unfairly tainted in the scandal, and makes a forceful argument: "I was introduced to Jackson by my uncle Grover, who had played a lot of textile ball and knew him. It was the only time I ever met him. It was at a textile league game. I was about nine years old. There was a great feeling in the state about the unfairness of Jackson's banishment from baseball.

"I was not aware until I got into this that a sportswriter testified about Charles Comiskey, the owner of the White Sox, and said that Shoeless Joe went to Comiskey the night before the World Series and asked him not to play him. Jackson said, 'There's been all these rumors out there and my name's been kicked around. Take me out of the game. Tell them I was drunk. Tell them what you want, but don't put me in the game.' Well, anybody found guilty of any wrongdoing would be banned. There were no specifications in Commissioner Landis's ruling. This was all in Landis's head.

"The eight players accused of taking bribes or conspiring with the gamblers were acquitted in the courtroom, but Landis's ruling superseded the legalities.

"The judge sitting in the case said that he never believed that Jackson was guilty. The first baseman for Cincinnati, Jake Daubert, said he never believed it because he said Jackson played flat-out baseball. In the Hall of Fame, they put you at the top of the heap by what you do on the field, and the idea that he was involved is beyond belief. He hit the only home run that was hit in the Series. He led in the batting and set a record for the number of hits—12—that lasted, what?—40 or 50 years. He threw a number of guys out. He had several cutoffs, but of course he had nothing to do with that. They felt the runner would have been out. He led both teams in total bases, slugging percentage, batting average—no errors in the field—and yet they say he was part of it. But to me, you look at what the guy did on the field and you can't believe that he was a part of it. The people that I knew in my early life, the people who knew him and saw him play, which I never did of course, you know they just said, 'Look, to him, the greatest thing in the world was to be out on that field.'

"Babe Ruth said that his swing was modeled after Shoeless Joe Jackson. I never sat down and talked to Jackson, and I don't know if he was aware that I was playing in the major leagues. He may have been, but I never heard from him, even though we were from the same hometown. Joe Anders, who's a good friend of mine and now in his eighties, grew up in Greenville and worked at a drugstore right down the street from Shoeless Joe Jackson's liquor store. The people down there never believed that he did it—that was not in his character."

As Anders grew up, Jackson worked with him on his hitting. Anders played in the Dodgers system several years (he also played third base for Greenville in the Sally League when Brissie played for Savannah). Anders recalled to this writer that when Ty Cobb came by to visit Joe Jackson, which he did fairly often over the years, "Jackson would call me and say, 'Come on down here. I got a guy I want you to meet.' He'd say, 'This is Ty Cobb. This is the best hitter who ever played the game.' Cobb would say, 'Oh, no. I might have been second, but this is the best hitter that ever played.' They were bantering, that type of thing."

Anders said that before Jackson died, and a friend of his asked him about the money—the $5,000 that he had gotten from the gamblers—Jackson said that when he tried to give the money to the team because he didn't know what else to do with it, and they wouldn't take it, he gave it to a hospital. "I think his attitude was that he'd always done the best that he could do—play as hard as he could play—and if the game didn't see fit to take care of him and look out for his well-being then he had no place in it," said Brissie.

Anders said that Jackson and his wife also had a good dry cleaning business in Savannah, Georgia, with some 30 employees. "He was doing well," said Anders. "I think he wasn't bitter. Yes, he felt that he'd been mistreated by baseball. But his attitude about it was kind of like most of the folks in the South: where you do me wrong you won't get the opportunity to do it twice. They just cut you off and you become a nonperson."

Brissie was aware that some people have disagreed with his and Anders' point of view. The late Eddie Collins, for one. Collins was a Hall of Fame second baseman on the 1919 White Sox team who was never implicated in the scandal and, as sports columnist Joe Williams of the *New York World-Telegram* wrote, "seemed to have no sympathy for any of them (those who purportedly sold out to the fixers), not even Jackson who was practically an illiterate." Jackson, Collins told Williams, "was old enough to know the difference between right and wrong." There were some people who believed that since Jackson was considered so unsophisticated, he was simply a dupe of the gamblers. "The bottom line is that they were all acquitted in a court of law," said Brissie. "But Landis banned them anyway. He could never get away with something like that today."

Brissie maintains an interest in the baseball season, and if his leg isn't bothering him to an unusually great extent, he enjoys the annual weekend at the Philadelphia A's Historical Society get-togethers with some of his former teammates. He also remembered going to the 1970 Old Timers' Day game at Shibe Park, which had been renamed Connie Mack Stadium, and which brought together vintage Phillies and A's players, one of them being Lefty Grove. (The A's had already left Philadelphia for Kansas City and old Shibe Park would soon be demolished to make way in 1971 for Veterans Stadium.)

"Richie Ashburn was leading off for the Phillies' old timers and Joe Coleman was pitching for the A's," recalled Brissie. "Ashburn tried to drag bunt the first pitch and he fouled it off. I called out to Joe, who had been a teammate of mine. I said, 'Okay, Joe, he wants to run. Stick it in his ear and knock him down.' Grove was sitting beside me. He had been a very mean pitcher—the word I had gotten was 'Don't ever get him upset when he's pitching because you're gonna eat dirt.' So when I hollered out, 'Go stick it in his ear,' Grove punched me in the ribs and said, 'You know, kid, I always knew I would like you.'"

He still follows baseball and admires a player like the Braves' pitcher John Smoltz, who can go from being a successful starting pitcher to a successful reliever, and then back again, the model of a good teammate and a great athlete. "Smoltz is a sharp cookie," said Brissie. "He makes a batter look like he's waiting for a bus sometimes. He throws them off and leaves them with their bat on their shoulder."

He expresses appreciation for Yankees shortstop Derek Jeter: "Should we call him an Old Yankee? Jeter rises to the occasion. He's a pleasure to watch. One of the things I've noticed about him is his range. To me he looks like a bigger Phil Rizzuto."

Jim Abbott was another player Brissie had great respect for. Abbott, a left-handed pitcher who was born without a right hand, pitched a no-hitter for the Yankees among his 87 wins (against 108 losses) in his 10-year major league career, from 1989 to 1999. Abbott, widely hailed as a "hero" for his efforts, said that the real heroes of his life were his parents. "They treated me like I was normal, no different than they'd treat a child born without the disability," said Abbott. "And that gave me confidence. They taught me to tie my shoe with my one hand, for example, but to do that, they first learned how to tie a shoe with one hand themselves."

"I admired Abbott just walking out to the mound," said Brissie. "People didn't take him seriously when he started. But his public attitude was, 'Just go out there and do the job—just get on with it.' He never took no for an answer. He showed a lot of moxie. And he was innovative, in that, like me, he had to make certain physical accommo-dations to deal with a handicap." (Abbott kept his glove on his right wrist and after delivering the pitch would smoothly and swiftly switch it to his left hand.)

In regard to overcoming a disability, however, Brissie did not relate to Abbott in a way that he did to some of the returning World War

II servicemen who couldn't regain their former abilities after suffering physical problems in battle. One in particular was Ernie White, who, like Brissie, was a left-hander from South Carolina. White had been a World Series star for the St. Louis Cardinals in 1942, shutting out the Yankees. At the wintry, monthlong Battle of the Bulge near war's end, the bloodiest battle ever fought by U.S. forces, with 19,000 soldiers killed and 62,000 wounded, White had been pinned down in icy water for most of a day, as Frederick Turner described in *When the Boys Came Back*. When he returned to the Cardinals in spring training 1946, he sought to get back his spot in the starting rotation. It didn't happen. He had a dead arm, which he believed was the result of that terrible day in Belgium. He was shortly traded to the Braves, but he was essentially finished as a pitcher. White was 30–18 for his career before he entered service, and 0–3 for the remainder. "In my mind, when I returned, I thought of Ernie White and some of the others who couldn't come back to play as they once had," said Brissie. "And when I began to establish myself in the big leagues, I felt I was hugely fortunate. Those guys were often in my thoughts."

• • •

Brissie, not alone, harbors suspicions about Barry Bonds: "You don't know if you're seeing him or his drugs." But, he adds, with respect, "It's still very hard to hit a major league fastball at 95 miles an hour, no matter what you put in your system."

On Mark McGwire: "I don't think he belongs in the Hall of Fame. I feel for baseball with that problem. They're taking some steps to fix the situation. McGwire hurt himself by not being forthcoming in the congressional hearings on steroids a few years ago. You owe it to the public to guarantee that you're in condition to play and that you don't go out there jacked up.

"A lot has changed. When I see balls hit to the outfield today, and some of these guys have such difficulty getting to them, I think of someone like Dom DiMaggio. He would just be standing there waiting for it. They just don't seem to have the range. I saw Dallas Green, who managed the Mets and Yankees and Phillies, on some television program. He was asked about the quality of the modern ballplayer and his answer was, 'Well, they invest money in these young fellows and they want to get them up to the major leagues and get them productive, and they don't have the years of experience to learn some of the finer points that'd put them on top to start with, and they're still learning.' That made a lot of sense to me.

"Maybe some of my observations are just an old man's dreams, or an old man's pride. But there have been a lot of changes in the game. And the ball has got to be livelier nowadays.

"The whole philosophy of pitching has changed. I don't know whether it's the training methods or the hitters have more strength or are better or more juiced up or the liveliness of the ball, but the strike zone is certainly smaller than it was years ago. There are several pitchers who I love to watch besides Smoltz. There's Tommy Glavine and Greg Maddux. Glavine reminds me of Shantz—his motion and delivery and the style he used to pitch. Glavine and Shantz would give you the same motion every time, but I think they're terrific in changing speeds, and both had a good curveball. They never overpower you, but when you ended up and you got to looking at that good curveball and they threw that fastball, it looked like a bullet.

"Speaking of bullets, there was Mickey Mantle. I think the first thing that impressed me about Mantle was the ease with which he appeared to run. He was like Jesse Owens. You know, how did a guy run so fast with so little effort? Well, it wasn't effort, it was coordination. When they clocked him—I guess Jim Busby of the White Sox was a little faster than Mantle and was the fastest to first base—but when Mantle was hitting left-handed, if that ball bounced three times, you couldn't throw him out. He hit a home run off of me, right-handed. It wasn't a record breaker. That was my consolation. At least to me, he always looked invincible as a left-handed batter. I always thought he swung much harder from the left side. When he first came up, he'd stand in center field blowing bubbles with bubble gum during a ballgame. Some of the guys would talk to him out of the bullpen—the visiting bullpen was in left center in Yankee Stadium. And Mickey would always respond. He was funny. He didn't ignore anybody. And then he'd get up and hit a home run out of sight.

"He was an extraordinary athlete. I loved him."

• • •

Though Brissie thought he would never marry again after Dot died, that changed after he met Diana Ingate Smith, in 1974.

He had taken notice of the attractive receptionist in a hotel restaurant in Augusta where he often ate. "I asked someone, 'Who is that? I'd like to meet her,'" recalled Brissie. "She had the most pleasant, intelligent way about her, and most unusual was that she spoke with an English accent—here in the deep South. It turned out that she was from Suffolk, England, had married a man from Augusta, moved here, had two children, and then got divorced. She was raising her two children by herself. She'd been without a husband for eight years, and I had been without a wife for eight years. I sort of made it a point to hang around her a little bit."

It took Brissie about six months to summon the courage to ask her out. He finally did, and she said "no." "I didn't want him to think I was too interested," she recalled. Six months later he tried again. This time it was a "yes." While dating, Lou introduced Diana to Vicki, living with a husband and two children in southeast South Carolina. "So," Vicki asked Lou, "when are you getting married?" It seemed that obvious. Diana became Mrs. Lou Brissie on December 30, 1975.

A year later, Diana gave birth to a daughter, Jennifer. From Brissie's six children (including Diana's two children by her previous marriage), there are nine grandchildren and 12 great-grandchildren.

Diana and Lou live in a well-appointed house on a quiet street in North Augusta, South Carolina, across the Savannah River from Augusta, Georgia. Brissie had worked as an industrial consultant for the State of South Carolina for 14 years, in which he supervised the technical training of a workforce to go into new industry. He retired from business in 2000 after undergoing a five-bypass heart surgery. Diana recently retired after 25 years as a staffing and recruiting specialist for a human resources company.

Brissie became the stepfather to Diana's two children, Aaron and Charlotte. "I was 12 when my mother and Lou got married," said Charlotte Klein. "And he became a big influence in my life. He made an impression on me not to take anything, especially health, for granted. And that nothing's impossible to achieve if you work hard enough. He'd say, 'Can't never could.' In high school, I had to write a paper on someone I admired. I wrote about Lou."

Aaron Smith was 10 when his mother married Brissie. "He'd go out to the ballfield behind our house and hit baseballs to my friends and me," said Smith. "He was fun, but if you stepped out of line he could be strict. He used to say that you are responsible for your actions. He never bragged, never talked about baseball unless he was asked. And I remember when his leg would flare up and he'd lie on the couch in the living room and go from shivering cold to pouring sweat. It was horrible for him, and horrible to see."

Brissie stayed in touch with a few of his former teammates, including Bob Savage and Charlie Harris, two former A's relief pitchers. Another he maintained a relationship with was his A's and Indians teammate Hank Majeski. Over the years, he and Majeski talked on the phone once a week, just to catch up on their lives and recall their baseball days together. Brissie said: "Hank told me about when his wife was institutionalized with Alzheimer's, 'When you get up in the morning and have a cup of coffee with the same little lady for 50 years, and then one morning she's not there, life can get hard.'"

Brissie, thinking of Dot, responded that he understood. Then one day in August of 1991 Brissie called Majeski's home several times, but no one answered. He tried again one morning and a young lady picked up the phone. It was Majeski's niece. Majeski was at her home, she informed him, and added, "You could call tomorrow and he may know you and he may not." About a week later Majeski, suffering from colon cancer, passed away, at age 74. His niece told Brissie, "Uncle Hank used to talk about you a lot." "I remember Hank fondly," said Brissie. "He was always alive on the bench, cheering people on."

In 1974, Brissie was elected to the South Carolina Sports Hall of Fame. Looking back on his life and times, Brissie said, "I believe in angels," for the doctors and others who aided him at the most unlikely times. He continued, "I think I'm the luckiest man to ever walk on a ballfield. I believe in angels because of the extraordinary people in my life who were there when I needed them. Morgan Waters engineered my reconstructive plastic surgery. And I've had so many folks like that in my life like Hilliard Nance, the Savannah shortstop, who visited me and encouraged me when I was in pain. And Joe Astroth, my catcher in Savannah, who gently imparted his experience to an inexperienced pitcher. I think that's a special gift.

"And the doctors, especially Suraci and Brubaker. Bru got the Surgeon General's Certificate of Commendation for his work in repairing my leg. He told me that the older he got the more he realized how extraordinary it was that they were able to do what they did (for me). That's another one of those angel things that you talk about. I'd gone to two hospitals before I got to the one in Naples and met Bru. I got the one guy that could do what he did or figured out what had to be done. Out of some 200 doctors in that hospital, he was the only one who believed he could save my leg—other doctors told me that—and he did. We maintained a lifelong friendship.

"Bru was such a dedicated doctor, it was just in his blood. When he'd come up to Cleveland to see me, or when I'd go to Elyria, about 20 miles from Cleveland, to visit him, he'd always take me aside or motion me into another room and say, 'Let me have a look at that leg.' Al Suraci would do the same. When Bru retired he moved to Cape Coral, Florida. He was in his late sixties. Then after about sixty days down there he reopened his practice. His wife, Marion, told me that she was surprised it took him *that* long.

"Again, Bru was one of my angels, my mortal angels. I don't know if there are any other kind. Am I religious? I go to church. Was God looking down on me through my life, I don't know. I mean, some guys made it out of the war, for example, and some didn't. Was God not looking down on them? If there is a God, and I've got to believe there is...there was, or is, a Creator. That I believe. I'm Protestant. I'm a deep-dyed double-dipped Baptist, Methodist, Presbyterian, Episcopal. Been to all of them. Now I go to the Methodist Church. My family was Baptist. But I don't think there's any religion in the world that says, 'Desert those that cannot help themselves.' That's what should concern us most of all. That was my father's belief. That's how he acted toward his black partner, Hunt, during those tough days for blacks in the South. Whether God up there is Baptist or whether he's Jewish or Catholic or Muslim or Methodist like me, that doesn't concern me. But I think basically the rules—the big rules—are the same. You may worship in a different way, you may do things in a different manner but basically there are two things—no matter how you look at it: tolerance and understanding. To me the nicest compliment in the world is when a man is different from another man and he invites me into his home and he knows that I'm different. He's not going try to convert me or try to change me. He's saying, 'You're a friend. I want you to see a part of what I am.' That doesn't make you hate him. That should make you understand."

• • •

While at the Veterans Administration Hospital in Augusta, Georgia, he sometimes engaged in conversation with some of the veterans from the Iraq war. He was horrified at the casualties. "Worse than World War II," he said. "With the advancement in explosives, even more damage is done to life and limbs.

"Those bombs that these people are being hit with are devastating. Those car bombs and the IEDs—the force of the explosions is so great, and the nails and metal splinters can tear you apart.

"You can see how discouraged some of them are," he continued. "No arm, no leg, faces burned. Not knowing what the future holds, and here they are feeling transformed. I try to be encouraging. I try to tell them that they can do more than they think they can." Without saying it, though some know his story, he is, of course, living proof of that notion.

Brissie passes out cards to veterans that he has had printed up, and which he feels are appropriate regardless of how anyone feels about the justification of the Iraq war. The cards, superimposed on a representation of the American flag, read, in part:

For more than 200 years Americans have answered our nation's call. Whatever the cause, whatever the duty, no matter the strength, or deadly nature of the enemy, they step forward. Coming from all walks of life, every culture and religion in defending our values and freedoms....With courage, loyalty and devotion to comrades in arms, they serve all Americans as guardians of the rights and freedoms we enjoy each day.

Thank you for all of us,

Lou Brissie, WWII Vet

Brissie also continues to speak to various handicapped groups, "If it can help people to see what they can do rather than what people *say* they can do."

From the same mortar attack that shattered his leg, there remains a ringing in Brissie's ears that has never left him. He became deaf in his left ear and has lost 30 percent of hearing in his right ear. A fragment of the mortar remains in the index finger of his left hand—doctors felt they could not successfully remove it—and the protrusion can be felt as well as seen, and remains tender at times.

Because of the pain in his leg he cannot remember ever sleeping through the night. He lives within minutes of the Augusta National Golf Club, home of The Masters, but he hasn't played golf in more than 20 years because walking on rough ground might flare up his chronic infection. He began using crutches full time in 1985.

"If I hadn't played baseball and put so much pressure on my leg, I might not have had to go on crutches as soon as I did. But my left leg and knee are so bad that eventually I would have had to go to crutches."

He was once asked if his is not, after all, a story of misfortune: a potentially great career reduced to 44 wins in the major leagues and a life of incessant pain.

He looked at his questioner. "I'm blessed," he said. "I've had good fortune. I'm here. Others, friends of mine in the war, never came back."

13

Return to Italy

In the summer of 1994, nearly 50 years after the end of World War II, and more than 50 years since his shelled body was carried from a creek in the Apennines and his life saved, Lou Brissie returned to Italy and Africa. He made a long-anticipated journey to the military cemeteries at Anzio and Florence, and Tunisia, where he visited with difficulty the grave of his uncle Robert Brissie, close to his age and his first catcher in boyhood pickup games in South Carolina.

He went first to Florence, where many of the people he served with were buried. Diana and their daughter, Jennifer, accompanied Brissie on the trip. In the cemeteries, they thought he would want to be alone with his thoughts and memories, and he appreciated that.

The Florence American military cemetery was a beautiful place, he recalled. Rolling hills, trees, manicured grass, white grave stones all neatly in order, and so well kept. It was a warm, lovely day, and quiet. So peaceful—unlike the terrible, incredible battlefield this site and the surrounding terrain had been a half century earlier, with the shattering sound of cannon fire and mortar shells, the piercing screams of the wounded, the spurting blood, and the sky aflame.

"The graves stretched beyond my vision," said Brissie. "Almost endlessly. All those crosses, the Stars of David. So many young men, some just kids, really. I found a lot of old friends there, and thought about those times." He paused for a moment. "It was overwhelming."

In the binder that is given to guests of the cemetery, these facts are presented: Burials 4,189. Unknown 213. Latin crosses 4,322. Stars of David 76. Four women—two lieutenants, one civilian volunteer, one member of the Red Cross. Five sets of brothers. One general. Total of known and unknown 5,811. There is also a "Wall of the Missing," memorializing soldiers lost in action.

"No matter what else we accomplished, fighting for our country was the most important thing we ever did in our lives," Brissie recalled. "You felt you were part of something big. And for those of us still here, we all look back in old age and feel fortunate to have survived at all. Bob Feller said that signing up with the navy the day after Pearl Harbor was the smartest thing he ever did. I never met a man who served who didn't feel that way."

In the summer of 2007, sitting in the den of his home in North Augusta, South Carolina, his left leg propped up on a chair to keep swelling down, his crutches standing in the corner near him, Brissie vividly remembered that visit of 13 years earlier.

"As you think back, some names you'll always remember, and a lot of names will escape you," he said. "Some events are shady, some aren't. But all the faces are clear, are forever fresh in memory. All the people you depended on, and who depended on you. They all look like they did 60 years ago.

"I went back as a tribute to the guys I soldiered with, and as a remembrance. I remembered them with a lot of affection."

Brissie made his way on crutches among the dead. It was, as Abraham Lincoln had said about the dead at Gettysburg, their "final resting place." Brissie had a list of who was buried where and the campaigns in which they had fought. A cemetery employee guided him to some of those places. There was, among others of his unit who were killed in the same action in which Brissie was wounded, Lt. John C. Clancy Jr. from Michigan. "We had about seven trucks when the shells fell," he said. "We lost three officers immediately, and nearly a dozen enlisted men." Lieutenant Clancy was one of those officers. And Brissie visited the grave of Pvt. William Bowen from Indiana, whom Brissie had urged to stay close to the house and didn't and was shot to death, and the grave of his college classmate and friend Tech Sgt. Charles Lawrence Aiken.

Brissie's visit coincided with the Italian Memorial Day. A small American flag and a small Italian flag were placed on every gravestone.

"The Italians had requested to put their flag on the graves, too," said Brissie. "The thought was that these American soldiers had died for their freedom the same as they had died for ours. They'd been fighting for all of us.

"I ran into some other visitors, children and grandchildren of those buried there. And I met a French couple who were there paying respects, and the woman said to me, 'The American military cemeteries are beautiful, except for the price you had to pay for them.'"

He moved from row to row among the graves. "Memories, incidents in combat, off-line hilarious things guys said and did, problems guys had—all of it came back to me," he said.

In his mind's eye, he was back with his fellow G.I.s in the mountains of northern Italy, in the snow and cold, with the sense of fear that they all surely had felt, sometimes suppressed, sometimes not, as he and they, in helmets and olive-drab uniforms and rifles, prepared to kill or be killed. His mind flashed back to the horrors of warfare, of seeing men shot full of holes just a few feet or yards away from him, their bodies blown apart, bodies that, just moments before, had been full of life, now strewn like cast-aside marionettes in the blood-soaked snow. "I felt a flood of emotion," he recalled. "I broke down. I just wasn't prepared for the way it hit me. I remember just standing there, leaning on my crutches, bent over, my eyes filled with tears."

Even now, so many years after all of it happened on the battlefield, and more than a decade after the visit to the cemeteries, Brissie's words got caught in his throat.

"I felt privileged just to have made it," he said, finally. "And very, very lucky. I think about that one part of my life, and the dreams I dreamed, and the realization of one of those dreams—to play baseball again—and I truly believe that there's never been a guy playing major league baseball as lucky as I am."

He said he stayed in the cemetery in Florence for a few hours. "But I couldn't finish walking among those buddies—they were all buddies, in a way—and I had to walk away," he said.

"There's not a day that passes that I don't think about it. How can I not?"

231

Epilogue

A few times a month, Lou Brissie places his aluminum crutches in the open rear of his black pickup truck parked in the driveway of his house in North Augusta, South Carolina, climbs into the cab, and drives across the 13th Street bridge to the handsome Veterans Administration Medical Center on 1 Freedom Way, in Augusta, Georgia, a few miles from his home. He goes there for treatment of his left leg, the one that was shattered by a mortar attack 60-plus years ago.

At the VA Hospital, he is often met by Dave James, a therapist at the hospital. James has introduced Brissie to a number of the wounded American Army soldiers from the war in Iraq who are patients in the Active Duty Rehab Unit. The soldiers have read some of the stories about Brissie—stories that James circulated to them from newspaper pieces found on the Internet, and stories that were published about Brissie in the *Augusta Chronicle* the previous Memorial Day.

Sometimes Brissie brings the soldiers autographed baseballs, sometimes he just sits and talks with them. They are interested in his experiences, how he dealt with what he saw and lived through in combat, how he dealt with his injuries when he returned home, and how he dealt with, well, home. And he is interested in their experiences.

One October afternoon in 2007 Brissie, moving through the corridors and past young men and women in wheelchairs and braces, sat down with six of these soldiers around a conference table in the hospital and traded questions and thoughts. Several of the men had met Brissie before; a couple of them, recent arrivals to the hospital, had not. The ice broke quickly, as the men perceived Brissie's genuineness, and the fact of soldierly kinship. At 6'4", Brissie is taller than any of the others, but the only one sporting gray hair.

When the conversation began, only three of the soldiers were seated at the table. After a while, when their rehab sessions concluded, a fourth showed up, then a fifth and, finally, the sixth.

Jason Capps, Spc-4, with short-cropped blond hair and wearing a black T-shirt, is 36 years old, the father of three, and from Muskogee, Oklahoma. He was the medic in a unit in Kalsu, Iraq, about 20 miles south of Baghdad, who suffered multiple injuries when, on June 10, 2007, a suicide bomber detonated a truck with 4,000 pounds of explosives under the checkpoint bridge he patrolled with fellow soldiers. The improvised explosive device (IED) killed three of the men and wounded the six others, including him. Specialist Capps is in rehabilitation, having sustained two spinal fractures, six pelvic fractures, and many facial lacerations including almost losing the tip of his nose. He was left with a hole in his lower lip through which he could stick his tongue.

Derman Simmons, 31, staff sergeant, from Swainsboro, Georgia, has a wife and three children. He was traveling in a truck along a road in southern Iraq in August 2007 when a roadside bomb exploded and broke his left arm and wrist. He wears a large cast from wrist to elbow. "I don't know if I'll ever move my arm," he said, "but I hope I will."

Luke Wrubel, a 23-year-old Spc-4 from Rochester, Minnesota, had the least serious and traumatic of war-related injuries, but his also gives a sense of the difficulties the soldiers deal with. He suffered broken ankle bones from the attrition of the equipment he regularly carried as an infantryman, totaling 100 pounds or more of body armor, side plates, ammunition, rifle, rucksack, medical kit, and so on. "My injury can hardly compare to some of the others," he said, "but it is part of what goes on in warfare."

Capps: "Everything was quiet, and then boom! We were blown up. Usually members of the Iraqi Army were stationed about 200 meters on either side of the checkpoints. And now there was no one there. They just disappeared."

Wrubel: "The problem is, you can't trust anybody over there, from 8 to 80. Anybody walking toward you is a potential enemy."

Simmons: "You see a kid riding a bicycle, and in his basket there could be a bomb. They don't wear uniforms that tell us they're the enemy. They wear civilian clothes. You can't tell someone who is a friend from someone intent on killing you—and himself."

Brissie: "That stress has to be terrible. We had stress, too—everyone in warfare has stress. I mean, people are trying to kill you. But in World War II, we knew who the enemy was and where he was."

Capps: "I can't be in a crowded room now. I can't stand it when someone is standing behind me. It comes from what I experienced as a soldier in Iraq. They come at you from all sides, often when you least expect it. And I have three kids. Not long ago I fell asleep in the front seat of our car when one of the kids popped some balloons. I almost went out of my skull. I actually hurt my back. My wife said, 'Oh, boys, you just can't do that around Daddy.'"

Simmons: "And things got worse and worse in Iraq. I was there when the war started in 2003, and you could sleep on the side of the road and not be concerned for your welfare. But six months later, we began experiencing the suicide bombers. And we started being viewed as occupiers; it all changed."

Wrubel: "And the enemy is amazing in the way they can adapt to anything. We put up one obstacle, and soon they found a way to get around it, to kill us, to blow us up. They can make anything out of anything."

At that point, M. Sgt. Tom Morrissey, 54, muscular, hair cut very short with sprigs of gray, in his third tour of duty in the army, entered the room. He was in special operations, an intelligence unit that gathered information from the populace. He had been wounded in Afghanistan, taking gun shots to eight parts of his body, two in the chest, and in both arms and legs.

Morrissey: "A lot of the problems that you have in Iraq, you have in Afghanistan. I was shot in an ambush. I had become friendly with civilians and the police there. But you never know when someone will turn on you. This one local policeman and I had had a good relation-ship. He was vetted and trained by the U.S. But one day, it was June 6 (2007), I saw him and I got this funny feeling. He was maybe 10 feet away from me. I looked him in the face and he drew his pistol and began shooting at me. I was left for dead, but luckily I was found by our guys and saved. This policeman—why did he do it? Was he intimidated by the Taliban that if he didn't kill me they'd kill members of his family? Were they held captive? Was there money involved, ideology? It's stuff like that that goes on. People over here just don't understand. You can't trust anybody."

Brissie: "I can remember the saying, 'If it feels wrong, it probably is.'"

Simmons: "We say the same thing. It's so true."

The door of the room opened and a young black man, baseball cap turned backwards on his head, entered the room, tapping with a red-and-white cane. This was Sergeant First Class Dexter Durrante, age 38, from Fayetteville, North Carolina. He had served in Afghanistan, then returned to the States and was in a training session on the demolition range in Fort Bragg, North Carolina, when, on August 10, 2007, explosive devices he was working with went off and blinded him.

He picked up on the discussion, "If it feels wrong, it probably is."

Durrante: "In Afghanistan, when we ran patrols we often used the kids as a gauge for trouble. If we took a road and saw kids playing on it, we knew things were probably okay. But if we're going down that same road and no one is there, we figure there's trouble ahead, that the townspeople have been alerted about a possible attack. We radio ahead for more help—'Hey, watch out, something not right is goin' down.' Or we take a different route."

In relation to difficulty of trust in the current war, Durrante told of the time that Laura Bush, the president's wife, visited Bagram, Afghanistan. "We were all made to leave our weapons locked in our barracks. We never were supposed to not carry our weapons. But this was different. The idea was that there can always be infiltrators on the post—you never know who, when, or where—and the brass was taking no chances on someone shooting her. The fact is, you can never be comfortable over there. It does play on your head."

Brissie: "It was my experience that when you come back after experiencing combat, it's hard for others at home to understand what you've gone through. How do you handle it when someone, your wife or your lover, say, is driving you up a wall?"

Simmons: "When I came back, I didn't want to talk about it. I felt no one would understand. I was kind of sullen. And then I had these nightmares about being back there, about all the explosions and chaos and, well, fears, and I'd thrash around in bed. I've hit my wife in my sleep. And then she and some others persuaded me to seek counseling. And I have, and it's been a big help."

Brissie: "Psychiatry wasn't such a big thing for returning veterans in World War II. If you had a serious problem, you were generally sent to Perry Point, in Maryland, where those cases usually were housed. And sodium pentothal was just coming into use. (Sodium pentothol is injected intravenously in a solution as a general anesthetic and hypnotic, and used in psychiatry to repress trauma.) I guess emotional or mental problems then were viewed by a majority of people more as a weakness than a sickness—we've made vast strides in that area, I think. But my dad was a big help. The women, my mother and my wife, seemed to understand it less, or at least worry more. My dad said, 'He'll be all right, just let him alone. Don't talk him into being sick.'"

Capps: "When people, like my wife, started asking questions about what it was like over there, it irritated me a lot. But now I try not to get upset. I'm getting better at it. I may cuss and gripe under my breath, but I just say, 'I love you, too.' When I was blown up, I remember going up and down in the air. I thought I was going to die. My philosophy is, Thank God I'm alive. Thank God I made it. A lot of my pals didn't—I saw them die—and that's a constant thought with me."

Morrissey: "Yeah, thank God I'm alive. Everything else is secondary. If you can keep it in that context, it makes everything simple."

Wrubel: "When I came back home, after 11 months in Iraq, my family greeted me at the Minneapolis airport. They all circled me and were loving me to death. It was the strangest feeling. When I was in Iraq, I'd talk to them on the phone, it was like they didn't really exist—our worlds were so far apart. But I had such anxieties built up, it was so overwhelming. I had to go talk to a therapist, a chaplain. I still do."

Joseph Creswell, 22, a baby-faced Spc-4 from St. Mary's, Georgia, came into the room on crutches and took a seat at the table. He had been shot by a sniper in Baghdad on August 13, 2007. The bullet went through his right arm and into his right thigh. Wearing a short-sleeve white T-shirt, the scars from several operations to save the arm are readily apparent. He wears a wrapping around his thigh.

Like every one of the others, Creswell said that he looks forward to the day when he will return to his unit in Iraq.

Creswell: "They're my brothers. We were together 24/7. We lived for each other; we looked after each other. There's an incredible bond that develops in situations like the one you're placed in."

Capps: "You patrol together; you mourn together."

Wrubel: "It's 'we'; it's rarely 'I.'"

Brissie: "A difference between your experience and mine in World War II is that many of you went over together from the same unit. You knew each other for a time before going to war, in the Reserves or the National Guard. That wasn't often the experience in World War II as replacements. We came together over there. And yes, you made friendships, you created bonds, no doubt about that, but you were often reluctant to get too close to someone because you could lose them the next day, or the next week. It happened regularly. In the 88th Division, where I served, in Italy, after the first 60 days we had 100 percent casualties in 14 months. And as you guys know, it's a shattering experience to lose a buddy—to see him get killed just a few feet from you.

"Another big difference is in the way medics were used then and now. Back in my day, a medic didn't carry a weapon and had a big red cross on his helmet, signifying who he was. He took care of the needs of the other guys, that's all he did."

Capps, a medic, laughed: "We don't have a red cross on our helmets. If we did, we'd be the first targets of the enemy. They figure, if they can take out a medic, then they can take two, three, four of his fellow soldiers, because he can't attend to them. It's like five for the price of one. And we carry weapons. In this war, medics are soldiers first, medics second."

Brissie: "In some respects, it may be said that ours was a more gentlemanly war, but there were instances when medics were fired upon."

Creswell: "We're still fighting by rules, but the enemy isn't. That's our problem."

Brissie: "Sometimes, guys coming back found the adjustment so difficult they resorted to alcohol. There was a big problem of drinking to excess. He was marked down as a bad guy—'a sinner.' People had a hard time comprehending what he had gone through."

Capps: "There's a lot of that now. Some guys resort to trying to drink away their problems. But it only gets you more depressed."

While all the others hope to return to their units—as unlikely as it might be for some of them—Sergeant Durrante will not.

Brissie: "What do you hope to do with the rest of your life?"

Durrante: "It's all so new to me—being blind for just the last two months—but I'm just now considering the future, what I can do. I think I'd like to be an advocate for servicemen with disabilities. Make other people aware. Until it happened to me, I didn't realize the type of discrimination that exists toward them. Like, just because you can't see means you can't do other things, which isn't true. Even talking to you. They talk louder."

Brissie: "That's a noble cause, trying to make others aware that just because you're disabled in one area doesn't make you a lesser person. I've had my own experiences with that, like with needing crutches. People have even suggested I shouldn't be going up and down on escalators, that it's too uncertain for me. They're going to lose that battle, I can tell you that."

Capps: "I'll tell you this: In P.T.—physical training—in rehab, Dexter runs every one of us into the ground. I mean, if he told me he was going into archery, I'd believe him."

Durrante: "In fact, I'm aware that you compensate. I really think that my hearing is getting better since I lost my eyesight, and this is even after the blast severed an ear drum!"

Brissie: "I think there's a power in all of us to compensate. I went to college with a guy who was blind. But if someone had a ladder up he could always sense it and avoid walking into it. Maybe there was an echo on the sidewalk as he approached it. I'm not sure how, but he was uncanny that way."

It was agreed that in World War II, the entire nation was behind the war, that virtually every American citizen had a friend or relative serving (or who had been killed) in the war. There was rationing of everything from food to gas. None of that is the case in this war, and, in polls, close to three-fourths of Americans are opposed to the war.

Morrissey: "You can't believe all the statistics you read. Maybe I'm sheltered, but almost all the people I talk to are for the war."

Durrante: "Tom, you are sheltered."

Brissie: "But whether Americans support the war or not, I think there's no question that they all support the troops. I wonder if one difference is that in World War II there was a draft. There is no draft now; it's all volunteer."

Durrante: "If there was a draft, you'd see a lot of young guys heading for Mexico."

Morrissey: "Or Canada! But I do think people support us because they see we're trying to do a job."

Durrante: "And we've done a helluva good one."

Morrissey: "People often don't understand the real threat, of what the terrorists are trying to do. They're committed to kill us wherever we may be."

Capps: "One reason I was over there, and want to go back, is that I have two boys, 15 and 11, and I'm fighting now so that they won't have to do it when they get of age. And if we leave now, they'll just get stronger over there."

Brissie: "Nothing disturbs me more than that the government won't let people see the coffins of soldiers coming back to America from the war. I think it should be a public event, to honor those who died for our country. Let our people see the price that is paid—the ultimate sacrifice."

Wrubel: "It makes it real, 300 coffins or bags, coming over at a time. While some of us are going about our business safely here, others are losing their lives in the war."

Morrissey: "Maybe the government is sincere in trying to protect the privacy of the families of the dead soldiers."

Capps: "I think the public needs to see it, needs a visual memory."

The men had to leave for a rehab session, but before doing so, Capps told a story to the group. He told of his 15-year-old son, Shane, who was a very good young pitcher. Shane hurt his arm and it looked like he would never be able to pitch again. "He had bone spurs and we thought he had torn tendons," said Capps. Capps gave Shane an article about Brissie.

"Lou, I have to tell you, he was impressed with how you overcame your disability," said Capps. "And he said to me, 'Dad, I think I'm going to learn to throw left-handed.' Well, his arm did get better and he is throwing again with his right arm."

Around the table, Capps' story brought understanding and empathetic nods from the other soldiers.

Brissie: "That's a great compliment, Jason, but don't let your son's enthusiasm override his limitations as they exist now. Be careful rushing it."

The others in the room nodded, and it was obvious that they seemed to be thinking about that story in relation to their own wounds.

At the conclusion of the session, the soldiers said good-bye to Brissie. Durrante, who had picked up his folding cane that he had placed on the table in front of him, reached out with his right hand.

"Mr. Brissie?" he said.

"Right here, Dexter," Brissie said. And Durrante shook his hand and gave him a hug.

"Thanks for coming—what you've done, what you've overcome means a lot to us," the blind sergeant said to the 83-year-old former pitcher and corporal. Then he added, with a smile and a wave, "See you around."

Selected Bibliography

Allen, Maury. *You Could Look It Up: The Life of Casey Stengel.* New York: Times Books, 1979.

Berkow, Ira. *Beyond the Dream.* New York: Atheneum, 1975.

Boyd, Brendan C., and Fred C. Harris. *The Great American Baseball Card Flipping, Trading and Bubble Gum Book.* Boston, Toronto: Little, Brown, 1973.

Carmichael, John P. *My Greatest Day in Baseball: as told to John P. Carmichael and other noted sportswriters.* Lincoln, NE: Bison Books, 1996.

Churchill, Winston S. *The Second World War: Closing the Ring.* Boston: Houghton Mifflin, 1951.

Cramer, Richard Ben. *Joe DiMaggio: The Hero's Life.* New York: Simon and Schuster, 2000.

Creamer, Robert W. *Stengel: His Life and Times.* New York: Simon and Schuster, 1984.

Dewey, Donald, and Nicholas Acocella. *The New Biographical History of Baseball.* Chicago: Triumph Books, 2002.

Einstein, Charles, ed. *The Fireside Book of Baseball.* New York: Simon and Schuster, 1956.

Eisenhower, Dwight D. *Crusade in Europe.* Garden City, NY: Doubleday, 1948.

Greenberg, Hank, and Ira Berkow. *The Story of My Life.* Chicago: Triumph Books, 2001.

Gershman, Michael. *Diamonds.* Boston, New York: Houghton Mifflin, 1993.

Halberstam, David. *Summer of '49.* New York: HarperCollins, 1989.

Halberstam, David. *The Fifties.* New York: Villard Books, 1993.

Honig, Donald. *When the Grass Was Real.* New York: Coward, McCann & Geoghegan, 1975.

Honig, Donald. *The All-Star Game.* St. Louis, MO: The Sporting News Publishing Co., 1987.

Kaiser, David: *Epic Season: The 1948 American League Pennant Race.* Amherst: University of Massachusetts Press, 1998.

Lowry, Philip J. *Green Cathedrals.* New York: Addison-Wesley Publishing, 1992.

Mead, William B. *Baseball Goes to War.* Washington, DC: Farragut Publishing Co., 1985.

Newell, Rob. *From Playing Field to Battlefield: Great Athletes Who Served in World War II.* Annapolis, MD: Naval Institute Press, 2006.

Paige, Satchel. *Maybe I'll Pitch Forever.* Garden City, NY: Doubleday, 1962.

Palmer, Peter, and Gary Gillette. *The Baseball Encyclopedia.* New York: Barnes and Noble Books, 2004.

Pietrusza, David, Matthew Silverman, and Michael Gershman, ed. *Baseball: The Biographical Encyclopedia.* New York: Total Sports Illustrated, 2000.

Reporting World War II: Part Two American Journalism 1944–1946. New York: Library of America, 1995.

Seidel, Michael. *Ted Williams: A Baseball Life.* Lincoln, NE: Bison Books, 2000.

Smith, Red. *Out of the Red.* New York: Alfred A. Knopf, 1950.

Smith, Red. *Red Smith on Baseball.* Chicago: Ivan R. Dee, 2000.

Turner, Frederick. *When the Boys Came Back: Baseball and 1946.* New York: Henry Holt, 1996.

Tygiel, Jules. *Baseball's Great Experiment: Jackie Robinson and His Legacy.* New York: Oxford University Press, 1983.

Veeck, Bill, with Ed Linn. *Veeck—as in Wreck.* New York: Bantam Books, 1962.

Vecchione, Joseph J., ed. *The New York Times Book of Sports Legends.* New York: Times Books, 1991.

Williams, Ted, with John Underwood. *My Turn at Bat, as told to John Underwood.* New York: Simon and Schuster, 1969.

Numerous magazine and newspaper stories were also used as reference, and many of them are cited in the book's text and the acknowledgments.

About the Author

IRA BERKOW was a sports columnist and feature writer for *The New York Times* for 26 years, from March of 1981 to his retirement from the paper on February 1, 2007. He shared the Pulitzer Prize for National Reporting in 2001 with his article "The Minority Quarterback," later published in *The Minority Quarterback and Other Lives in Sports,* a collection of his feature stories. He was a finalist for the Pulitzer Prize for Distinguished Commentary in 1988, and he has received numerous awards and citations for his work.

Mr. Berkow's work has appeared in many sports and literary anthologies, and he is the only writer to be represented for five decades in the prestigious annual *Best Sports Stories* and its successor, *Best American Sports Writing.* A column of his was also included in *Best American Sports Writing of the Century,* edited by David Halberstam (1999).

Mr. Berkow was born in Chicago on January 7, 1940. He is a gradu-ate of Miami University in Ohio (1963) and Northwestern University's Medill Graduate School of Journalsm (1964). He received the Distinguished Achievement Medal from Miami University and is a charter member of Medill's Hall of Achievement. He also attended Roosevelt University (1958–60) and was honored with that school's Professional Achievement Award.

A sportswriter and book reviewer for the *Minneapolis Tribune* from 1965 to 1967, Mr. Berkow then served as a sports columnist, sports editor, and general columnist for the Newspaper Enterprise Association (1967–76). He worked as a freelance writer (1976–81), before engaging in his long tenure with *The New York Times* (1981–2007). He was named a senior writer at both NEA and *The New York Times.*

Mr. Berkow is the author of 18 books, including the 2006 memoir, *Full Swing: Hits, Runs and Errors in a Writer's Life,* and the best-sellers *Red: A Biography of Red Smith* (1987) and *Maxwell Street: Survival in a Bazaar* (1977). *The Man Who Robbed the Pierre* (1987) was a finalist for the Edgar Award for Best

True Crime Book of the Year. His memoir, *To the Hoop*, as well as *Red*, were *New York Times* Notable Books of the Year.

His collaboration with basketball star Walt Frazier, *Rockin' Steady: A Guide to Basketball and Cool* (1974), was named by the American Library Association as one of the Best Books for Young Adults in the last 75 years—the only sports book so honored. His book *The DuSable Panthers* was chosen by the New York Public Library among its Distinguished Books for Young Adults. He collaborated on the autobiography *Hank Greenberg: The Story of My Life* (2001), which was made into an award-winning documentary, *The Life and Times of Hank Greenberg* (2001), and for which Mr. Berkow was the major consultant as well as an on-screen interviewee.

Beyond the Dream: Occasional Heroes of Sports, Mr. Berkow's first collection of columns, was reissued in 2008—33 years after it was first published by Atheneum (1975). "The best of these stories are as good as any ever written," commented Rick Kogan of the *Chicago Sun-Times*. *Pitchers Do Get Lonely* (1988) and *The Minority Quarterback, and Other Lives in Sports* (2002) are two other collections of his columns.

Mr. Berkow lives in New York City.

Other Books by Ira Berkow

Full Swing
The Minority Quarterback
Court Vision
To the Hoop
The Gospel According to Casey (with Jim Kaplan)
How to Talk Jewish (with Jackie Mason)
Hank Greenberg: Hall of Fame Slugger (juvenile)
Hank Greenberg: The Story of My Life (editor)
Pitchers Do Get Lonely
The Man Who Robbed the Pierre
Red: A Biography of Red Smith
Carew (with Rod Carew)
The DuSable Panthers
Maxwell Street
Beyond the Dream
Rockin' Steady (with Walt Frazier)
Oscar Robertson: The Golden Year

Index